KU-798-508

lonely planet

NEW ZEALAND

TOP SIGHTS, AUTHENTIC EXPERIENCES

Tasmin Waby, Brett Atkinson, Andrew Bain,
Peter Dragicevich, Monique Perrin,
Charles Rawlings-Way

Contents

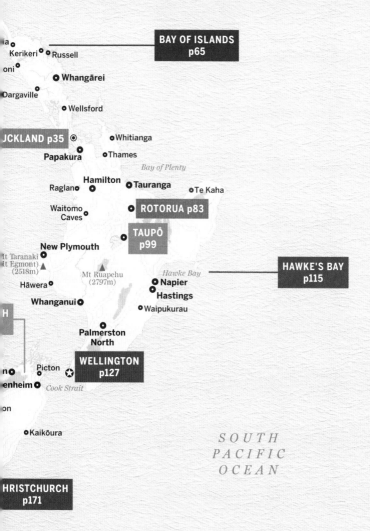

Kerikeri ○ ○ Russell
○oni ○

BAY OF ISLANDS
p65

○ia ○

○ **Whangārei**

○Dargaville

○ Wellsford

○CKLAND p35 ◎ ○Whitianga
Papakura ○ ○Thames

Bay of Plenty

Hamilton
Raglan ○ ○ ○ **Tauranga** ○Te Kaha

Waitomo ○
Caves

ROTORUA p83

New Plymouth ○
○ **TAUPŌ**
p99

○t Taranaki ○
t Egmont) ▲
(2518m)
Hāwera ○
▲ Mt Ruapehu
(2797m)
Hawke Bay
○ **Napier**
Hastings

HAWKE'S BAY
p115

Whanganui ○
○Waipukurau

H

○
Palmerston
North

○n ○
Picton
○ ○
enheim ○ *Cook Strait*

WELLINGTON
p127
✪

on

○Kaikōura

S O U T H
P A C I F I C
O C E A N

HRISTCHURCH
p171

OTAGO PENINSULA
p253

⊛ 0 ■■■■■■■■ 200 km
Ⓝ 0 ■■■■■■■■ 100 miles

Welcome to New Zealand

Epic national parks, indigenous Māori culture, compact and creative cities, and world-class outdoors activities... Your trip to New Zealand can be as relaxed or as action-packed as you want to make it, but it will always be memorable.

There are just 4.8 million New Zealanders, scattered across 268,021 sq km: bigger than the UK with one-fourteenth of the population. With plenty of room to explore, tackle one of the epic 'Great Walks' or spend a few hours wandering along a beach, paddling a kayak or mountain biking through some easily accessible wilderness.

Hungry yet? NZ chefs borrow influences from as far afield as South Pacific islands and Western Europe for creative takes on locally sourced lamb and seafood like abalone, oysters and scallops. Wash it down with craft beer and legendary cool-climate wines (sublime sauvignon blanc and pinot noir).

Next, immerse yourself in the indigenous culture: across NZ you can hear Māori language, watch Māori TV, join in a *hāngi* (Māori feast) or catch a cultural performance with song, dance and a spine-tingling *haka* (war dance).

But fear not – New Zealanders these days are far from warlike. This forward-looking Pacific nation is a dynamic, friendly and increasingly eco-conscious place to explore.

Your trip to New Zealand can be as relaxed or action-packed as you want to make it.

Queenstown (p205)
SANGKHOMHUNGKHUNTHOD/GETTY IMAGES ©

Kait

Opo

*Tasman
Sea*

A

MARLBOROU
p149

Takaka○

Karamea○ **Nels**

B

Westport ○   ○
                Murchis
Punakaiki ○

THE WEST COAST
p189

Hokitika

                ○ **Arthur's Pass**

Franz
Josef
Fox ○ ○ Glacier
Glacier   Methven ○

                C

QUEENSTOWN
p205

▲
Aoraki/
Haast Mt Cook
        (3754m)   ○
(Haast   Ashburton
  Pass

            ○ **Timaru**

    ○ Wānaka   ○ **Waimate**

                ○ **Ōamaru**

FIORDLAND
p231

                ○ **Palmerston**

Te Anau ○

        Lumsden   **Dunedin**
          ○   ○

Tuatapere ○   ○ Gore ○ Balclutha

        ○ Invercargill
Bluff ○

    ○ Oban

Leabharlann Dhún Laoghaire - Ráth an Dúin

COVID-19

We have re-checked every business in this book before publication to ensure that it is still open after 2020's COVID-19 outbreak. However, the economic and social impacts of COVID-19 will continue to be felt long after the outbreak has been contained. Therefore many businesses, services and events referenced in this guide may experience ongoing restrictions. Some businesses may be temporarily closed, or have changed their opening hours and services; some unfortunately could have closed permanently. We suggest you check with venues before visiting for the latest information.

New Zealand's Top 12

RUDY BALASKO/SHUTTERSTOCK ©

Auckland

Pacific culture and city buzz

Built on the remnants of long-extinct volcanoes, Auckland (p35) isn't your average metropolis. It's regularly rated one of the world's most liveable cities. It's blessed with subtropical weather, good beaches and thriving dining, drinking and live music scenes. However it's the culture of this ethnically diverse city (which has the biggest Polynesian population of any city in the world) that makes Auckland stand out on the global stage.

SHELLY MACK/SHUTTERSTOCK ©

1

Bay of Islands

Sailing between islands with dolphins

Turquoise waters lapping in pretty bays and dolphins frolicking at the bows of boats: chances are these are the kinds of images that drew you to New Zealand in the first place. The Bay of Islands (p65) delivers this idyll with myriad options to tempt you out on the water to explore the 150-odd islands that dot this beautiful bay. Back on dry land you can delve into the region's rich history, in which successions of migrants descended on these shores.

RUTH BLACK/SHUTTERSTOCK ©

Rotorua

Māori culture and geothermal wonders

The first thing you'll notice about Rotorua (p83) is the sulphuric smell – from gushing geysers, bubbling mud, steaming cracks in the ground and boiling pools of mineral-rich water. The other key draw: the many cultural experiences, curated and run by local Māori, where you can learn about Aotearoa from its indigenous peoples. Expect everything in this tourism playground from *hāngi* and hot springs to mountain biking and luging.

3

4

Taupō

Lakeside playground with stunning vistas

The heart of the North Island, hip little Taupō (p99) sits on the doorstep of Tongariro National Park – an alien landscape of alpine desert punctuated by three smouldering volcanoes. The brilliant one-day Tongariro Alpine Crossing hike skirts past craters and iridescent lakes, with views across the vast Central Plateau. Lakeside Taupō itself offers hot springs, trout fishing, skydiving, mountain biking... and plenty of great places to wine and dine.

5

Hawke's Bay

Art-deco architecture and coastal vineyards

It's curious that more New Zealanders don't choose to live on the North Island's sunny East Coast. With a backdrop of chardonnay vines in the Hawke's Bay Wine Region (p120), and the picture-perfect cache of art-deco architecture in Napier (pictured; p122), the living here is most definitely easy. You're the beneficiary: without the crowds there's plenty of room for you to venture out and enjoy your holiday.

MOHD FUAD RAHIM/SHUTTERSTOCK ©

BOYLOSO/SHUTTERSTOCK ©

ROBERT CHG/SHUTTERSTOCK ©

Wellington

One of the world's coolest little capitals

Windy Wellington (p127) is synonymous with cinema thanks to
local boy Peter Jackson. But residents are also proud of its vibrant
arts-and-music scene and special events schedule (from Fringe to
WOW), plus dining choices that range from innovative food trucks
to high-end gastronomy. For visitors to the capital, its proximity
to mountain biking and walking trails, not to mention a glistening
harbour, score just as highly. Don't miss it.

6

TOMAS PAVELKA/SHUTTERSTOCK ©

Marlborough

Sublime wine and wilderness

After a few days overindulging in Marlborough (p149) sauvignon blanc or Nelson craft beer made with locally grown hops, Abel Tasman National Park offers tramping, kayaking and swimming in golden sandy coves with gin-clear seas. The Marlborough Sounds are an impossibly photogenic wilderness, while seaside Kaikōura is the place for spying whales, seals and local bird life.

Christchurch

Manicured streetscapes and gardens

It's an understatement to say that Christchurch (p171) – a city of 375,000 people that was shaken to its core first by two massive earthquakes and then by unbelievable violence – is a resilient town. Today, new architecture and street art spell creativity, businesses are busy again and the city's heritage sites are a marvel to see. Despite all the heartache, the locals welcome visitors to this proud South Island city.

TRAVELLIGHT/SHUTTERSTOCK ©

NIRADJ/SHUTTERSTOCK ©

The West Coast

Glaciers to inspire awe

Hemmed in by the Tasman Sea and the Southern Alps, Westland Tai Poutini National Park is like nowhere else in New Zealand, and nowhere else on earth. Fed by upwards of 3m of annual rainfall, Franz Josef (pictured left; p192) and Fox (pictured right; p196) Glaciers are truly awe-inspiring remnants from another time. Book a helihike for an icy close encounter, or a scenic flight for an aerial assessment of their previous vast proportions.

ASIATRAVEL/SHUTTERSTOCK ©

Queenstown

Extreme adventures in stunning landscapes

Queenstown (p205) may be world-renowned as the birthplace
of bungy jumping, but there's more to NZ's adventure hub. The
Remarkables provide a jagged indigo backdrop to days spent skiing,
hiking or mountain biking, before dining in cosmopolitan restaurants
or partying in some of NZ's best bars. Keep the adrenaline flowing
with hang gliding, kayaking or river rafting, before heading to 'quieter'
Wānaka and taking your vertigo into overdrive on the via ferrata.

10

MAWARDIBAHAR/SHUTTERSTOCK ©

Fiordland

Mountains meet the sea

Whatever the weather, Milford Sound (pictured; p238) will dazzle you with its collage of waterfalls, forbidding cliffs and dark cobalt waters, with the iconic profile of Mitre Peak rising above. Fiordland's waterfalls are most spectacular when fed by rain, but blue-sky days set rainbows sparkling from their mist. Either way, keep your eyes peeled for seals, dolphins and the elusive Fiordland crested penguin, especially if you're exploring NZ's most famous fiord by kayak.

VLADISLAV T. JIROUSEK/SHUTTERSTOCK ©

Otago Peninsula

Rugged coast & wildlife

With a constant backdrop of glorious coastal vistas, the Otago Peninsula (p253) offers some of NZ's best wildlife encounters. Dozens of little penguins achieve peak cuteness in their nightly beachside waddle, while their much rarer yellow-eyed cousin, the hoiho, can be glimpsed standing sentinel on deserted coves. Sea lions and seals laze on rocks while albatrosses from the world's only mainland colony soar above.

Plan Your Trip

Need to Know

When to Go

Auckland
GO Nov–Apr

Rotorua
GO Oct–Dec

Wellington
GO Dec–Feb

Christchurch
GO Jan–Mar

Queenstown
GO Jun–Aug

High Season (Dec–Feb)
○ Summer brings busy beaches and sporting events.

○ Accommodation prices rise – book ahead.

○ High season in ski towns is winter (Jun–Aug).

Shoulder (Mar–May & Sep–Nov)
○ Fine weather, warmish ocean.

○ Queues are shorter; popular road-trip routes are clear.

○ March to May brings the autumn colours, while spring (Sep–Nov) means the end of snow season.

Low Season (Jun–Aug)
○ Brilliant skiing and snowboarding from mid-June.

○ Good accommodation deals; a seat in any restaurant (outside of ski towns).

○ Warm-weather beach towns may be half asleep, so book accommodation ahead.

Currency
New Zealand dollar ($)

Languages
English, Māori, NZ Sign Language

Visas
Visitors need an NZeTA (NZ$12 online). Tourists are also expected to pay an International Visitor Conservation and Tourism Levy (IVL; $35).

Money
Bank cards are used for most purchases, and are accepted in most hotels and restaurants. ATMs are widely available in cities and larger towns.

Mobile Phones
It's simple to buy a local SIM card and prepaid account at outlets in airports and large towns (provided your mobile is unlocked).

Time
New Zealand time (GMT/UTC plus 12 hours)

Daily Costs

Budget: Less than $150

- Dorm beds or campsites per night: $20–45

- Main course in a budget eatery: up to $20

- Hop-on hop-off bus pass (12 to 28 days): $699–1779

Midrange: $150–250

- Double room in a midrange hotel/ motel: $130–200

- Main course in a midrange restaurant: $20–35

- Car rental per day: from $45

Top end: More than $250

- Double room in an upmarket hotel: $200–350

- Three-course meal in a classy restaurant: from $80

- Domestic flights: from $100

Useful Websites

100% Pure New Zealand (www.new zealand.com) Comprehensive government tourism site.
Department of Conservation (www.doc. govt.nz) DOC parks, trail and camping info.
Lonely Planet (www.lonelyplanet.com/ new-zealand) Destination information, hotel bookings, traveller forum and more.
Te Ara (www.teara.govt.nz) Online encyclopedia of NZ.

Opening Hours

Opening hours vary seasonally depending on where you are. Most places close on Christmas Day and Good Friday.

Banks 9am to 4.30pm Monday to Friday; some also 9am to noon Saturday
Cafes 7am or 8am to 3pm or 4pm
Post offices 8.30am to 5pm Monday to Friday; larger branches also 9.30am to 1pm Saturday

Pubs and bars noon to late ('late' varies by region and by day)
Restaurants noon to 2.30pm and 6pm to 9pm
Shops and businesses 9am to 5.30pm Monday to Friday; 9am to noon or 5pm Saturday
Supermarkets 7am to 9pm

Arriving in New Zealand

Auckland Airport Airbus Express buses (adult/child $17/2) run into the city every 10 to 30 minutes, 24 hourly. Prebooked door-to-door shuttle buses (from $25) run 24 hours. A taxi into the city costs around $100 (45 minutes).
Wellington Airport Airport Flyer buses ($12) run into the city every 10 to 20 minutes from around 7am to 9pm. Door-to-door shuttles (from $20) run 24 hours. A taxi into the city costs around $30 (20 minutes).
Christchurch Airport Christchurch Metro Purple Line runs into the city ($8.50 when paying in cash) regularly from around 7am to 11pm. Door-to-door shuttles (from $25) run 24 hours. A taxi into the city costs around $50 to $75 (20 minutes).

Getting Around

New Zealand is long and skinny, and many roads are two-lane country byways: getting from A to B requires some planning.

Car Travel at your own tempo, explore remote areas and visit regions with no public transport. Hire cars in major towns. Drive on the left; the steering wheel is on the right (...in case you can't find it).

Bus Reliable, frequent services to most destinations around the country (usually cheaper than flying), though services thin out in rural areas. To get further than main cities, you'll need to rely on tours.

Plane Fast-track your visit with affordable, frequent, fast internal flights.

Train Reliable, regular services (if not fast or cheap) along specific routes on both islands.

For more on **getting around**, see p306

Plan Your Trip

Hotspots For...

YEVGEN BELICH/SHUTTERSTOCK ©

Māori Culture

New Zealand's indigenous Māori culture is accessible and engaging. Museums are crammed with Māori artefacts, but this is a living culture: vibrant, potent and contemporary.

Rotorua (p83)
Catch a cultural performance featuring a *haka* (war dance) and a *hāngi* (Māori feast).

Te Puia (p87)
Dynamic performances in an active geothermal zone.

Bay of Islands (p65)
Māori knew it as Pēwhairangi centuries before the first permanent British settlers arrived.

Waitangi Treaty Grounds (p68)
Pākehā negotiated with Māori to create the NZ nation.

The West Coast (p189)
From mountains to sweeping beaches and primordial forests.

Hokitika (p199)
The primary source of *pounamu* (greenstone).

DMITRY NAUMOV/GETTY IMAGES ©

The Great Outdoors

Glaciers leak into rainforests, volcanoes spike through green hills, and ice-tipped mountains stretch towards the starry skies.

Marlborough (p149)
The sunny forested tip of the South Island is perfect for kayaking and hiking.

Queen Charlotte Track (p152)
One of New Zealand's classic walks.

The West Coast (p189)
Untamed coastal wilderness and epic touring routes, with surprisingly accessible glaciers.

Franz Josef Glacier (p192)
Discover by guided walk or a sightseeing flight.

Queenstown (p205)
You'll be immersed in stunning surrounds at this lake-side town surrounded by snowcapped mountains.

Adventure Sports (p208)
Try bungy jumping from Kawarau Bridge.

Wine Regions

New Zealand's world class wine industry also produces great tourism experiences from cellar-door tastings to vineyard restaurants and cycling tours.

JSVIDEOS/SHUTTERSTOCK ©

Auckland Region (p35)
The weekend playgrounds around Auckland produce amazing syrah, pinot gris and chardonnay.

Waiheke Island (p42)
Ideal climate for Bordeaux-style reds and rosés.

Marlborough (p149)
The country's biggest wine region just keeps on turning out superb sauvignon blanc.

Blenheim (p162)
The hub of the Marlborough scene, with 35-plus wineries.

Hawke's Bay (p115)
Warm days shift into chardonnay nights on the sun-stroked East Coast.

Napier Wineries (p120)
Bike between vineyards around this art-deco town.

Aquatic Adventures

From canoeing to yachting, an armada of boaties turn New Zealand's bays, rivers and harbours into a watery playground.

SERGEY-73/ SHUTTERSTOCK ©

Bay of Islands (p65)
Sail, cruise or kayak between 150 unspoiled islands.

Urupukapuka Island (p71)
Spend the day walking to secluded beaches.

Waitomo Caves (p78)
Waitomo's astonishing cave systems are ripe for adventure.

Black-Water Rafting (p81)
Don a wetsuit and surge along an underground river.

Fiordland (p231)
Keep your eyes peeled for marine life on a waterfall cruise in Fiordland.

Real Journeys (p240)
Scenic cruises and nature tours on Milford Sound.

Plan Your Trip

Essential New Zealand

Activities

From mid-air adventures to deep dives, New Zealand's activity tourism is fuelled by adrenaline. Inspired by NZ's rugged landscape, even the meekest travellers muster the courage to dangle on a bungy rope, skydive above mountains or thunder down river rapids. Hiking is a big deal here, too, with 10 epic Great Walks and myriad short hikes on offer – a magnificent way to explore the country's abundant natural beauty and feast your eyes on mountain vistas, hidden waterfalls and rare wildlife. NZ is also a premier destination for snow sports, with family-friendly ski areas, cross-country (Nordic) skiing, snowboarding and pulse-quickening heliskiing. The ski season varies but it's usually mid-June to September, running as late as mid-October in a good season.

Shopping

New Zealand has much to tempt the shopper. Its vibrant and unique fashion scene, especially its Wearable Art, features natural materials like possum fur and merino wool. Māori arts and crafts include gorgeous hand-carved jewellery with powerful symbols and motifs. Kiwi artisans also sell beautiful acrylic and watercolour paintings to remind you of this wonderful country, and epic landscape photographs to get lost in back home. Sometimes the best buys are edible: at farmers markets stock up on things you can take home such as feijoa jam and mānuka honey, plus wines and spirits that are the best in their class.

Eating

New Zealand is a gastronomic nirvana with top-shelf ingredients and a hospitality industry that takes itself seriously – even a small-town barista will know their way around an espresso machine or a cold-press. From country pubs to modern restaurants, the emphasis is on home-grown and local ingredients like lamb, seafood and venison, but with a thriving vegetarian and

CHRIS MELVILLE/SHUTTERSTOCK ©

vegan food scene to keep all culinary persuasions more than satisfied. You're spoilt for choice in the big cities, and although small towns will have less variety and earlier closing times, you can still expect a great meal out.

Drinking & Nightlife

New Zealanders love a drink. And if it's locally made, even better. Cool-climate wines (sauvignon blanc and pinot noir) do well here and the craft beer scene is going strong. Most pubs have excellent local beers on tap or in the fridge. Bars and pubs are busy in most major regional centres, but outside of Auckland, there's not much of a clubbing vibe going on. Nights out are geared towards quality drinks, tapas and friendly conversation. Don't be afraid to go out after dark on your own; you're likely to find a local to have a chat with over a drink. And no one will bat an eyelid if it's just you having a pinot noir by candlelight with a good book.

★ Best Eats

Rātā (p226)

Mister D (p122)

Pasture (p56)

5th Street (p184)

Noble Rot (p143)

Entertainment

As the world now knows, thanks to artists like Taika Waititi, New Zealanders know how to entertain themselves on a rainy day (or night). They also get their fair share of major touring performers and festivals, cranking up the decibels in summer time. Independent cinemas, theatres and live music keep cities and regional towns abuzz all year round. In smaller towns you'll be limited to open-mic or a sports screening in the local pub. Check out local media to see what's happening.

From left: Kawarau Bridge (p208), Queenstown; Auckland bar scene (p57)

Plan Your Trip
Month by Month

January

With perfect weather and the cricket season in full swing, it's holiday time for the locals.

February

Kids are back at school and the 'sauv blanc' is chillin' in the fridge; this is high summer.

✤ Waitangi Day

On 6 February 1840 the Treaty of Waitangi was first signed between Māori and the British Crown. Waitangi Day remains a public holiday across NZ, but in Waitangi itself (the Bay of Islands) there's a lot happening: guided tours, concerts, market stalls and family entertainment.

☆ Fringe

New Zealand Fringe, Wellington, is where unusual, emerging and controversial acts come to play. We're talking cabaret, comedy, spoken word...and pavement chalking.

✤ Art Deco Weekend

Napier, levelled by an earthquake in 1931 and rebuilt during the art-deco era, celebrates its architectural heritage with this high-steppin' fiesta (p119), featuring music, food, wine, vintage cars and costumes over a long weekend in February.

March

A hint of autumn and harvest time in the vineyards and orchards.

☆ Te Matatini National Kapa Haka Festival

This spine-tingling *haka* competition (www.tematatini.co.nz) happens in early March/ late February in odd-numbered years, with much gesticulation, eye-bulging and tongue extension. But it's not just the *haka*: expect traditional Māori song, dance, storytelling and other performing arts. Host cities vary.

Above: Art Deco Weekend (p119)

MARUEDOM/GETTY IMAGES ©

✖ Wildfoods Festival

Eat insects, baby octopi and 'mountain oysters' at Hokitika's comfort-zone-challenging foodie fest. Local classics like whitebait patties are represented too, if you aren't hungry for pork-blood casserole. Tip: NZ brews and wines are available to wash down the worst taste-bud offenders.

✤ Pasifika Festival

With upwards of 140,000 Māori and strong communities of Tongans, Samoans, Cook Islanders, Niueans, Fijians and other South Pacific Islanders, Auckland has the largest Polynesian community in the world. These vibrant cultures come together at this annual fiesta at Western Springs Park.

April

The ocean is still swimmable and the weather still mild, with nary a queue in sight.

★ Top Events

Te Matatini National Kapa Haka Festival, March

Fringe, Wellington February

Beervana, August

Pasifika Festival, March

Art Deco Weekend, February

May

Chilly winter beckons, but that doesn't stop the festivals.

☆ New Zealand International Comedy Festival

Local and international acts perform across Auckland, Wellington and various regional centres over three weeks in May. With stand-up, improv, clowning and children's events, you'll find something to tickle your funny bone.

Above: Queenstown Winter Festival (p215)

June

It's ski season! Queenstown and Wānaka come to life in winter.

✦ Matariki

Māori New Year (www.matarikifestival.org.nz) is heralded by the rise of Matariki (aka the Pleiades star cluster) in May. Three days of astronomy, education, ritual, music and community days take place, mainly around Auckland, Wellington and Northland.

July

Ski season reaches its peak. Hit Mt Ruapehu on the North Island to avoid crowds.

✦ Queenstown Winter Festival

This southern snow-fest (p215) has been running since 1975, and now attracts more than 57,000 visitors. It's a four-day party, with fireworks, live music, comedy, a community carnival, masquerade ball, and wacky ski and snowboard activities on the mountain slopes.

August

Land a good deal on accommodation pretty much anywhere except ski towns.

♟ Beervana

Attain beery nirvana at this annual craft-beer guzzle fest (www.beervana.co.nz) in Wellington – it's freezing outside; what else is there to do? Sample the best of NZ's booming beer scene. Not loving beer is heresy, but yes, it also has cider and wine.

September

Spring is sprung. The amazing and surprising World of WearableArt is always a hit.

✦ World of WearableArt

A bizarre (in the best possible way) two-week Wellington event featuring amazing hand-crafted garments. Entries from the show are displayed at the World of WearableArt & Classic Cars Museum in Nelson after the event (Cadillacs and corsetry?). Sometimes spills over into October.

October

October is 'shoulder season' – reasonable accommodation rates, minimal crowds and no competition for the best campsites.

November

Across Northland, the Coromandel Peninsula, the Bay of Plenty and the East Coast, NZ's iconic pohutukawa trees bloom, the weather picks up and tourists start to arrive.

✦ Ōamaru Victorian Heritage Celebrations

The good old days; when Queen Vic sat dourly on the throne, when hems were low and collars were high. Old Ōamaru thoroughly enjoys this tongue-in-cheek historic homage (www.vhc.co.nz): expect dress-ups, penny-farthing races, choirs, guided tours and more.

December

Summertime! Office workers surge towards the finish line. Everyone gears up for Christmas and shopping centres are packed out.

Plan Your Trip
Get Inspired

Read

The Luminaries (Eleanor Catton; 2013) Man Booker Prize winner; crime and intrigue on West Coast goldfields.

Mister Pip (Lloyd Jones; 2006) Tumult on Bougainville Island, intertwined with Dickens' *Great Expectations*.

The Bone People (Keri Hulme; 1984) Feminist magic realism novel set against a backdrop of violence and isolation.

The Collected Stories of Katherine Mansfield (2006) The greatest hits of one of NZ's most famous writers.

The Wish Child (Catherine Chidgey; 2016) Harrowing, heart-breaking WWII novel; NZ Book Awards winner.

Watch

Lord of the Rings trilogy (2001–03) Hobbits, dragons and magical rings – Tolkien's vision comes to life.

The Piano (1993) A piano and its owners arrive on a mid-19th-century West Coast beach.

Whale Rider (2002) Magical tale of family and heritage on the East Coast.

Once Were Warriors (1994) Brutal relationship dysfunction in South Auckland.

Boy (2010) Taika Waititi's bittersweet coming-of-age drama set in the Bay of Plenty.

Listen

Six60 (Six60; 2015 & 2019) Award-winning Kiwi roots, funk, reggae and pop fusion with Māori instrumentation.

True Colours (Split Enz; 1980) Urgent riffs, bittersweet lyrics and this rock outfit's only number-one single.

Woodface (Crowded House; 1991) Upbeat singalongs define the easy-going third album of this acclaimed pop-rock band.

Submarine Bells (The Chills; 1990) Punkish energy and swoon-worthy soundscapes layered through a near-perfect indie-rock record.

Melodrama (Lorde; 2017) Soaring vocals, hypnotic electronica, from a former teen superstar.

Above: Hobbiton, *The Lord of the Rings* filming location (p62)

Five-Day Itineraries

Auckland vs Wellington

With a population of 1.4-million and access to two oceans and vibrant Polynesian culture, Auckland is happening; but bohemian Wellington is arguably the hippest little city on the planet. Split five days between the two and decide which comes out on top.

Auckland (p35) Big-city essentials: Ponsonby Rd eating and drinking, Auckland Art Gallery and Auckland Museum.
⚓ 40 mins to Waiheke Island

Waiheke Island (p42) Paradise found: wineries, cafes, beaches... Hello holiday! ⚓ 40 mins to Auckland, ✈ 1 hr to Wellington

Wellington (p127) NZ's capital is raffish, arty and soulful. Hit the craft-beer bars, eat on Cuba St and plan your next novel.

FROM LEFT 1. IVO ANTONIE DE ROOIJ/SHUTTERSTOCK ©; 3. NATALIA RAMIREZ ROMAN/SHUTTERSTOCK ©; DESIGNED BY BURREN AND KEEN

Southern Scenic

Feeling like less city, more pretty? Take a five-day jaunt across NZ's deep south for an eyeful of unforgettable mountain and seaside scenery. This is NZ at its most scenic – snowy peaks, dazzling coastline and bottomless fiords. And the wildlife down here is rampant!

Milford Sound (p238)
Rain, shine or misty drizzle, Milford Sound is an unbelievably atmospheric place to explore.

Queenstown (p205)
Scenic mountain biking or fine food and wine...maybe both.
🚗 3¾ hrs to Milford Sound

Otago Peninsula (p253)
Way down south, the wildlife-rich Otago Peninsula is pretty as a picture.
🚗 4 hrs to Queenstown

FROM LEFT: SHASSELER/SHUTTERSTOCK ©; WESTEND61/GETTY IMAGES ©

10-Day Itinerary

Winter Wanderer

Yes, yes, we know – a whole bunch of you are here for one thing and one thing only: snow! But there's plenty more to see and do on a 10-day tour around NZ's chilly southern zones.

The West Coast (p189)
Gargantuan Franz Josef Glacier and Fox Glacier are ice-age time-travellers. Take a helihike to assess their mass.

Christchurch (p171)
Spend a day or two finding your feet at upbeat bars and restaurants.
🚗 20 mins to Lyttelton

Lyttelton (p176)
Christchurch's harbour town is a soulful little enclave.
🚗 20 mins to Christchurch then ✈ 1 hr to Queenstown

Queenstown (p205)
Bungy? Jetboat? Skydive? As if there wasn't enough fun to be had skiing...
🚗 25 mins to Gibbston Valley

Gibbston Valley (p216)
Break from the snow to tour this nearby wine region.
🚗 4½ hrs to the West Coast

FROM LEFT: CHAMELEONSEYE/SHUTTERSTOCK ©, SIMON LASS/SHUTTERSTOCK ©, MATT MAKES PHOTOS/SHUTTERSTOCK ©

Two-Week Itinerary

North & South

From the top of the north to halfway down the south, here's a playlist of New Zealand's greatest hits. Tune in to vibrant city scenes, bewitching islands, volcanic hubbub, eye-popping mountain scenery, sublime wine and lonesome wilderness – all the things NZ does best (other than rugby).

Auckland (p35) Hike up One Tree Hill (Maungakiekie) before drinks on K Rd.
🚌 3¼ hrs to Bay of Islands

Bay of Islands (p65) Show-stopping island scenery and a window into NZ's bicultural history.
🚌 6 hrs to Rotorua

Rotorua (p83) Geysers! Bubbling mud! Sulphurous gas! Rotorua is unique; Māori cultural performances equally so.
🚌 2 hrs to Tongariro National Park

Tongariro National Park (p102) Truck through progressive Taupō to hike among otherworldly peaks.
🚌 2 hrs to Napier

Napier (p122) Under the East Coast sun, little Napier is all art-deco facades and chardonnay.
🚌 4 hrs to Wellington

Marlborough Wine Region (p154) Tour the Blenheim wineries and sip some superb sauvignon blanc.
🚌 4¼ hrs to Christchurch

Wellington (p127) The hilly, windy NZ capital oozes charm and character.
⛴ 3¾ hrs to Picton then 🚌 30 mins to Marlborough Wine Region

Christchurch (p171) Swinging further south, cruise into 'ChCh' to enjoy some southern hospitality in a city of rapid reinvention.

FROM LEFT: SORANG/SHUTTERSTOCK ©, TOM JASTRAM/SHUTTERSTOCK ©, NOLOMO/SHUTTERSTOCK ©

Plan Your Trip

Family Travel

New Zealand is a dream for family travel: kid-centric activities, family-friendly accommodation, a moderate climate and very little danger. Unadventurous palates can always be accommodated and food servers are clued up on dietary requirements. Base yourself in a sizeable town for amenities galore and excursions within a short drive.

Keeping Costs Down

Accommodation

Campgrounds, holiday parks and kid-friendly motels are all great options for bedding down the family on the cheap with large shared kitchens to cook in. Coastal campgrounds are often sited near beaches and/or offer other free outdoor activities. Motels sometimes include a kitchenette for self-catering.

Sightseeing

Most museums, galleries, entertainment parks, wildlife sanctuaries and similar attractions offer discounts to families – in the form of kids' concessions and/or family tickets that let the whole tribe in for less.

Eating

Most midrange restaurants and pubs will offer a kids' menu, with choices, portions and prices sensibly adapted to the needs of younger diners. When the weather's good, hit supermarkets and farmers markets to piece together a picnic to enjoy alfresco where kids don't need to sit still.

Transport

Urban transport networks all offer discounts to children and students, with infants usually travelling for free. When weather, terrain and your plans allow it, consider kitting the family out with rental bikes to take advantage of New Zealand's fantastic cycling infrastructure or the flat topography of cities like Christchurch.

HOBBITON MOVIE SET ©

Good to Know

Look out for the 🚼 icon for family-friendly suggestions throughout this guide.

Babies and toddlers Attitudes to public breast-feeding are pretty enlightened throughout New Zealand, while infant formula, nappies and other essentials are readily available in supermarkets, pharmacies and smaller groceries.

Dining out The golden rule is 'be considerate': kids are welcome in most eating establishments, but their behaviour is your responsibility, and fine-dining patrons will expect to enjoy an adults-only environment. Generally, licenced establishments such as pubs welcome well-behaved kids, but not after dinner time.

Prams and strollers New Zealand's cities are well-paved, well-lit and easy to negotiate for parents pushing prams and strollers.

Seat belts Everyone must wear seat belts while in moving vehicles, with appropriately-anchored chairs and capsules mandated by law for the very youngest.

★ Best for Kids

Te Papa (p130), Wellington

Hobbiton (p63), Matamata

West Coast Wildlife Centre (p195), Franz Josef Glacier

Canterbury Museum (p179), Christchurch

Auckland Zoo (p50), Auckland

Public transport Kids' discounts of different kinds exist for all mass transit systems in New Zealand. Infants travel free.

Hire vehicles If your kids are little, check that your car-hire company can supply the right-sized car seat for your child, and that the seat will be properly fitted. Some companies legally require you to fit car seats yourself. Consider hiring a campervan. These formidable beasts are everywhere in NZ, kitted out with beds, kitchens, and even toilets and TVs.

From left: Hiking toward Mt Cook (p197), South Island; Hobbiton, *The Lord of the Rings* filming location (p62)

AUCKLAND

City Centre
Newly energised with Britomart and Wynyard Quarter for dining, shopping and waterfront strolling.

Devenport
Well-preserved Victorian and Edwardian architecture and plenty of cafes, all just a short ferry ride from the city.

Motutapu Island

Oneroa Bay

WAIHEKE ISLAND

Huruhi Bay

Putiki Bay

Motukorea Channel

Motuihe Island

Waitematā Harbour

Ponsonby
Buzzing restaurants and bars and fashion in Auckland's hippest suburb.

AUCKLAND MUSEUM

Parnell
One of Auckland's oldest areas, with cafes, restaurants, fancy retailers, and outdoor saltwater pools.

Tamaki Strait

ONE TREE HILL

Mt Eden
Cool villagey feel nestled below Auckland's highest volcanic cone.

Manukau Harbour

Tasman Sea

Auckland International Airport

City Centre & Ponsonby Map (p48)
Mt Eden, Newmarket & One Tree Hill Map (p54)

0 5 km
0 2.5 miles

Auckland at a Glance...

Auckland's harbourfront bustles with restaurants overlooking yachts and ferries, framing the edge of the city's high-rise centre. Rolling out from the cityscape, historic and cosmopolitan inner suburbs, with weatherboard buildings reminiscent of San Francisco, hug hills studded with green volcanic cones. The world's largest Polynesian city has a strong Pacific Islander and Māori population, bringing a distinctive mix of arts, culture and languages.

The water is never far away: from the rugged west-coast surf beaches to the Hauraki Gulf with its myriad islands – one of the closest to the mainland, Waiheke Island, is home to secluded bays and world-class wineries.

Two Days in Auckland

Acquaint yourself with the city on a **walk** (p44) from Karangahape Rd (K Rd) to the Wynyard Quarter, stopping at the **Auckland Art Gallery** (p46). Catch a ferry to check out nautical **Devonport**, before ferrying back to the city for dinner. On day two, head up **One Tree Hill** (p43) then visit the **Auckland Museum** (p39). Drive along **Tamaki Drive** (p51) then spend the night bar-hopping, starting at **Freida Margolis** (p57).

Four Days in Auckland

On the third day, get out on the Hauraki Gulf. Catch the ferry to **Waiheke Island** (p42) and divide your time between the beaches and the wineries. For your final day, throw caution to the wind with a bungy jump off the **Auckland Bridge** (p50) or a **SkyJump** (p51) from the Sky Tower. Regroup for a night on the town at **Wynyard Pavilion** (p58).

Previous page:
GEORGECLERK/GETTY IMAGES ©

Opposite page:
FROM LEFT CLOCKWISE; JOSE ANTONIO MACIEL/GETTY IMAGES ©, ROBERT CHG/SHUTTERSTOCK ©, GR8/SHUTTERSTOCK ©, MASTAPIECE/ SHUTTERSTOCK ©, TI1993/GETTY IMAGES ©

Auckland Harbour Bridge (p50)

Arriving in Auckland

Auckland Airport New Zealand's main international gateway is 21km south of the city centre. Dedicated SkyBus services, pre-bookable shuttles, and taxis run into the city.

SkyCity Coach Terminal The terminus for InterCity bus services. Other companies arrive at 172 Quay St, opposite the Ferry Building.

Auckland Strand Station *Northern Explorer* trains depart from Wellington.

Where to Stay

Auckland's city centre has plenty of luxury hotels, with several international chains catering to wandering business bods (and those who like predictability). There's plenty of budget accommodation in the city centre, too, but it can be noisy and shabby – you'll find better hostels in the inner suburbs (p61). Historic Devonport is worth considering, if only for the fun ferry ride to/from the city!

ALARICO/SHUTTERSTOCK ©

Auckland Museum

One of Auckland's more distinctive buildings, the Auckland Museum sits proudly in Auckland Domain. Auckland is the world's biggest Polynesian city: it follows that the museum's Pacific Island displays are compelling viewing.

Great For...

☑ **Don't Miss**

The views across the harbour and central Auckland from the museum's entrance.

This imposing neoclassical temple (1929), capped with an impressive copper-and-glass dome (2007), dominates the Auckland Domain and is a prominent part of the Auckland skyline, especially when viewed from the harbour. More importantly, Auckland Museum is culturally prominent – it's the repository of the city's stories and heritage and occupies a special place in Aucklanders' hearts, minds and memories (just ask the colourful troupes of school kids as they shuffle through the front door).

The displays of Pacific Island and Māori artefacts on the museum's ground floor are essential viewing. Highlights include a 25m war canoe and an extant carved meeting house (remove your shoes before entering). There's also a fascinating display about Auckland's volcanic field, including an eruption simulation, and the upper

ℹ️ Need to Know

Map p48; 📞09-309 0443; www.auckland museum.com; Auckland Domain, Parnell; adult/child $25/10; 🕙10am-5pm

✕ Take a Break

A cool cafe, **Winona Forever** (p57), patiently awaits in nearby Parnell.

★ Top Tip

Check the museum website for concerts, shows and events, often featuring local musicians.

---

floors showcase military displays, fulfilling the building's dual role as a war memorial. Auckland's main Anzac commemorations take place at dawn on 25 April at the cenotaph in the museum's forecourt.

Admission & Tours

Admission packages incorporating a highlights tour and a Māori cultural performance cost from $45 to $55. Here's your chance to see twirling *poi* dances and a hair-raising *haka* (the Māori ceremonial war dance) and to meet and chat with the performers (the war stuff is all for show).

What's Nearby

Around 1.5km south of the museum, **Newmarket** is a buzzy retail district with some of Auckland's best fashion and designer shopping, especially around Teed and Nuffield Streets.

Karen Walker (Map p54; 📞09-522 4286; www.karenwalker.com; 6 Balm St, Newmarket; 🕙10am-6pm) is a world-renowned designer whose cool (pricey) threads have been worn by Madonna and Kirsten Dunst; **Zambesi** (Map p48; 📞09-308 0363; www. zambesi.co.nz; 287 Parnell Rd, Parnell; 🕙10am-6pm Mon-Fri, 11am-5pm Sat & Sun) is another iconic NZ label, much sought after by local and international celebs. For interesting art and design from a collective of 100 local artists, visit **Texan Art Schools** (Map p54; 📞09-529 1021; www.creativeandbrave.co.nz; 366 Broadway, Newmarket; 🕙9.30am-5.30pm Mon-Sat, 10am-5pm Sun).

Newmarket also offers good cafes and restaurants. At the **Teed St Larder** (Map p54; 📞09-524 8406; www.teedstreetlarder.co.nz; 7 Teed St, Newmarket; mains $14-27; 🕙7am-4pm Mon-Fri, from 8am Sat & Sun) it's hard to go past the delicious sandwiches and tarts.

MICHAEL SCHOLLUM/GETTY IMAGES ©

One Tree Hill

Auckland is a city of volcanoes, with ridges of lava flows forming thorough-fares and volcanic cones providing islands of green in the suburbs. And the most famous cone is One Tree Hill.

The volcanic cone of One Tree Hill was the isthmus' key *pā* (fortified village) and the greatest fortress in the country. A walk around the top proffers 360-degree views and the grave of John Logan Campbell, who gifted the land to the city in 1901 and requested that a memorial be built to the Māori people on the summit. Allow time to explore surrounding **Cornwall Park** with its mature trees and historic Acacia Cottage (1841).

The **Cornwall Park Information Centre** (Map p54; ☏09-630 8485; www.cornwallpark.co.nz; Huia Lodge, Michael Horton Dr; ☺10am-4pm) has fascinating interactive displays illustrating what the *pā* would have looked like when 5000 people lived here. Near the excellent **children's playground**, the **Stardome** (Map p54; ☏09-624 1246; www.stardome.org.nz; 670 Manukau Rd;

Great For...

☑ Don't Miss

Inspecting the stand of new native trees at the summit – which will be the 'one'?

One Tree Hill monument

PATRIKSTEDRAK/GETTY IMAGES ©

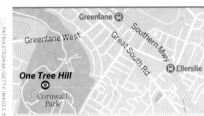

ℹ️ Need to Know

Maungakiekie; Map p54

✕ Take a Break

There aren't many places in which to eat or drink around here. Pack a picnic and enjoy the view.

★ Top Tip

The view from One Tree Hill (182m) is good, but Mt Eden's (p46) (196m) is even better.

After much consultation with local Māori and tree experts, a grove of six pohutukawa and three totara was planted on the summit in mid-2016. In an arboreal version of the *X Factor,* the weaker-performing trees will be eliminated, with only one tree left standing by 2026.

shows adult/child from $12/10; ⏱10am-5pm Mon, to 9.30pm Tue-Thu, to 11pm Fri-Sun) `FREE` offers regular stargazing and planetarium shows that aren't dependent on Auckland's fickle weather (usually 7pm and 8pm Wednesday to Sunday, with extra shows on weekends).

Where's the Tree?

Looking at One Tree Hill, your first thought will probably be 'Where's the bloody tree?' Good question. Up until 2000 a Monterey pine stood at the top of the hill. This was a replacement for a sacred totara tree that was chopped down by British settlers in 1852. Māori activists first attacked the foreign usurper in 1994, finishing the job in 2000. The stump of this last 'one tree' is near John Logan Campbell's grave.

No, It's Not a Joshua Tree

Auckland's most beloved landmark achieved international recognition in 1987 when U2 released the song 'One Tree Hill' on their acclaimed *The Joshua Tree* album. It was only released as a single in NZ, where it went to number one for six weeks.

Getting There

To get to One Tree Hill from the city take a train to Greenlane and walk 1km along Green Lane West. By car, take the Greenlane exit off the Southern Motorway and turn right into Green Lane West.

TROY/ANA/GETTY IMAGES ©

Waiheke Island

World-class wineries, superb dining with sweeping ocean views and a few of the region's best beaches collude to make Waiheke Island a favourite weekender for city-weary Aucklanders.

On the island's landward side, emerald waters lap at rocky bays, while its ocean flank has excellent sandy beaches. And indeed, beaches are Waiheke's biggest drawcard...but wine is a close second. There are around 30 boutique wineries scattered about here. The island also boasts plenty of quirky galleries and craft stores, a lasting legacy of its hippyish past.

Great For...

☑ Don't Miss

The ferry ride is part of the experience, with memorable views of the gulf, the city and Waiheke.

Beaches

Waiheke's two best beaches are **Onetangi**, a long stretch of white sand at the centre of the island, and **Palm Beach**, a pretty little horseshoe bay between **Oneroa** and Onetangi. Both have nudist sections; head west just past some rocks in both cases. Oneroa and neighbouring **Little Oneroa** are also excellent, but you'll be sharing the waters

ⓘ Need to Know

Waiheke is 40 minutes by ferry from downtown Auckland. Online, see www.tourismwaiheke.co.nz, www.waiheke.co.nz and www.aucklandnz.com.

✕ Take a Break

Dragonfired (☎021 922 289; www.dragonfired.co.nz; Little Oneroa Beach; mains $12-16; �10am-8pm daily Nov-Mar, 11am-7pm Fri-Sun Apr-Oct; ☑) is a pizza caravan by a beach – perfectly Waiheke!

★ Top Tip

Pick up the *Waiheke Art Map*, listing galleries and craft stores, from the **Tourist Information Booth** (Matiatia Wharf; �9am-4pm).

---

with moored yachts in summer. Reached by an unsealed road through farmland, **Man O' War Bay** is a compact sheltered beach that's excellent for swimming.

Vineyard Restaurants

Many Waiheke wineries have tasting rooms, swanky restaurants and breathtaking views. Some of the best:

Cable Bay (☎09-372 5889; www.cablebay.co.nz; 12 Nick Johnstone Dr; meze $12-22, pizza $26-29, shared plates $22-36; ☑11am-late; ☎) Impressive mod architecture and beautiful views.

Shed at Te Motu (☎09-372 6884; www.temotu.co.nz/the-shed; 76 Onetangi Rd; shared plates $20-26; ☑11am-5pm daily, 6pm-late Fri & Sat Nov-Apr, reduced hours May-Oct; ☑) Rustic courtyard and shared plates.

Tantalus Estate (☎09-372 2625; www.tantalus.co.nz; 70-72 Onetangi Rd; mains $38-44; ☑11am-5pm) ✐ Waiheke's newest vineyard.

Walking

The island's beautiful coastal walks (ranging from one to three hours) include the 3km **Cross Island Walkway** (from Onetangi to Rocky Bay). Other tracks traverse **Whakanewha Regional Park**, a haven for rare coastal birds and geckos, and the Royal Forest & Bird Protection Society's three reserves: **Onetangi** (Waiheke Rd), **Te Haahi-Goodwin** (Orapiu Rd) and **Atawhai Whenua** (Ocean View Rd).

Te Ara Hura is a 100km network of connected trails taking in coastline, forests, vineyard stops and historic places. Route markers indicate the way ahead on the island. See www.aucklandcouncil.govt.nz for more info; search for 'Waiheke Island Walkways'.

City Centre Ramble

This walk aims to show you some hidden nooks and architectural treats in Auckland's somewhat scrappy city centre – there's more here than meets the eye!

Start St Kevins Arcade, Karangahape Rd
Distance 4.5km
Duration Three hours

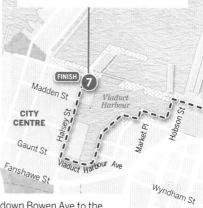

7 Finish your ramble at the vamped-up **Wynyard Quarter**, via Viaduct Harbour's buzzy bars and cafes.

FINISH **7**

Madden St

Viaduct Harbour

CITY CENTRE

Halsey St

Gaunt St

Viaduct Harbour Ave

Market Pl

Hobson St

Fanshawe St

Wyndham St

Albert St

5 Head down Bowen Ave to the High St shops, then hang left into **Vulcan Lane**, lined with historic pubs.

2 Heading down Queen St, pass **Auckland Town Hall** and **Aotea Sq**, the city's civic heart.

Aotea Sq

2

Queen St

Queen St

Scotia Pl

START **1**

Karangahape Rd

1 Explore the shops in **St Kevins Arcade**, then take the stairs down to Myers Park.

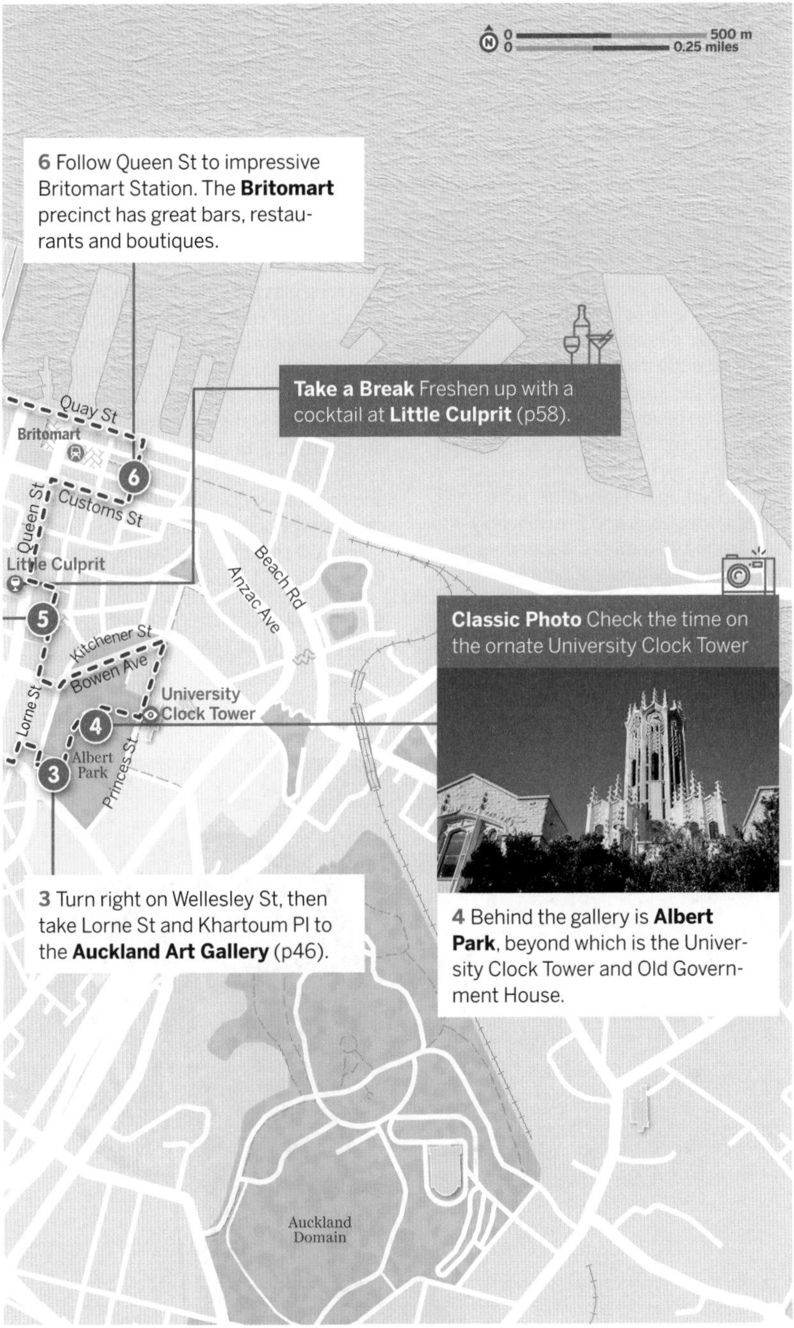

N
0 ____ 500 m
0 ____ 0.25 miles

6 Follow Queen St to impressive Britomart Station. The **Britomart** precinct has great bars, restaurants and boutiques.

Quay St

Britomart

Customs St

Queen St

6

Little Culprit

5

Kitchener St

Bowen Ave

Lorne St

4

University Clock Tower

Princes St

3

Albert Park

Beach Rd

Anzac Ave

Take a Break Freshen up with a cocktail at **Little Culprit** (p58).

Classic Photo Check the time on the ornate University Clock Tower

3 Turn right on Wellesley St, then take Lorne St and Khartoum Pl to the **Auckland Art Gallery** (p46).

4 Behind the gallery is **Albert Park**, beyond which is the University Clock Tower and Old Government House.

Auckland Domain

4 CHAMELEONSEYE/GETTY IMAGES ©

◎ SIGHTS

Mt Eden
Volcano

(Maungawhau; Map p54; 250 Mt Eden Rd) From
the top of Auckland's highest volcanic
cone (196m), the entire isthmus and both
harbours are laid bare. The symmetrical
crater (50m deep) is known as Te Ipu Kai
a Mataaho (the Food Bowl of Mataaho, the
god of things hidden in the ground) and is
considered *tapu* (sacred). Do not enter it,
but feel free to explore the remainder of the
mountain. The remains of *pā* terraces and
food-storage pits are clearly visible.

Until recently it was possible to drive
right up to the summit, but concerns
over erosion have led to vehicle access
being restricted to travellers with limited
mobility.

Paths lead up the mountain from six
different directions and the walk only
takes around 15 minutes, depending on
your fitness. A network of boardwalks was
established in mid-2020 to help protect
the historical and cultural significance
of the site. Catching bus 27 from Britomart to stop 1870 near Tahaki Reserve is
recommended.

Auckland Art Gallery
Gallery

(Toi o Tāmaki; Map p48; ☑09-379 1349; www.
aucklandartgallery.com; cnr Kitchener & Wellesley
Sts; adult/student/child $20/17/free; ☺10am-
5pm) Auckland's premier art repository has
a striking glass-and-wood atrium grafted
onto its 1887 French chateau frame. It
showcases the best of NZ art, along with
important works by Pieter Bruegel the
Younger, Guido Reni, Picasso, Cézanne,
Gauguin and Matisse. Highlights include
the intimate 19th-century portraits of tat-
tooed Māori subjects by Charles Goldie,
and the starkly dramatic text-scrawled
canvases of Colin McCahon.

Free 60-minute tours depart from the
foyer daily at 11.30am and 1.30pm.

Sky Tower
Tower

(Map p48; ☑09-363 6000; www.skycityauck
land.co.nz; cnr Federal & Victoria Sts; adult/

*Spectacular lighting renders
it space age at night*

Sky Tower

MATIASCAUSA/SHUTTERSTOCK © MOLLER ARCHITECTS

child $32/13; ⊙8.30am-10.30pm Sun-Thu, to
11.30pm Fri & Sat Nov-Apr, 9am-10pm May-Oct)
The impossible-to-miss Sky Tower looks
like a giant hypodermic giving a fix to the
heavens. Spectacular lighting renders it
space age at night and the colours change
for special events. At 328m it is the southern hemisphere's tallest structure. A lift
takes you up to the observation decks in
40 stomach-lurching seconds; look down
through the glass floor panels if you're after
an extra kick. Consider visiting at sunset
and having a drink in the Sky Lounge Cafe
& Bar.

Auckland Domain   Park
(Map p48; Domain Dr, Parnell; ⊙24hr) Covering about 80 hectares, this green swath
contains the Auckland Museum (p107),
sports fields, interesting sculpture,
formal gardens, wild corners and the
Wintergarden (Map p48; Wintergarden Rd,
Parnell; ⊙9am-5.30pm Mon-Sat, to 7.30pm Sun
Nov-Mar, 9am-4.30pm Apr-Oct) **FREE**, with its
fernery, tropical house, cool house, cute
cat statue, coffee kiosk and neighbouring
cafe. The mound in the centre of the park
is all that remains of Pukekaroa, one of
Auckland's volcanoes. At its humble peak,
a totara tree surrounded by a palisade
honours the first Māori king.

Wallace Arts Centre   Gallery
(⊉09-639 2010; www.wallaceartstrust.org.nz;
Pah Homestead, 72 Hillsborough Rd, Hillsborough;
⊙10am-3pm Tue-Fri, 8am-5pm Sat & Sun) **FREE**
Housed in a gorgeous 1879 mansion with
views to One Tree Hill (p111) and the Manukau Harbour, this arts centre is endowed
with contemporary NZ art from an extensive private collection, which is changed
every four to six weeks. Have lunch on the
veranda at the excellent **Homestead Cafe**
and wander among the magnificent trees
in the surrounding park. The art is also very
accessible, ranging from a life-size skeletal
rugby ruck to a vibrant Ziggy Stardust
painted on glass.

Bus 305 or 295 (Lynfield) departs every
15 minutes from Queen St – outside the

Civic Theatre – and heads to Hillsborough
Rd ($5.50, 40 minutes).

New Zealand
Maritime Museum   Museum
(Map p48; ⊉09-373 0800; www.maritime
museum.co.nz; 149-159 Quay St, Viaduct Harbour;
adult/child $20/10, incl harbour cruise $53/27;
⊙10am-5pm, free tours 10.30am & 1pm Mon-
Fri) This museum traces NZ's seafaring
history, from Māori voyaging canoes to
the America's Cup. Recreations include a
tilting 19th-century steerage-class cabin
and a 1950s beach store and bach (holiday
home). 'Blue Water Black Magic' is a tribute
to Sir Peter Blake, the Whitbread-Round-
the-World and America's Cup–winning
yachtsman who was murdered in 2001 on
an environmental monitoring trip in the
Amazon. Packages incorporating harbour
cruises on heritage boats, including a
ketch-rigged scow and a vintage motor
launch, are also available.

Civic Theatre   Theatre
(Map p48; ⊉09-309 2677; www.aucklandlive.
co.nz/venue/the-civic; cnr Queen & Wellesley
Sts) The 'mighty Civic' (1929) is one of only
seven 'atmospheric theatres' remaining in
the world and a fine survivor from cinema's
Golden Age. The auditorium has lavish
Moorish decoration and a starlit southern-
hemisphere night sky in the ceiling, complete with cloud projections and shooting
stars. It's mainly used for touring musicals,
international concerts and film-festival
screenings.

Even if nothing is scheduled, try and
sneak a peek at the foyer, an Indian
indulgence with elephants and monkeys
hanging from every conceivable fixture.
Buddhas were planned to decorate the
street frontage but were considered too
risqué at the time – neoclassical naked
boys were chosen instead!

Kelly Tarlton's
Sea Life Aquarium   Aquarium
(⊉09-531 5065; www.kellytarltons.co.nz;
23 Tamaki Dr, Orakei; adult/child $39/27;
⊙9.30am-5pm) ✐ In this topsy-turvy

City Centre & Ponsonby

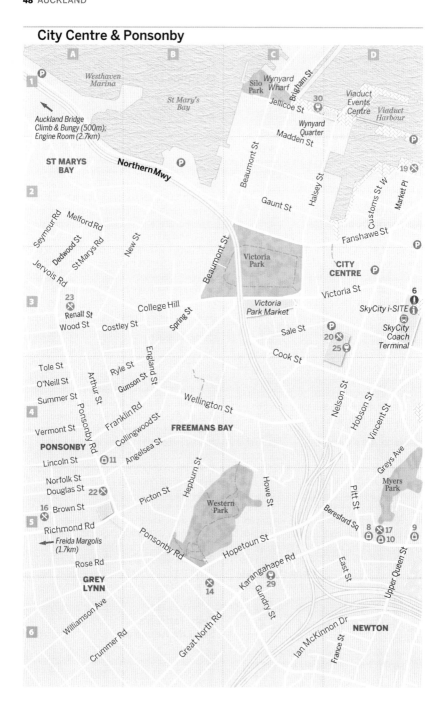

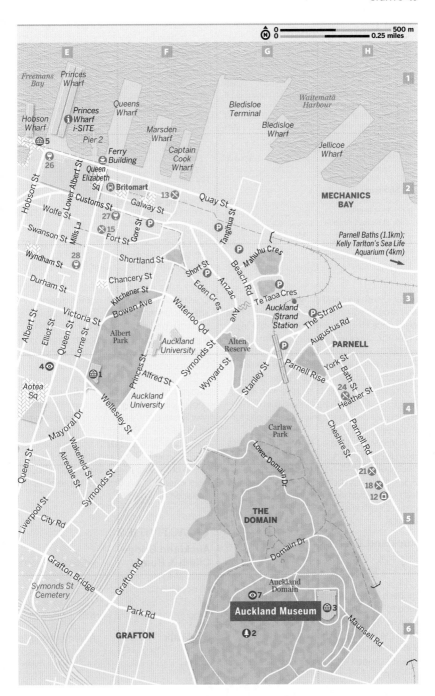

City Centre & Ponsonby

Sights

1 Auckland Art Gallery ... E4
2 Auckland Domain ... G6
3 Auckland Museum ... H6
4 Civic Theatre ... E4
5 New Zealand Maritime Museum ... E2
6 Sky Tower ... D3
7 Wintergarden ... G6

Activities, Courses & Tours

SkyJump ... (see 6)
SkyWalk ... (see 6)

Shopping

8 Crushes ... D5
9 Real Groovy ... D5
10 St Kevin's Arcade ... D5
11 Zambesi ... A4
12 Zambesi ... H5

Eating

13 Amano ... F2
14 Azabu ... B6
15 Cassia ... E2
16 Cocoro ... A5
17 Gemmayze St ... D5
18 Gerome ... H5
19 Hello Beasty ... D2
20 Odette's ... D3
21 Pasture ... H5
22 Saan ... A5
23 Sidart ... A3
24 Winona Forever ... H4

Drinking & Nightlife

25 Brothers Beer ... D3
26 Dr Rudi's ... E2
27 La Fuente ... E2
28 Little Culprit ... E3
29 Madame George ... C5
30 Wynyard Pavilion ... C1

aquarium sharks and stingrays swim over and around you in transparent tunnels that were once stormwater tanks. You can also enter the tanks in a shark cage with a snorkel ($89). Other attractions include the Penguin Passport tour (10.30am Tuesday, Thursday and Saturday; $179 per person) where visitors can get up close with Antarctic penguins. For all tickets, there are significant discounts online, especially for midweek visits.

A free shark-shaped shuttle bus departs from the Britomart Transport Centre hourly on the half-hour from 9.30am to 3.30pm. Check the website for the exact location, as construction was taking place around central Auckland at the time of writing.

Auckland Zoo — Zoo

(Map p54; 09-360 3805; www.aucklandzoo.co.nz; Motions Rd; adult/child $24/13; 9.30am-5pm, last entry 4.15pm) At this modern, spacious zoo, the big foreigners tend to steal the attention from the timid natives, but if you can wrestle the kids away from the tigers and orangutans, there's a well-presented NZ section. Called Te Wao Nui, it's divided into six ecological zones: Coast (seals, penguins), Islands (mainly lizards, including NZ's pint-sized dinosaur, the tuatara), Wetlands (ducks, herons, eels), Night (kiwi, naturally, along with frogs, native owls and weta), Forest (birds) and High Country (cheekier birds and lizards).

Check the website for the times of zookeepers' talks, Behind the Scenes experiences and ongoing progress of the zoo's new South East Asia display (scheduled to open in late 2020). Catch the number 18 bus (adult/child $5.50/3) from bus stop 1362 (corner Victoria and Albert Sts) in the city to bus stop 8124 on Great North Rd, from where it's a 700m walk to the zoo's entrance.

ACTIVITIES

Auckland Bridge Climb & Bungy — Adventure Sports

(09-360 7748; www.bungy.co.nz; 105 Curran St, Westhaven; adult/child climb $130/90, bungy $165/135; 9am-3.30pm) Climb up or jump off the Auckland Harbour Bridge.

SkyWalk — Adventure Sports

(Map p48; 0800 759 925; www.skywalk.co.nz; Sky Tower, cnr Federal & Victoria Sts; adult/child

$150/120; ⊘10am-4.30pm) The SkyWalk involves circling the 192m-high, 1.2m-wide outside halo of the Sky Tower (p46) without rails or a balcony. Don't worry, it's not completely crazy – there is a safety harness.

SkyJump
Adventure Sports

(Map p48; ✆0800 759 586; www.skyjump.co.nz; Sky Tower, cnr Federal & Victoria Sts; adult/child $225/175; ⊘10am-5.15pm) This thrilling 11-second, 85km/h base wire leap from the observation deck of the Sky Tower (p46) is more like a parachute jump than a bungy. Combine it with the SkyWalk (p50) in the Look & Leap package ($290).

Silo Cinema & Markets
Film

(www.silopark.co.nz; Silo Park, Wynyard Quarter; ⊙Dec-Easter) Classic movies screened outdoors on Friday nights, and markets with food trucks, DJs and craft stalls on Friday nights and Saturday and Sunday afternoons.

Coast to Coast Walkway
Walking

(www.aucklandcity.govt.nz) Heading right across the country from the Tasman to the Pacific (which is actually only 16km), this walk encompasses One Tree Hill (p111), Mt Eden (p46), the Domain (p47) and the university, keeping mainly to reserves rather than city streets.

Do it in either direction: starting from the Viaduct Basin and heading south, it's marked by yellow markers and milestones; heading north from Onehunga there are blue markers. Our recommendation? Catch the train to Onehunga and finish up at the Viaduct's bars. From Onehunga station, take Onehunga Mall up to Princes St, turn left and pick up the track at the inauspicious park by the motorway.

Parnell Baths
Swimming

(✆09-373 3561; www.parnellbaths.co.nz; Judges Bay Rd, Parnell; adult/child $6.40/free; ⊘6am-8pm Mon-Fri, 8am-8pm Sat & Sun Nov-Easter) Outdoor saltwater pools with an awesome 1950s mural.

 Tamaki Drive

This scenic, pohutukawa-lined road heads east from the city, hugging the waterfront. In summer it's a jogging/cycling/rollerblading blur. A succession of child-friendly, peaceful swimming beaches starts at **Ohaku Bay**. Around the headland is **Mission Bay**, a popular beach with an electric-lit art-deco fountain, historic mission house, restaurants and bars. Safe swimming beaches **Kohimarama** and **St Heliers** follow.

Further east along Cliff Rd, the **Achilles Point Lookout** (Cliff Rd, St Heliers) offers panoramic views and Māori carvings. At its base is **Ladies Bay** (or is it Lady's Bay?), popular with nudists (ie clothing is optional). You've been warned.

Buses 767 and 769 from behind Britomart station follow this route, while buses 745 to 757 go as far as Mission Bay.

GRACETHANG2/SHUTTERSTOCK ©

TOURS

Tāmaki Hikoi
Cultural

(✆021 146 9593; www.tamakihikoi.co.nz; 1/3hr $55/99) Guides from the Ngāti Whatua *iwi* (tribe) lead various Māori cultural tours, including walking and interpretation of sites such as Mt Eden (p46) and the Auckland Domain (p47).

Toru Tours
Bus

(✆027 457 0011; www.torutours.com; per person $89) The three-hour Express Tour

 Devonport Detour

With well-preserved Victorian and Edwardian buildings and loads of cafes, Devonport is an extremely pleasant place to visit and only a short ferry trip from the city. There are also two volcanic cones to climb and easy access to the first of the North Shore's beaches.

Ferries to Devonport (adult/child return $15/7.50, 12 minutes) depart from the Ferry Building at least every 30 minutes from 6.15am to 11.30pm (until 1am Fridays and Saturdays), and from 7.15am to 10pm on Sundays and public holidays. Some Waiheke Island and Rangitoto ferries also stop here.

CHAMELEONSEYE/SHUTTERSTOCK ©

will depart with just one booking – ideal for solo travellers.

Big Foody Food Tour Tours
(☏021 481 177, 0800 366 386; www.thebig foody.com; per person $85-185) Small-group city tours, including visits to markets and artisan producers, and lots of tastings. Also on offer are hop-fuelled explorations of Auckland's burgeoning craft-beer scene and behind-the-scenes tours of **Eden Park** (Map p54; ☏09-815 5551; www.edenpark.co.nz; Reimers Ave, Mt Eden), home of rugby and cricket in Auckland.

Brewbus Beer
(☏027 583 2484; www.brewbus.co.nz; per person $80-220) Operates craft beer-focused tours taking in microbreweries and bars in

Auckland, Waikato, Tauranga, the Bay of Plenty and Wānaka.

🛍 SHOPPING

Real Groovy Music
(Map p48; ☏09-302 3940; www.realgroovy. co.nz; 520 Queen St; ⊗9am-7pm) Masses of new, secondhand and rare releases in vinyl and CD format, as well as concert tickets, giant posters, DVDs, books, magazines and clothes.

St Kevin's Arcade Shopping Centre
(Map p48; www.stkevinsarcade.co.nz; 183 Karangahape Rd) Built in 1924, this historic, renovated shopping arcade has interesting stores selling vintage clothing and organic and sustainable goods. The arcade also has excellent cafes and restaurants.

Royal Jewellery Studio Jewellery
(Map p54; ☏09-846 0200; www.royaljewellery studio.com; 486 New North Rd, Kingsland; ⊗10am-4pm Tue-Sun) Work by local artisans, including beautiful Māori designs and authentic *pounamu* (greenstone) jewellery.

Huffer Clothing
(Map p54; www.huffer.co.nz; 309 Broadway, Westfield Newmarket; ⊗9am-7pm Mon-Wed, Fri & Sat, to 9pm Thu, 10am-7pm Sun) Stylish technical apparel and streetwear from a hip NZ company with its roots in snowboarding and skateboarding.

Zambesi Clothing
(Map p48; ☏09-360 7391; www.zambesi.co.nz; 169 Ponsonby Rd, Ponsonby; ⊗10am-6pm Mon-Fri, 11am-5pm Sat & Sun) Designed by Liz and Neville Findlay, the iconic Zambesi label offers sought-after NZ clothing coveted by both locals and internationals.

Crushes Arts & Crafts
(Map p48; ☏09-940 5065; www.crushes.co.nz; 225 Karangahape Rd; ⊗10am-6pm Mon-Fri, to 5pm Sat, 11am-5pm Sun) Sells an excellent selection of arts, crafts, foodstuffs and homewares from local NZ designers. Also an interesting array of vintage clothing.

⊗ EATING

Henderson Night Market
Market $

(www.aucklandnightmarket.co.nz; Waitakere Mega Centre, under Kmart; ⊗5.30-11pm Thu) Of Auckland's bustling night markets, held in a different suburban car park each night of the week, the Henderson market is the most convenient for travellers to reach. Expect dozens of stalls serving food from all over the world, from Argentina and Samoa to Hungary and Turkey. Catch a western-line train from Britomart to Henderson and walk 650m to underneath the Kmart department store.

Nanam
Filipino $$

(☑09-488 9976; www.nanam.co.nz; 178 Hurst-mere Rd, Takapuna; tapas $11, mains $26-33; ⊗5-10pm Tue-Wed, 11.30am-10pm Thu-Sat, 5-9pm Sun) Modern Filipino food is the star at Nanam in the North Shore suburb of Takapuna. Dine on innovative updates of traditional Filipino food that made UK chef Marco Pierre White a big fan. Especially good is the *longganisa* sausage combining

Wagyu beef and lemongrass and the lamb *adobo* croquettes. Menu options include tapas style, main dishes and set sharing menus.

Bus 82 (30 to 35 minutes) from the Civic Theatre in central Auckland will drop you on Hurstmere Rd right outside the restaurant.

Engine Room
Modern NZ $$$

(☑09-480 9502; www.engineroom.net.nz; 115 Queen St, Northcote; mains $36-43; ⊗noon-3pm Fri, 5.30-11pm Tue-Sat) One of Auckland's best restaurants, this informal eatery serves up lighter-than-air goats'-cheese soufflés, inventive mains and oh-my-God choco-late truffles. It's worth booking ahead and catching the ferry to Northcote Point; the restaurant is a further 1km Uber or walk away.

Amano
Italian $$

(Map p48; ☑09-394 1416; www.amano.nz; 66-68 Tyler St; mains $22-35; ⊗restaurant 7am-late,

> *Expect dozens of stalls serving food from all over the world*

St Kevin's Arcade

CHAMELEONSEYE/SHUTTERSTOCK ©

Mt Eden, Newmarket & One Tree Hill

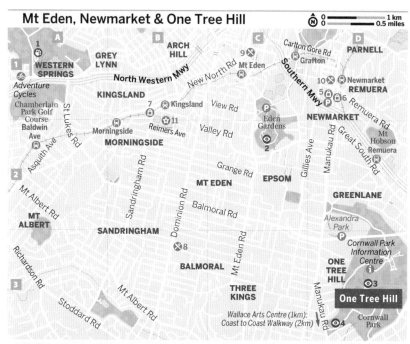

Mt Eden, Newmarket & One Tree Hill

bakery 6.30am-6pm Mon-Sat, to 4pm Sun) 🥐
Rustic Italian influences underpin this
bistro-bakery in a repurposed warehouse
in Auckland's Britomart precinct, but
there's real culinary savvy evident in
the open kitchen. Many dishes harness
seasonal produce and ingredients from
the owners' farm in West Auckland, and
Amano effortlessly transitions from a
buzzy caffeine-fuelled daytime cafe to a
sophisticated evening bistro featuring NZ
wines and craft beers.

The attached bakery has superb sourdough and wood-fired ciabatta sandwiches.
Order an Italian meatball sandwich, grab a
takeaway espresso and adjourn to a comfy
beanbag in nearby Takutai Sq.

Saan Thai $$

(Map p48; ☏ 09-320 4237; www.saan.co.nz;
160 Ponsonby Rd, Ponsonby; dishes $12-38;
⊙5pm-late Sat-Thu, noon-3pm & 5pm-late Fri)
Hot in both senses of the word, this super-
fashionable restaurant focuses on the fiery
cuisine of the Isaan and Lanna regions of

northern Thailand. The menu is conveniently sorted from least to most spicy and split into smaller and larger dishes for sharing. Be sure to order the soft-shell crab.

Odette's
Modern NZ $$

(Map p48; ☑09-309 0304; www.odettes.co.nz; Shed 5, City Works Depot, 90 Wellesley St; dishes $19-40; ☺8am-3pm Sun & Mon, 7am-11pm Tue-Sat) Nothing about Odette's is run of the mill. Not the bubbly light fixtures or the quirky photography, and certainly not the menu. How about lamb meatballs with saffron mustard for brunch? Or wild mushrooms served with a truffle pancake and cashew cream? In the evening the more cafe-ish items are replaced with dishes for sharing. It gets hectic on weekends.

Gemmayze St
Lebanese $$

(Map p48; ☑09-600 1545; www.gemmayze street.co.nz; St Kevin's Arcade, 15/183 Karangahape Rd; meze & mains $10-35; ☺5.30-10pm Thu-Sat; ✐) Located amid the restored heritage architecture of St Kevin's Arcade, Gemmayze St presents a stylish update on Lebanese cuisine. Mint, orange blossom and rosewater cocktails are prepared at the beaten-copper bar, while shared tables encourage lots of sociable dining on meze and expertly grilled meats. The optional 'Jeeb' menu (per person $65) is a brilliant choice for a leisurely feast.

Azabu
Japanese $$

(Map p48; ☑09-320 5292; www.azabuponsonby. co.nz; 26 Ponsonby Rd, Grey Lynn; mains & shared plates $16-39; ☺noon-late Wed-Sun, from 5pm Mon & Tue) Nikkei cuisine, an exciting blend of Japanese and Peruvian influences, is the focus at Azabu. Amid a dramatic interior enlivened by striking images of Tokyo, standout dishes include the tuna sashimi tostada, Japanese tacos with wasabi avocado, and king prawns with a jalapeño and ponzu dressing. Arrive early and enjoy a basil- and chilli-infused cachaca cocktail at Azabu's Roji bar.

Hello Beasty
Asian $$

(Map p48; ☑021 554 496; https://hellobeasty. nz; 95-97 Customs St W, Viaduct Harbour; shared plates $12-38; ☺11am-11pm; ✐) Japanese, Korean and Chinese flavours are all filtered through a fun contemporary vibe near Auckland's Viaduct Harbour. Secure a spot with ocean views, and fill your table with shared plates, including steamed bao buns, smoky Japanese-style *tsukune* sausage and barbecued eggplant. The concise drinks list includes sake cocktails and spritzes, and NZ lamb and seafood is regularly featured.

Gerome
Greek $$

(Map p48; ☑09-373 3883; www.gerome.nz; 269 Parnell Rd, Parnell; shared plates $14-34; ☺11.30am-late) Greek cuisine is rare in Auckland, but Gerome's modern interpretation of traditional Hellenic flavours make it one of Auckland's best restaurants. Highlights include the pork and lamb *manti* (dumplings) with fermented chilli, and the superb slow-roasted lamb *kleftiko* with watermelon jelly and pine nuts. On a warm summer's afternoon or evening, sit in the open-air pavilion out front.

Cocoro
Japanese $$$

(Map p48; ☑09-360 0927; www.cocoro.co.nz; 56a Brown St, Ponsonby; dishes $22-49, degustation menus $150-240; ☺noon-2pm & 5.30-10pm Tue-Sat) Japanese elegance infuses everything at this excellent restaurant, from the soft lighting and chic decor to the delicate flavours of the artistically arranged food. At lunchtime it offers an affordable *donburi* rice bowl ($24 to $29) and a multiplate option ($45), while in the evening multicourse degustation menus showcase the chefs' skills.

French Cafe
French $$$

(Map p54; ☑09-377 1911; www.sidatthe frenchcafe.co.nz; 210 Symonds St, Newton; mains $36-48, 5-/7-course tasting menus $140/180; ☺noon-3pm Fri, 6pm-late Tue-Sat) ✐ The French Cafe has been rated one of Auckland's top restaurants for more than 30 years. Now helmed by one of the city's

From left: Amano (p53); Winona Forever; Wynyard Pavilion (p58)

finest chefs, Sid Sahrawat, there's a subtle and seamless blending of French, Asian and Pacific cuisine. Foraged ingredients regularly feature, as do excellent vegetarian à-la-carte and tasting-menu options.

Pasture
Modern NZ $$$

(Map p48; ☑09-300 5077; www.pastureakl.com; 3/235 Parnell Rd, Parnell; menu per person $230; ⊙5.45pm-late Wed-Sun; 🖊) 🌮 Pasture is unlike any other dining experience in the city. You'll need to book a few months ahead – the compact space has just two seatings per night and room for only six diners – to enjoy chef Verner's intensely seasonal multicourse menu harnessing foraging, fermentation and wood-fired cooking. Look forward to an eclectic soundtrack, also of the chef's choosing.

Sidart
Modern NZ $$$

(Map p48; ☑09-360 2122; www.sidart. co.nz; Three Lamps Plaza, 283 Ponsonby Rd, Ponsonby; mains $32-38, 5-/7-course tasting menus $120/179; ⊙6pm-late Tue-Sun, noon-3pm Fri) No one in Auckland produces creative degustations quite like Sid Sahrawat. It's food as both art and science but, more importantly, food to fire up the taste buds, delight the brain, satisfy the stomach and put a smile on the face. The restaurant is a little hard to find, tucked away at the rear of what was once the Alhambra cinema.

Expect high-end and innovative combinations of European, Asian and Indian flavours. The Chef's Table dinner experience (per person $195) is a personalised insight into some of NZ's finest dining.

Cassia
Indian $$$

(Map p48; ☑09-379 9702; www.cassiares taurant.co.nz; 5 Fort Lane; mains $30-39; ⊙noon-3pm Wed-Fri, 5.30pm-late Tue-Sat) Occupying a moodily lit basement, Cassia serves modern Indian food with punch and panache. Start with a *pani puri,* a bite-sized crispy shell bursting with flavour, before devouring a decadently rich curry. The Delhi duck is excellent, as is the Goan-style snapper. Artisan gins and NZ craft beer are other highlights. Cassia is often judged Auckland's best restaurant.

Cazador
International $$$

(Map p54; ☑09-620 8730; www.cazador.co.nz; 854 Dominion Rd, Balmoral; tapas $7-10, mains

$36; ⊗5-10pm Wed-Sat) ✐ The Persian heritage of the Lolaiy family combines with game meat and foraged ingredients at Cazador. Decor such as stuffed animal heads is largely unchanged since the 1980s, but the food is delicious and includes housemade charcuterie and interesting proteins like venison and wild hare. And don't worry, it's not heavy and stodgy, but rather light and delivered with an innovative touch.

Winona Forever
Cafe $$

(Map p48; ☑09-974 2796; www.winonaforever. co.nz; 100 Parnell Rd, Parnell; mains $20-26; ⊗7am-4pm Mon-Fri, 8am-4pm Sat & Sun) Some of Auckland's best counter food – including stonking cream doughnuts – partners with innovative cafe culture at this always-busy eatery near good shopping and art galleries along Parnell Rd. Locals crowd in with travellers for coffee, craft beer and wine, and one of the cafe's signature dishes: the tempura soft-shell-crab omelette.

Alluding to actor Winona Ryder, the cafe's name is both one of Johnny Depp's

tattoos – now amended to 'Wino Forever' apparently – and a Vancouver indie-rock band.

🍷 DRINKING & NIGHTLIFE

Freida Margolis
Bar

(☑09-378 6625; www.facebook.com/freida margolis; 440 Richmond Rd, Grey Lynn; ⊗4-11pm Sun-Wed, to 2am Thu-Sat) Formerly a butcher's – look for the Westlynn Organic Meats sign – this corner location is now a great little neighbourhood bar with a backstreets Bogotá ambience. Loyal locals sit outside with their well-behaved dogs, supping on sangria, wine and craft beer, and enjoying eclectic sounds from the owner's big vinyl collection.

La Fuente
Cocktail Bar

(Map p48; ☑09-303 0238; www.lafuente.co.nz; 23 Customs St E, Snickel Lane; ⊗11am-late) Auckland's only bar specialising in the potent Mexican spirit *mezcal*, La Fuente (The Fountain) is also a fine spot to partner an excellent selection of wine and craft beer with Latin American–inspired snacks,

 **Volcanic Auckland**

Some cities think they're tough just by living in the shadow of a volcano. Auckland is built on 50 of them and, no, they're not all extinct. The last one to erupt was Rangitoto about 600 years ago and no one can predict when the next eruption will occur. Auckland's quite literally a hotspot – with a reservoir of magma 100km below, waiting to bubble to the surface. But relax: this has only happened 19 times in the last 20,000 years.

Some of Auckland's volcanoes are cones, some are filled with water and some have been completely quarried away. Moves are afoot to register the field as a World Heritage site and protect what remains.

Most of the surviving cones show evidence of terracing from when they formed a formidable series of Māori *pā* (fortified villages). The most interesting to explore are Mt Eden (p46), One Tree Hill (p111), North Head and Rangitoto, but Mt Victoria, Mt Wellington (Maungarei), Mt Albert (Owairaka), Mt Roskill (Puketāpapa), Lake Pupuke, Mt Māngere and Mt Hobson (Remuera) are all also worth a visit.

Mt Eden (p46)
KRITSANA LAROQUE/SHUTTERSTOCK ©

including ceviche and cheese-and-jalapeño croquettes. The knowledgeable bartenders will guide you through more than 20 different *mezcals* from the Mexican region of Oaxaca.

Little Culprit Cocktail Bar

(Map p48; www.littleculprit.co.nz; cnr Wyndham & Queen Sts; ⊘noon-1am Mon-Thu, to 2am Fri & Sat) Some of Auckland's most interesting cocktails feature at this stylish bar, and the owners' background in restaurants also shines through. Graze on a platter of cheese and charcuterie or indulge in a savoury waffle with duck-liver parfait. People-watch at pavement level or adjourn to the more intimate lower lounge downstairs. There's a good selection of natural wines too.

Wynyard Pavilion Bar

(Map p48; ☏09-303 1002; www.facebook.com/wynyardpavilion; 17 Jellicoe St, Wynyard Quarter; ⊘11am-11pm) Formerly a harbourside warehouse, Wynyard Pavilion's high-ceilinged heritage space is now one of the area's most versatile spots to eat, drink and take in maritime views. Oysters and kingfish feature from the raw bar; pizza ingredients include smoked salmon or spicy *njuda* sausage; and the watermelon and feta salad is perfect for warmer days. Try to snaffle a seat outside.

Dr Rudi's Microbrewery

(Map p48; ☏021 048 7946; cnr Quay & Hobson Sts, Viaduct Harbour; ⊘8am-4am Mon-Fri, from 11am Sat & Sun) Viaduct Harbour's best views – usually including a bevy of visiting superyachts – combine with Dr Rudi's very own craft beers and a menu featuring wood-fired pizza and excellent seafood and barbecue platters designed to defeat even the hungriest group. There are also a couple of tenpin bowling lanes to get active on.

Madame George Bar

(Map p48; ☏09-308 9039; www.madamegeorge.co.nz; 490 Karangahape Rd; ⊘5pm-late Tue-Sat) Two patron saints of cool – Elvis Presley and Marlon Brando – look down in this compact space. Shoot the breeze with the friendly bar staff over a craft beer or Auckland's best cocktails, or grab a shared table out front and watch the passing theatre of

Dr Rudi's microbrewery

K Rd. It's just like hanging at your hippest mate's place.

Madame George also offers a classy Peruvian-influenced food menu, either at the bar or in a cosy dining room out back.

Brothers Beer Craft Beer
(Map p48; ☑09-366 6100; www.brothersbeer. co.nz; City Works Depot, 90 Wellesley St; ⏱noon-10pm) This beer bar combines quirky decor with 18 taps crammed with Brothers' own brews and guest beers from NZ and further afield. Hundreds more bottled beers are chilling in the fridges, and bar food includes pizza. There are occasional movie and comedy nights, and beers are available to take away. The adjacent City Works Depot has other good eating options.

Galbraith's Alehouse Brewery
(Map p54; ☑09-379 3557; http://alehouse. co.nz; 2 Mt Eden Rd, Mt Eden; ⏱noon-11pm) Brewing real ales and lagers on-site, this cosy English-style pub in a grand heritage building offers bliss on tap. There are always more craft beers from around NZ and the world on the guest taps, and the

food's also very good. From April to September, Galbraith's Sunday roast is one of Auckland's best.

ℹ INFORMATION

Auckland International Airport i-SITE (☑09-365 9925; www.aucklandnz.com; International Arrivals Hall; ⏱6.30am-10pm)

Princes Wharf i-SITE (Map p48; ☑09-365 9914; www.aucklandnz.com; Princes Wharf; ⏱9am-5pm) Auckland's main official information centre, incorporating the **DOC Auckland Visitor Centre** (☑09-379 6476; www.doc.govt.nz)

SkyCity i-SITE (Map p48; ☑09-365 9918; www. aucklandnz.com; SkyCity Atrium, cnr Victoria & Federal Sts; ⏱9am-5pm)

ℹ GETTING THERE & AWAY

Auckland Airport (p305) is 21km south of the city centre and accessible by SkyBus, Super-Shuttles or taxis.

Coaches depart from 172 Quay St, opposite the **Ferry Building** (Map p48; 99 Quay St), except

Ferry Building

for InterCity and SKIP services, which depart from **SkyCity Coach Terminal** (Map p48; 102 Hobson St). Many southbound services also stop at the airport.

Northern Explorer (☑0800 872 467; www. greatjourneysofnz.co.nz) ⚑ trains leave from **Auckland Strand Station** (Map p48; Ngaoho Pl) several days a week. Standard fares range from $139 to $219.

ℹ GETTING AROUND

Bike Auckland Transport (p60) publishes free cycle maps. Bikes can be taken on most ferries and trains for free. **Adventure Cycles** (Map p54; ☑09-940 2453; www.adventure-auckland.

co.nz; 9 Premier Ave, Western Springs; per day $30-40, per week $120-160, per month $260-350; ⏱7.30am-7pm Thu-Mon) hires road, mountain and touring bikes.

Car Auckland's car hire agencies are clustered around Beach Rd and Stanley St close to the city centre, and at the airport.

Public Transport The **Auckland Transport** (☑09-366 6400; www.at.govt.nz) information service covers buses, trains and ferries, and has an excellent trip-planning feature. AT HOP smartcard (www.athop.co.nz) provides discounts of at least 20% on most buses, trains and ferries, but cards cost $10 (nonrefundable), so are only worthwhile if you're planning an extended stay in Auckland.

Where to Stay

Befitting a burgeoning international city, Auckland has a wide range of accommodation. Booking ahead can secure better deals. Keep an eye out for when international concerts and big rugby games are scheduled as accommodation around the city can fill up.

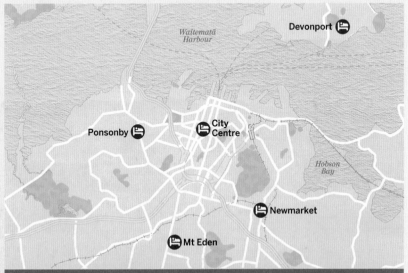

Neighbourhood	Atmosphere
City Centre	The central business district features luxury hotels, international chains and hostels of varying repute. Convenient but lacking character.
Ponsonby	Near to good restaurants, bars and shops with a good selection of B&Bs and hostels. A short distance from central Auckland.
Mt Eden	A leafy suburb on the fringe of the city with good hostels and B&Bs. Good transport links to the CBD and harbour ferries.
Devonport	A salubrious seaside suburb reached by ferry from downtown Auckland with beautiful Edwardian B&Bs.
Newmarket	Good-value motels along Great South Rd and near to good shopping. An easy bus ride into central Auckland.

ANDRE HEITER/EYEEM/GETTY IMAGES ©

Matamata

Rolling green hills, a pretty lake and well-kept gardens around compact Hobbit holes all make it very easy to suspend reality in Matamata's make-believe Middle-earth world of Hobbiton.

Matamata was just one of those pleasant, horsey country towns you drove through until Peter Jackson's epic film trilogy *The Lord of the Rings* put it on the map. During filming, 300 locals got work as extras (hairy feet weren't a prerequisite).

Following the subsequent filming of *The Hobbit,* the town has now ardently embraced its Middle-earth credentials, and given the local information centre an appropriately extreme makeover, including a spooky statue of Gollum .

Most tourists who come to Matamata are dedicated Hobbit-botherers. For everyone else there's a great cafe and bar, avenues of mature trees and undulating green hills.

Great For...

☑ Don't Miss

Slurping an Oakbarton Brew or Sackville Cider at Hobbiton's Green Dragon Inn.

Hobbiton Movie Set & Tours

Due to copyright, all the movie sets around NZ were dismantled after the

Wairere Falls

❶ Need to Know

Matamata i-SITE (☑07-888 7260; www.
matamatanz.co.nz; 45 Broadway; ⊙9am-
5pm) is housed in a Hobbit gatehouse.
Hobbiton tours leave from here.

✖ Take a Break

For a pre-Hobbit bite, stop for pizzas named after LOTR characters at
Redoubt Bar & Eatery (☑07-888 8585;
www.redoubtbarandeatery.co.nz; 48 Broadway; ⊙11am-1am).

★ Top Tip

Book ahead, especially for Hobbiton's
Evening Banquet Tours on Wednesday
and Sunday.

filming of *The Lord of the Rings*, but the
owners of **Hobbiton** (☑0508 446 224 866,
07-888 1505; www.hobbitontours.com; 501
Buckland Rd, Hinuera; adult/child tours $84/42,
dinner tours $195/153; ⊙tours 10am-4.30pm)
negotiated to keep their hobbit holes,
which were then rebuilt for the filming
of *The Hobbit*. Tours include a drink at
the wonderful Green Dragon Inn. Free
transfers leave from the Matamata i-SITE
– check timings on the Hobbiton website.
Booking ahead is strongly recommended.
The popular Evening Dinner Tours on
Wednesday and Sunday include a banquet
dinner.

To get to Hobbiton with your own
transport, head towards Cambridge from
Matamata, turn right into Puketutu Rd and
then left into Buckland Rd, stopping at the
Shire's Rest Cafe.

Non-Hobbit Stuff

Firth Tower   Historic Building
(☑07-888 8369; www.firthtower.co.nz; Tower
Rd; grounds free, buildings adult/child $10/5;
⊙grounds 10am-4pm daily, buildings to 4pm Thu-
Mon; 🚗) Firth Tower was built by Auckland
businessman Josiah Firth in 1882. The 18m
concrete tower was then a fashionable
status symbol; now it's filled with Māori and
pioneer artefacts. It's 3km east of town.

Wairere Falls   Waterfall
About 15km northeast of Matamata are the
spectacular 153m Wairere Falls. From the
car park it's a 45-minute walk through native
bush to the lookout or a steep 1½-hour climb
to the summit.

Getting There & Away

Matamata is on SH27, 160km south of
Auckland. **InterCity** (☑09-583 5780; www.
intercity.co.nz) runs buses from Auckland,
usually via Hamilton and Rotorua.

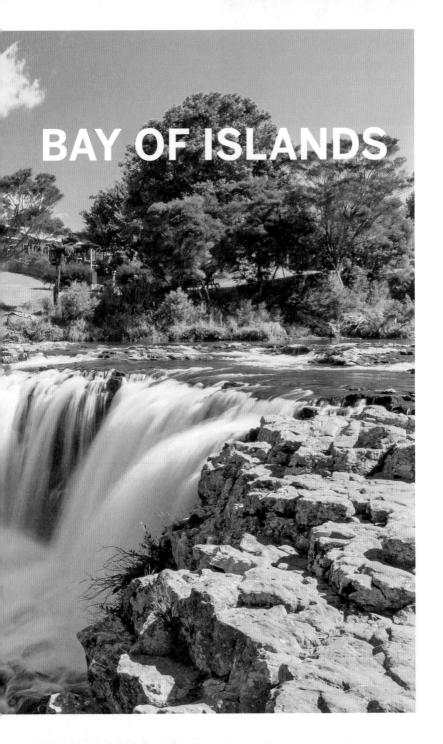

BAY OF ISLANDS

Bay of Islands at a Glance...

With turquoise waters and 150 undeveloped islands, the Bay of Islands ranks as one of New Zealand's top summertime destinations. Most of the action is out on the water: yachting, fishing, kayaking, diving or spying whales and dolphins. It's also a place of enormous historical significance. Māori knew it as Pēwhairangi and settled here early in their migrations. It's also the site of NZ's first permanent British settlement (at Russell). It was here that the Treaty of Waitangi was drawn up and first signed in 1840; the treaty remains the linchpin of race relations in NZ today.

Two Days in the Bay of Islands

Check out historic Russell (p72) in the morning, then ferry across to **Paihia** (p75) and spend the afternoon at the **Waitangi Treaty Grounds** (p107). Head out to dinner at one of Paihia's many great diners. The next morning hook up with an exciting **boat trip** (p70) exploring the Bay of Islands. Then relax with absolute waterfront drinks at **Zane Grey's** (p77).

Four Days in the Bay of Islands

Kick off the following morning with great coffee and a breakfast burrito at **El Cafe** (p76), before continuing the history theme in Kerikeri at the **Kerikeri Mission Station** (p74) and nearby **Kororipo Pā** (p74). Duck back to Paihia and join a cycling tour on the Twin Coast Cycle Trail (p77) or get out on the water again in a **kayak** (p71).

Previous page: Haruru Falls (p75), Paihia
ianwool/Getty Images ©

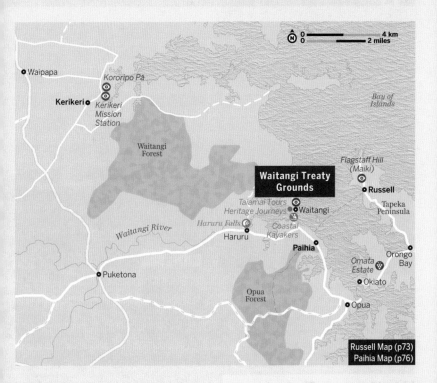

Russell Map (p73)
Paihia Map (p76)

Arriving in the Bay of Islands

Bay of Islands (Kerikeri) Airport (KKE; ☎09-407 6133; www.bayofislandsairport. co.nz; 218 Wiroa Rd) The airport is 8km southwest of Kerikeri. The only scheduled flights are Air New Zealand services from Auckland. SuperShuttle connects you to Kerikeri and Paihia.

Bus Services InterCity travels to Paihia and on to Kerikeri.

Ferry Car and passenger ferry from Paihia to Russell (via Opua).

Where to Stay

There's a wide range of accommodation available up here in the Bay of Islands. Motels and backpacker hostels are clustered in Paihia, while Russell and Kerikeri have a solid range of friendly bed and breakfast accommodations, and as well as tidy motels to choose from.

VALL_7/GETTY IMAGES ©

Waitangi Treaty Grounds

Occupying a lawn-draped headland, this is NZ's most significant historic site. Here, on 6 February 1840, the first 43 Māori chiefs signed the Treaty of Waitangi with the British Crown; eventually, over 500 chiefs would sign it.

Great For...

☑ Don't Miss

The beautiful carvings and *tukutuku* (woven panels) at Waitangi's Whare Rūnanga (meeting house).

Te Kōngahu Museum of Waitangi

Opened in 2016, Te Kōngahu Museum of Waitangi is a modern and comprehensive showcase of the role of the treaty in the past, present and future of Aotearoa New Zealand. It provides a warts-and-all look at the early interactions between Māori and Europeans, the events leading up to the treaty's signing, the long litany of treaty breaches by the Crown, the wars and land confiscations that followed, and the protest movement that led to the current process of redress for historic injustices. Many *taonga* (treasures) associated with Waitangi were previously scattered around NZ, and this excellent museum is now a safe haven for a number of key historical items. One room is devoted to facsimiles of all the key documents, while another screens

HOLGER LEUE/GETTY IMAGES ©

❶ Need to Know

☏09-402 7437; www.waitangi.org.nz; 1 Tau Henare Dr, Waitangi; adult/child $50/free; ⏰9am-5pm

✕ Take a Break

Overlooking the Treaty Grounds, the **Whare Waka** (mains $15-19.50; ⏰8am-4pm, shorter hours in winter; P ♿) offers good cafe fare.

★ Top Tip

Experience a *hāngi* dinner and concert at Whare Waka on Tuesday, Thursday and Sunday evenings, December to March.

a fascinating short film dramatising the events of the initial treaty signing.

Treaty House

The Treaty House was shipped over as a kit-set from Australia and erected in 1834 as the four-room home of the official British Resident James Busby. It's now preserved as a memorial and museum containing displays about the house and the people who lived here.

Whare Rūnanga

Across the lawn, the magnificently detailed Whare Rūnanga was completed in 1940 to mark the centenary of the treaty. The fine carvings represent the major Māori tribes. It's here that the cultural performances take place, starting with a *haka pōwhiri* (challenge and welcome) and then heading inside for *waiata* (songs) and spine-tingling *haka* (war dances).

Ngātokimatawhaorua

Near the cove is the 35m, 6-tonne *waka taua* (war canoe) Ngātokimatawhaorua, also built for the centenary. A photographic exhibit details how it was fashioned from gigantic kauri logs. There's also an excellent gift shop selling Māori art and design, with a carving studio attached.

Tours & Admission

Tours leave on the hour from 10am to 3pm. Admission (adult/child $50/free; discounted to $25 for NZ residents upon presentation of a passport or driver's licence) incorporates a guided tour and spirited cultural performance, and entry to the Museum of Waitangi, the Whare Rūnanga and the historic Treaty House.

Tall ship

CLOUDIA SPINNER/SHUTTERSTOCK ©

Marine Adventures

Getting out onto the water is the best way to experience the Bay of Islands. There are myriad opportunities here for sailing, cruising, jetboating, sea kayaking and marine mammal-watching amid the bay's eye-popping scenery.

Great For...

☑ Don't Miss

Subtropical diving on the wreck of the *Rainbow Warrior*, an hour north of Paihia by boat.

Boat tours leave from either Paihia or Russell, calling into the other town as their first stop.

Out on the bay, one of the most striking islands is Piercy Island (Motukokako) off Cape Brett, at the bay's eastern edge. This steep-walled rock fortress features a vast natural arch – the famous Hole in the Rock. If conditions are right, most boat tours pass right through the heart of the island. En route it's likely you'll encounter bottlenose and common dolphins, and you may see orcas, other whales and penguins.

A fabulous way to explore the bay is under sail. Either help crew the boat (no experience required), or sit back and spend the afternoon island-hopping, swimming and snorkelling.

CORNERSTA/GETTY IMAGES ©

ⓘ Need to Know

The Bay of Islands i-SITE (p77) at Paihia can help you book your water-based adventures.

✕ Take a Break

Hell Hole (☏022 175 7847; www.facebook.com/hellholecoffee; 19 York St; snacks $6-14; ⊙7am-5pm Jan & Feb, 8am-3pm Mar, Apr, Nov & Dec) in Russell brews hellishly good coffee.

★ Top Tip

Booking boat tours a few days ahead, especially during summer and school holidays.

child $149/90 including barbecue lunch) heads to the Hole in the Rock and stops at Urupukapuka Island.

Fullers Great Sights — Cruise

(☏09-402 7421; www.dolphincruises.co.nz; Maritime Bldg, Marsden Rd, Paihia) ✔ The four-hour Hole in the Rock Cruise heads out to the famous sea arch and stops at Urupukapuka Island on the way back. Boats stop at Russell wharf for pickups on all trips.

Tours

Phantom — Boating

(☏0800 224 421; www.yachtphantom.com; day sail $125) A fast 15m racing sloop, known for its great platters. It has a licensed cash bar on board for local wines and beers.

R Tucker Thompson — Boating

(☏09-402 8430; www.tucker.co.nz; ⊙Nov-Mar) Run by a charitable trust with an education focus, the *Tucker* is a majestic tall ship offering day sails (adult/child $159/79.50, including a barbecue lunch) and late-afternoon cruises (adult/child $67/33.75).

Explore NZ — Cruise

(☏09-359 5987; www.exploregroup.co.nz; cnr Marsden & Williams Rds, Paihia) ✔ Explore's four-hour Discover the Bay cruise (adult/

Coastal Kayakers — Kayaking

(☏0800 334 661; www.coastalkayakers.co.nz; Te Karuwha Pde, Paihia) Runs guided tours (half-/full day from $75 per person, minimum two people) and multiday adventures. Kayaks (half-/full day $50/70) can also be rented for independent exploration.

Russell

Proudly remembered as 'the hellhole of the Pacific', there's little in the way of depravity and debauchery here now. Instead you'll find a historic town made of weatherboard-style colonial buildings dotted with boutiques, souvenir stores and places to eat. The tree-covered hills beyond the harbour overlook fine homes and holiday accommodation – it's hard not to envy the friendly locals who call this slice of paradise home.

Before it was known as a hellhole (you'll read that word a lot before your trip is done), or even as Russell, this was Kororāreka (Sweet Penguin), a fortified Ngāpuhi village. In the early 19th century *iwi* (tribes) permitted this spot to become Aotearoa's first European settlement, but it quickly became a magnet for fleeing convicts, whalers, enterprising prostitutes and drunken sailors. You can imagine how the Māori must have viewed their new residents!

⊙ SIGHTS

Pompallier Mission   Historic Building
(☑09-403 9015; www.pompallier.co.nz; 5 The Strand; adult/child $15/free; ⊘10am-4pm by guided tour) Built in 1842 to house the Catholic mission's printing press, this rammed-earth building is the mission's last remaining building in the western Pacific, and NZ's oldest industrial building. Over its seven years of operation, a staggering 40,000 books were printed here in Māori. Admission includes extremely interesting hands-on tours that lead you through the entire bookmaking process, from the icky business of tanning animal hides for the covers to setting the type and stitching together the final books. You can visit the gardens only ($7) if you miss out on the tour.

Flagstaff Hill   Hill
(Maiki; Flagstaff Rd) Overlooking Russell, this is the hill where Hōne Heke chopped down the British flagpole four times. You can drive up, but the epic view over Russell and the harbour rewards a good 1.6km climb. Take the track west from the boat ramp along the beach at low tide, or head up Wellington St.

Long Beach   Beach
(Oneroa; Long Beach Rd) About 1.5km behind Russell (an easy walk or cycle) is this placid, child-friendly beach. Turn left (facing the sea) to visit **Donkey Bay**, a small cove that is an unofficial nudist beach.

Omata Estate   Winery
(☑09-403 8007; www.omata.co.nz; 212 Aucks Rd; ⊘11am-6pm Oct-May, by appointment Jun-Sep) With a growing reputation for red wines – especially its old-growth syrah – Omata Estate is one of Northland's finest wineries. To complement the tastings and sea views, pizzas and shared platters are available. The winery is on the road from Russell to the car ferry at Okiato.

✪ ACTIVITIES

There are some excellent walks in the area, such as a hike up to **Maiki (Flagstaff Hill)** or the day-long full-circle loop via **Opita** and **Opua** to **Paihia** then back to **Russell** incorporating two ferry journeys (see www.boiwalkways.co.nz for more information).

On the ocean coast, **Rāwhiti** is the starting point for the tramp to **Cape Brett lighthouse**, a strenuous eight-hour, 16.3km walk to the top of the peninsula (slippery when wet) where overnight stays are possible.

For those looking for something more sedate, head down to **Oke Bay** (best when the tide is out) for a picture-perfect white-sand swimming beach.

Another good walk near Rāwhiti leads through Māori land and Whangamumu Scenic Reserve to **Whangamumu Harbour**. There are more than 40 ancient Māori sites on the peninsula and the remains of an unusual whaling station.

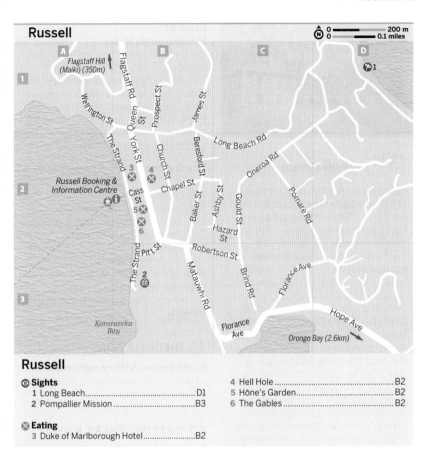

Russell

⊗ EATING & DRINKING

Hōne's Garden   Pizza $$

(☏022 466 3710; www.facebook.com/hones
garden; 10 York St; pizza $18-25; ⊙noon-10pm
Wed-Mon Nov-Apr; 🐾) Head out to Hōne's
shaded lantern-lit courtyard for wood-fired
pizza (gluten-free available), cold craft
beer on tap and a thoroughly easy-going
vibe. An expanded menu features tasty
wraps and healthy salads. Antipasto
platters are good for groups and indecisive
diners.

Sage @ Paroa Bay   Bistro $$

(www.thelindisgroup.com/paroabaywinerysage;
31 Otamarua Rd; ⊙noon-5pm Wed & Thu, to
8pm Fri-Sun) With hilltop views over the turquoise waters of the Bay of Islands, this
winery restaurant overlooking manicured
lawns is worth the drive. A limited mains
menu has all the bases covered with quality ingredients and surprising flavours. A
side salad comes with *dukkah* spice mix,
pickled vegetables and balsamic beetroot,
for example. The cheese tasting board is a
great afternoon grazing option.

Kerikeri Detour

Kerikeri, a quick 23km jaunt northwest of Paihia, is famous for its oranges, but it also offers a snapshot of early Māori and Pākehā interaction. Two of the nation's most significant buildings nestle side-by-side at **Kerikeri Mission Station** (☑09-407 9236; www.historic.org.nz; 246 Kerikeri Rd; museum $8, house tour $12, combined $15, children free; ☺10am-5pm Nov-Apr, to 4pm May-Oct; ⊞). Start at the Stone Store, NZ's oldest stone building (1836). Upstairs there's an interesting little museum, while downstairs the shop sells the type of goods that used to be stocked here in the 19th century. Tours of neighbouring Kemp House depart from here. Built by the missionaries in 1822, this humble yet pretty wooden Georgian-style house is NZ's oldest building. In summer, the Honey House Cafe operates from a neighbouring cottage. Just up the hill from the Mission Station is a marked historical walk that leads to the site of Hongi Hika's Kororipo *Pā* (fortress) and village on Kerikeri Rd. Little remains aside from the terracing that once supported wooden palisades. Huge war parties once departed from here, terrorising much of the North Island and slaughtering thousands during the Musket Wars. The role of missionaries in arming Ngāpuhi remains controversial. The walk emerges near the cute wooden St James Anglican Church (1878).

Stone Store
JUNKI ASANO/SHUTTERSTOCK ©

Duke of Marlborough Hotel — Pub Food $$

(☑09-403 7829; www.theduke.co.nz; 35 The Strand; mains lunch $20-39, dinner $26-42; ☺11.30am-9pm) There's no better spot in Russell to while away a few hours, glass in hand, than the Duke's sunny deck. Thankfully the upmarket bistro food matches the views, plus there's an excellent wine list and a great selection of NZ craft beers.

The Gables — Contemporary $$

(☑09-403 7670; www.thegablesrestaurant.co.nz; 19 The Strand; mains lunch $22-28, dinner $27-35; ☺noon-3pm & 5.30-10pm Wed-Mon) Serving Kiwi classics (lamb, beef, seafood), the Gables occupies an 1847 building (formerly a colonial brothel) on the waterfront built using whale vertebrae for foundations. Book a table by the windows for maritime views, and look forward to excellent service and top-notch local produce, including local cheeses.

ⓘ INFORMATION

Russell Booking & Information Centre (☑09-403 8020; www.russellinfo.co.nz; Russell Wharf; ☺8am-5pm, extended hours summer)

ⓘ GETTING THERE & AWAY

The quickest way to reach Russell by car is via the Fullers car ferry (car/motorcycle/passenger $13.50/5.90/1), which runs every 10 minutes from Opua (5km from Paihia) to Okiato (8km from Russell), between 6am and 9.50pm. Buy your tickets on board. If you're travelling from the south, a detour with walks and other diversions can be taken via the coastal route, Russell Rd.

On foot, the easiest way to reach Russell is on one of several **passenger ferry** operators from Paihia (adult/child return $12/6). These run hourly from 7am to 9pm (until 10pm in the peak season). Buy your tickets on board, or at the i-SITE (p77) in Paihia.

Paihia

Paihia is a gentle tourism-focused town, with an abundance of accommodation and good restaurants, plenty of tours as well as DIY options to get you out on the water, and a strong community spirit that lifts the vibe a few notches. Its name is said to be a mix of Māori and English, from *'pai'* (good) and here.

To Paihia's north is the birthplace of New Zealand (as opposed to Aotearoa): Waitangi inhabits a special but somewhat complex place in the national psyche.

 SIGHTS

Haruru Falls
Waterfall

 (Haruru Falls Rd, Haruru) A walking track (one way 1½ hours, 5km) leads from the Treaty Grounds along the Waitangi River to these attractive horseshoe falls. Part of the path follows a boardwalk through the mangroves. Otherwise you can drive here, turning right off Puketona Rd onto Haruru Falls Rd.

Williams House & Gardens
Historic Building

(www.williamshousepaihia.com; Williams Rd, Paihia) FREE The historic buildings and gardens of Paihia's first mission station include a restored stone store, and now house a community library and a community secondhand bookshop. Free public wi-fi is available here too.

 ACTIVITIES

Taiamai Tours Heritage Journeys
Cultural

(☏09-405 9990; www.taiamaitours.co.nz; 3hr tour $135; ☺departs 9am Tue, Thu, Sat & Sun Oct-Apr) Paddle a traditional 12m carved *waka* (canoe) from the Waitangi bridge to the Haruru Falls. The Ngāpuhi hosts wear traditional garb, and perform the proper *karakia* (incantations) and share stories. The price includes admission to the Waitangi Treaty Grounds (p67) at your leisure (which is otherwise $50).

Paihia

/GETTY IMAGES ©

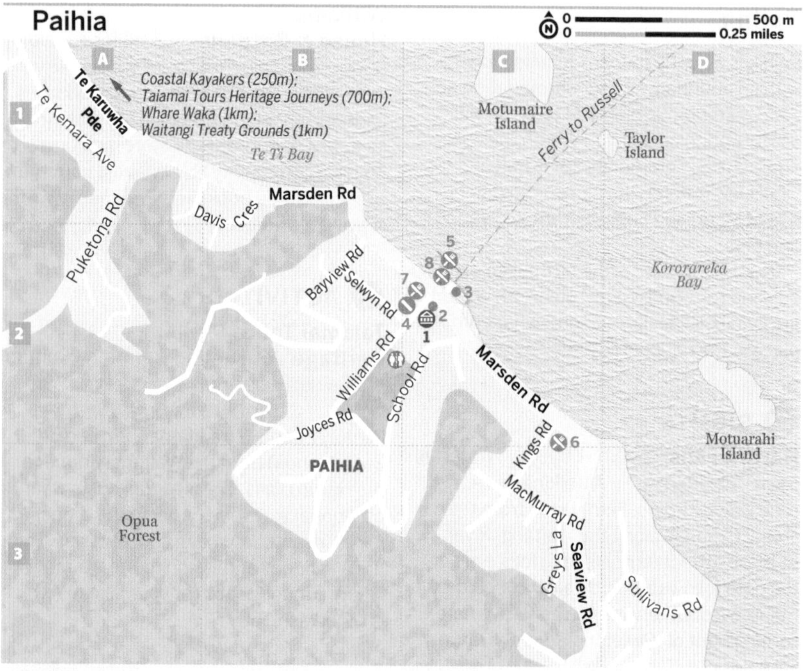

Paihia

Sights

1 Williams House & Gardens........................ C2

Activities, Courses & Tours

2 Explore NZ........................ C2
3 Fullers Great Sights........................ C2
4 Paihia Dive........................ C2

Eating

5 Charlotte's Kitchen........................ C2
6 El Cafe........................ C2
7 Terra........................ C2
8 Zane Grey's........................ C2

Paihia Dive Diving

(☎09-402 7551; www.divenz.com; 7 Williams Rd, Paihia; dives from $180; ⊙daily Oct-May, Mon-Sat Jun-Sep) This five-star PADI dive crew offers combined reef and wreck trips to either the *Canterbury* or the *Rainbow Warrior*. It also sells fishing gear and snorkelling sets.

EATING & DRINKING

El Cafe Latin American $

(☎09-402 7637; www.facebook.com/elcafepaihia; 2 Kings Rd, Paihia; mains $11-14.50; ⊙8am-4pm;) This excellent Chilean-owned cafe has the best coffee in town and terrific breakfast burritos, tacos and baked-egg dishes, such as spicy *huevos rancheros*. The Cuban pulled-pork sandwich is truly a wonderful thing. The fruit smoothies are also great on a warm Bay of Islands day.

Charlotte's Kitchen Contemporary $$

(☎09-402 8296; www.charlotteskitchen.co.nz; Paihia Wharf, 69 Marsden Rd, Paihia; mains lunch $16-27, dinner $20-35; ⊙11.30am-10pm Mon-Fri, to 11pm Sat & Sun) Named after an escaped Australian convict who was NZ's first white female settler, this hip restaurant-bar occupies a cheeky perch on the main pier. Bits of Kiwiana decorate the walls, while the menu takes a swashbuckling journey around the world and includes steamed pork buns, Vietnamese rolls, fresh oysters and pizzas.

Zane Grey's   Seafood $$
(☑09-402 6220; https://zanegreys.co.nz; 69 Marsden Rd, Paihia; mains $15-38; ⊘8am-10pm) Named after a local fishing legend, and with possibly the biggest deck in all of Northland, Zane Grey's has you covered all day, from traditional breakfasts through to a seafood-focused dinner menu with Asian and Pacific influences. Half of the venue transforms into an enviable bar in the evening with comfy modern lounges ready for conversations fuelled by cocktails or cold beer.

Terra   Seafood $$$
(☑09-945 8376; info@terrarestaurant.co.nz; 76 Marsden Rd, Paihia; mains $20-38; ⊘5.30pm-late Tue-Sun) Muted colours give way to sea views at this new upstairs seafood restaurant across from Paihia pier. The seasonal menu is largely seafood-focused (who can resist Orongo Bay oysters with lemon, seaweed, horopito and sherry mignonette?), but promises to take care of fine-dining vegetarians on request. Be advised to leave room for the cheese-tasting menu featuring a mix of French and local cheeses.

ⓘ INFORMATION
Bay of Islands
i-SITE   Tourist Information
(☑09-402 7345; www.northlandnz.com; 69 Marsden Rd, Paihia; ⊘8am-5pm Mar-Dec, to 7pm Jan & Feb) Information and bookings.

ⓘ GETTING THERE & AWAY
All **buses** (Maritime Building, Paihia) serving Paihia stop at the Maritime Building by the wharf.

InterCity (www.intercity.co.nz) has three or four coaches a day to and from Auckland (from $29, four hours), Waipu (from $25, 1¾ hours), Whangārei (from $12, 1¼ hours),

🚲 Twin Coast Cycle Trail (Pou Herenga Tai)

The inspiring Twin Coast Cycle Trail (Pou Herenga Tai) stretches from the Bay of Islands right across the country to the Hokianga Harbour. It's only 87km, but it definitely gives you boasting rights when you get home. The complete route takes two days and travels from Opua to Kawakawa, Kaikohe, Okaihau and Horeke before finishing at Mangungu Mission Station.

The most popular day ride is the 14km section from **Kaikohe** to **Okaihau**, which passes through an abandoned rail tunnel before skirting **Lake Omapere**.

If you are cycling to **Horeke**, be aware the **pub** (☑09-401 9133; www.horekehotel.nz; 2118 Horeke Rd; ⊘pre-booked meals only, call ahead) there is only open to staying and paying customers; book ahead if you want a meal or a place to sleep.

The trail is best described at www.twincoastcycletrail.kiwi.nz, where you'll find all the information on bike hire (including e-bikes for the less fit among us, we won't tell!) from various towns and shuttle transport to bring you back if you run out of puff.

STEVE TODD/SHUTTERSTOCK ©

Kawakawa (from $15, 20 minutes) and Kerikeri (from $15, 20 minutes).

Ferries (Paihia Wharf) depart regularly for Russell, and there are seasonal services to Urupukapuka Island.

Waitomo Caves

Even if damp, dark tunnels are your idea of hell, head to Waitomo anyway. The limestone caves and glowing bugs here are one of the North Island's premier attractions.

Great For...

Ōtorohanga

Waitomo Caves ◉

◉ Hangatiki

Oparure ◉

◉ Te Kuiti

ⓘ Need to Know

Waitomo Wanderer (p81) has a daily return service from Rotorua or Auckland with tour options.

★ **Top Tip**

There's no petrol in town, but there's an ATM at **Kiwi Paka** (☎ 07-878 3395; www. waitomokiwipaka.co.nz; Hotel Access Rd; @ 🛜). Stock up on cash, groceries and petrol in Te Kuiti or Ōtorohanga.

PHILARTPHACE/GETTY IMAGES ©

The name Waitomo comes from *wai* (water) and *tomo* (hole or shaft): dotted across this region are numerous shafts dropping into underground cave systems and streams. There are 300-plus mapped caves in the area; the three main caves – Glowworm, Ruakuri and Aranui – have been bewitching visitors for more than 100 years.

Caves

Book tours for the three main caves at the **Waitomo Caves Visitor Centre** (⌕0800 456 922; www.waitomo.com; Waitomo Caves Rd; ⏱9am-5pm).

Glowworm Cave

The guided tour of the **Glowworm Cave** (⌕0800 456 922; www.waitomo.com/experiences/ waitomo-glowworm-caves; adult/child $55/25; ⏱45min tours half-hourly 9am-5pm; 👪), which is

behind the visitor centre, leads past impressive stalactites and stalagmites into the large Cathedral cavern. At the tour's end you board a boat and float along beneath a Milky Way of little lights – these are the glowworms. The acoustics are so good here that Dame Kiri Te Kanawa and the Vienna Boys' Choir have given concerts here.

Ruakuri Cave

Ruakuri Cave (⌕0800 782 587, 07-878 6219; www.waitomo.com/glowworms-and-caves/ ruakuri-cave; adult/child $79/30; ⏱2hr tours half-hourly from 9am-4pm; 👪) has an impressive 15m-high spiral staircase, bypassing a Māori burial site at the cave entrance. Tours lead through 1.6km of the 7.5km system, taking in caverns with glowworms, subterranean streams and waterfalls, and intricate limestone structures. Some claim the cave is haunted – it's customary to

Glowworm Cave

wash your hands when leaving to remove the *tapu* (taboo).

Aranui Cave

Three kilometres west from the Glowworm Cave is **Aranui Cave** (☑0800 456 922; www.waitomo.com/experiences/aranui-cave; adult/child $55/25; ⊙1hr tours depart 9am-4pm). This cave is dry (hence no glowworms), but compensates with an incredible array of limestone formations. Thousands of tiny 'straw' stalactites hang from the ceiling. There's transport to the cave entrance from the visitor centre. A 15-minute bush walk is also included.

★ **Top Tip**

Waitomo i-SITE (☑07-878 7640, 0800 474 839; www.waitomocaves.com; 21 Waitomo Caves Rd; ⊙9am-5.30pm) has internet access and a post office, and is a booking agent for tours.

MARCEL STRELOW/GETTY IMAGES ©

Going Underground

Waitomo excels with challenging and unique ways to explore the area's subterranean wonders. Recommended operators include the following:

Legendary Black Water Rafting Company (☑0800 782 5874; www.waitomo.com/experiences; 585 Waitomo Caves Rd) The Black Labyrinth tour ($150, three hours) involves floating in a wetsuit on an inner tube down a river through Ruakuri Cave. The highlight is leaping off a small waterfall and then floating through a long, glowworm-covered passage. The trip ends with showers, soup and bagels in the cafe. There's also the more adventurous Black Abyss tour ($260, five hours).

CaveWorld (☑07-878 6577, 0800 228 396; www.caveworld.co.nz; cnr Waitomo Caves Rd & Hotel Access Rd) The Footwhistle Glowworm Cave tour ($64, one hour) incorporates a stop in a forest shelter for a mug of restorative kawakawa tea, a natural tonic made with leaves from an indigenous bush plant. Twilight Footwhistle tours exploring the cave at night are $69.

Waitomo Adventures (☑0800 924 866, 07-878 7788; www.waitomo.co.nz; 1227 Waitomo Valley Rd; ⊕) The Lost World trip ($425/595, four/seven hours) combines a 100m abseil with walking, rock climbing, wading and swimming. TumuTumu Toobing ($160, four hours) is a walking, climbing, swimming and tubing trip. St Benedict's Cavern ($235, three hours) includes abseiling and a subterranean flying fox.

Waitomo Wanderer (☑03-477 9083, 0800 000 4321; www.travelheadfirst.com) Has optional caving, glowworm and tubing add-ons. It'll even integrate Hobbiton into the mix if you're a JRR Tolkien or Sir Peter Jackson fan.

✕ **Take a Break**

The **Waitomo General Store** (☑07-878 8613; www.facebook.com/waitomogeneralstore; 15 Waitomo Caves Rd; snacks & mains $10-22; ⊙7.30am-8.30pm; 🛜) has pre- and post-caving sustenance: hearty burgers, good coffee and tap beer.

ROTORUA

Rotorua at a Glance...

A whiff of Rotorua's sulphurous air will probably be your first encounter with New Zealand's most dynamic thermal area, home to spurting geysers, steaming hot springs and exploding mud pools. Māori revered this place; today 35% of the population is indigenous, and their cultural performances and hāngi (feasts) are hugely popular with visitors.

Rotorua also delivers some of the best mountain biking in the country, plus a raft of adrenaline-charged outdoor activities. The town itself is fairly touristy, but the lake it presides over is gorgeous.

Two Days in Rotorua

Explore Rotorua's geothermal landscape at **Te Puia** (p87) and **Whakarewarewa** (p86) before a Māori concert and *hāngi* in the evening. Kick off day two with breakfast at **Artisan Cafe** (p94) before mountain biking at **Redwoods Whakarewarewa Forest** (p88) or **Skyline Rotorua MTB Gravity Park** (p93). In the evening take a **glowworm paddle boarding tour** (p94) before recounting your adventures over dinner at **Abracadabra** (p95).

Four Days in Rotorua

Have a walk around the lakefront then fuel up on brunch at **Third Place** (p96) before further outdoor adventures. Dangle from a forest zipline with **Rotorua Canopy Tours** (p93), **paddleboard** (p94) to caves in Lake Okareka, or jetboat with **Velocity Valley** (p94), before relaxing each evening in the mineral pools at **Polynesian Spa** (p94).

Previous page: Tamaki Māori dancers at Whakareware Village (p86)
Bob Hilscher/Shutterstock ©

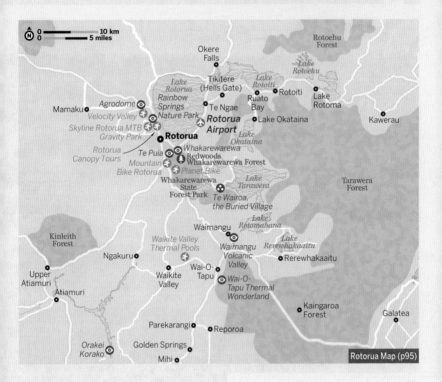

Rotorua Map (p95)

Arriving in Rotorua

Rotorua Airport (p97) is 9km north-east of town. **Super Shuttle** (www.supershuttle.co.nz) offers a door-to-door airport service (first passenger $22, each additional passenger $5). **Baybus** (www.baybus.co.nz) route 10 stops at the airport hourly ($2.80, 8am to 6pm). A taxi to/from the town centre costs about $32.

Where to Stay

Rotorua has plenty of motels (especially along Fenton St, which is something of a motel alley), plus some great holiday parks, big chain hotels and an ever-changing backpacker scene. If you're looking for some peace and quiet, Ngongotahā, 7km northwest of the town centre, has some good B&Bs in its rural hinterland.

Whakarewarewa Village

Geothermal Rotorua

Rotorua's main drawcard is Whakarewarewa (fah-kah-reh-wah-reh-wah), a geothermal reserve 3km south of the city centre. Local Māori have lived on this bubbling and steaming terrain for hundreds of years.

Great For...

☑ Don't Miss

A tour of Whakarewarewa with Māori guides, many descended from the area's first families.

Whakarewarewa Village

Whakarewarewa Village (☎07-349 3463; www.whakarewarewa.com; 17 Tryon St; adult/child $45/20, incl *hāngi* $70/40; ◷8.30am-5pm) is a living community where the local Tūhourangi/Ngāti Wāhiao people have resided for centuries. Villagers lead the tours (hourly, 9am to 4pm) amid steamy bubbling pools, silica terraces and geysers.

Admission includes a **cultural performance** (daily at 11.15am and 2pm, with an additional show at 12.30pm from November to March) and a self-guided nature walk. Village shops sell authentic arts and crafts, and you can learn more about Māori traditions such as flax weaving, carving and *tā moko* (tattooing). Nearby you can eat buttery sweetcorn ($2) pulled straight out of the hot mineral pool.

Pōhutu geyser

ALIZADA STUDIOS/SHUTTERSTOCK ©

ⓘ Need to Know

The active area is split between the still-lived-in Māori village of Whakarewarewa and the Te Puia complex, separated by a fence.

✖ Take a Break

The onsite cafe Pataka Kai at Te Puia has dishes infused with Māori flavours among its buffet offerings.

★ Top Tip

Whakarewarewa Village offers a good view of the Pōhutu geyser next door at Te Puia, for a few dollars less.

mud. **Cultural performances** (10.15am, 12.15pm and 3.15pm) incorporate a traditional welcome into the *wharenui* and a 45-minute *kapa haka* (traditional song and dance) concert.

The three-hour night experience (*Te Pō*) starts at 6pm and includes a cultural show and a *hāngi*, followed by a tour through the thermal zone.

Te Puia

Te Puia (☑07-348 9047; www.tepuia.com; Hemo Rd, Whakarewarewa; adult/child $60/30, incl performance $76/38, Te Pō $136/68; ⊙8am-6pm Oct-Mar, to 5pm Apr-Sep) dials up the heat on *Māoritanga* (things Māori) with explosive cultural performances and **Pōhutu** (Big Splash), the famous geyser that erupts 20 times a day, spurting hot water 30m skyward. The adjacent **Prince of Wales' Feathers** geyser starts up shortly before Pōhutu blows its top. The **National Carving School** and the **National Weaving School** are also here.

Daytime visits (*Te Rā*) include a guided tour (hourly), visiting a *wharenui* (carved meeting house), a re-created precolonial village, a nocturnal kiwi enclosure, three major geysers and a huge pool of boiling

Kuirau Park

Just west of central Rotorua **Kuirau Park** (Ranolf St) is a volcanic area you can explore for free. Steam hisses from fenced-off sections, while occasional eruptions smother the park in mud, thwarting the gardeners' best efforts. Keep your toddlers on a tight rein.

What's Nearby?

Don't miss big-ticket geothermal attractions including the amazing Wai-O-Tapu Thermal Wonderland (p93) and Waimangu Volcanic Valley (p93), both south of Rotorua.

Rotorua thermal areas

SHELLS | GETTY IMAGES ©

Mountain Biking

Welcome to one of the southern hemisphere's finest destinations for mountain biking, offering a range of experiences for everyone from families and beginners through to gung-ho two-wheeled downhill lunatics.

Great For...

☑ Don't Miss

Catching the gondola up Mt Ngon-gotahā then hurtling along downhill tracks.

Redwoods Whakarewarewa Forest

On the edge of town, the **Redwoods Whakarewarewa Forest** (☎07-350 0110; www.redwoods.co.nz; Long Mile Rd, Whaka-rewarewa) is home to some of the best mountain-bike trails in the country. There are close to 100km of tracks to keep bikers of all skill levels happy for days on end. Note that not all tracks in the forest are designated for bikers, so adhere to the signposting. Pick up a trail map at the for-est visitor centre. At the time of research, a professional-standard BMX track was also being constructed in the park.

Skyline Rotorua MTB Gravity Park

More evidence of Rotorua's status as a world-class mountain-biking destination

Whakarewarewa Forest

WITR/SHUTTERSTOCK ©

is the Skyline Rotorua MTB Gravity Park (p93), a network of 11 MTB tracks coursing down Mt Ngongotahā. There are options for riders of all experience levels, and access to the top of the park is provided by the Skyline gondola (p93). Bike rental is available on-site.

Te Ara Ahi (Thermal by Bike)

The two-day, 48km Te Ara Ahi (Thermal by Bike) trail starts in Rotorua and heads south via various geothermal attractions to the **Waikite Valley Thermal Pools** (☏07-333 1861; www.hotpools.co.nz; 648 Waikite Valley Rd; adult/child $20/11, private pools 40 min per person $24; ☺10am-9pm) ☛ 35km away. This intermediate-level route is designated as one of the New Zealand Cycle Trail's Great Rides (www.nzcycletrail.com).

ⓘ Need to Know

See www.riderotorua.com for loads of information on Rotorua's mountain-biking scene.

✕ Take a Break

The craft beer-fuelled good times at Brew (p96) are a hit with the local mountain-biking community.

★ Top Tip

Visit in March for the annual Crankworx (www.crankworx.com) mountain-biking festival.

Bike Hire & Tours

Mountain Bike Rotorua (p93) hires out bikes at the Waipa Mill car park entrance to the Redwoods forest. Its new central **Rotorua Adventure Hub** (☏07-348 4290; www.mtbrotorua.co.nz; 1213 Fenton St; ☺9am-5pm) offers rentals and info, and also has a cool cafe.

Planet Bike (☏027 280 2817, 07-346 1717; www.planetbike.co.nz; 8 Waipa Bypass Rd, Whakarewarewa; hardtail hire 2hr/day from $35/60, dual suspension $60/130, ebike 2/4hr $70/100; ☺9am-5pm) offers bike hire and guided mountain-bike rides (from $150) in Redwoods Whakarewarewa Forest.

Māori performance in Mitai Māori Village

TONKLA FOTO/SHUTTERSTOCK ©

Māori Rotorua

Māori culture is a big-ticket item in Rotorua and, although the experiences are largely commercialised and packaged-up neatly for visitor consumption, they're still a great introduction to authentic Māori traditions.

Great For...

☑ Don't Miss

The heavenly scents of meat-and-veg, cooked in an *umu* (earth oven).

Haka & Hāngi

Rotorua's Māori cultural experiences focus on two big activities: *kapa haka* (traditional performing arts) concerts and earth-cooked *hāngi* (feasts), often packaged together in an evening's entertainment featuring a *pōwhiri* (welcoming ceremony), the famous *haka* (war dance), *waiata* (songs) and *poi* dances, where women showcase their dexterity by twirling balls of flax.

Tamaki Māori Village (☏07-349 2999; www.tamakimaorivillage.co.nz; booking office 1220 Hinemaru St; adult/child $130/75) is an established favourite, offering a 3½-hour twilight Māori cultural experience to its re-created precolonial village, 15km south of Rotorua (free transfers from town). The concert is followed by a *hāngi*.

St Faiths Anglican Church

CEZARY WOJTKOWSKI/SHUTTERSTOCK ©

ⓘ Need to Know

Transfers to/from Māori cultural experiences beyond the city centre (Mitai, Tamaki) are available.

✖ Take a Break

Most of Rotorua's Māori cultural experiences involve plenty of food – you won't go hungry!

★ Top Tip

Both Whakarewarewa (p86) and Te Puia (p87) offer cultural performances along with geothermal action.

Ōhinemutu

Ōhinemutu is a lakeside Māori village that is home to around 260 people. Highlights include the 1905 **Tama-te-Kapua Meeting House** (not open to visitors), many steaming volcanic vents, and the wonderful Māori-British mash-up that is **St Faith's Anglican Church** (⏺07-348 2393; Korokai St, Ōhinemutu; admission by donation; ⏰10am-3pm, services 9am Sun) ⏹. Be respectful if you visit the village: the residents don't appreciate loud, nosy tourists wandering around taking photos of their private property.

Family-run **Mitai Māori Village** (⏺07-343 9132; www.mitai.co.nz; 196 Fairy Springs Rd, Fairy Springs; adult $123, child $25-61; ⏰6.30pm) offers a popular three-hour evening event with a concert, *hāngi* and glowworm bush walk. The experience starts with the arrival of a *waka taua* (war canoe) and can be combined with a nighttime tour of Rainbow Springs (p92) next door, including a walk through the kiwi enclosure. Pick-ups and a concert-only option are available.

Te Puia (p87) and Whakarewarewa (p86) offer the added thrill of being situated within an active geothermal zone. Both stage daytime shows; Te Puia also has an evening *hāngi*-and-show package while Whakarewarewa serves *hāngi*-cooked lunches.

◎ SIGHTS

Rainbow Springs Nature Park
Nature Centre

(☏07-350 0440; www.rainbowsprings.co.nz; 192 Fairy Springs Rd, Fairy Springs; adult/child $40/20; ☉8.30am-5.30pm) ⚑ The natural springs here are home to wild trout and eels, which you can peer at through an underwater viewer, and plenty of animals, including tuatara (a native reptile) and native birds. The star feature is the **National Kiwi Hatchery** (tour only $24, with park admission $10), which hatches around 120 chicks a year. Excellent 30-minute tours, departing on the hour, take you backstage to view the incubator and hatchery areas and three adult kiwi.

The centre also has interpretive walkways and a Big Splash water ride.

Rainbow Springs is right beside Skyline Rotorua.

The natural springs here are home to wild trout and eels

Government Gardens
Gardens

(Hinemaru St) The manicured Government Gardens surrounding the Rotorua Museum are a wonderful example of the blending of English (rose gardens, ponds, croquet lawns and bowling greens) and Māori traditions (carvings at the entrance and subtly blended into the buildings). Being Rotorua, there are thermal pools bubbling away, and it's well worth taking a walk along the active geothermal area at the lake's edge.

Agrodome
Farm

(☏07-357 1050; www.agrodome.co.nz; 141 Western Rd, Ngongotahā; adult/child shows $36/19, tours $49/25, show & tour $70/37; ☉8.30am-5pm) Learn everything you need to know about farming at this 140-hectare model farm. Shows (9.30am, 11am and 2.30pm) include a parade of champion rams, lamb feeding, and shearing, milking and doggy displays. Yes, some of the jokes are corny, but it's still very entertaining. Farm tours on a tractor train depart at 10.40am, 12.10pm, 1.30pm and 3.40pm, allowing you to see

Wai-o-tapu Thermal Wonderland

KIERAN STONE/SHUTTERSTOCK ©

Agrodome's sheep, deer, alpacas, llamas, cows, ostriches and emus.

Wai-O-Tapu
Thermal Wonderland   Natural Feature

(☑07-366 6333; www.waiotapu.co.nz; 201 Waiotapu Loop Rd; adult/child $33/11; ☺8.30am-6pm summer, to 5pm winter) The most colourful of the region's geothermal attractions, Wai-O-Tapu (Sacred Waters) has a variety of features packed into a relatively compact, heavily cratered area, with the highlights being the orange-rimmed, fizzing **Champagne Pool** and the unearthly lemon-lime-hued **Roto Kārikitea**. Just down the road (but included in the entry fee) is the **Lady Knox Geyser**, which erupts (with prompting from an organic soap) punctually at 10.15am and gushes up to 20m – follow the park exodus just before 10am to witness it.

All the headline acts are on the shortest (1.5km) of three interconnecting walking loops, but you're best to set aside at least a couple of hours for the full 3km track, which leads down to a waterfall spilling into **Lake Ngakoro**.

Wai-O-Tapu is 27km south of Rotorua along SH5 (towards Taupō), and a further 2km from the marked turn-off.

Waimangu
Volcanic Valley   Natural Feature

(☑07-366 6137; www.waimangu.co.nz; 587 Waimangu Rd; adult/child walk $42/14, cruise $45/14; ☺8.30am-5pm, last admission 3.30pm, to 6pm Jan) The most visible wound from Mt Tarawera's 1886 eruption, the Waimangu geothermal area spreads down a valley to **Lake Rotomahana** (Warm Lake). The experience is quite different from the other ticketed thermal areas as it involves a stroll down the lush, bush-lined valley, with a return by shuttle bus from either the 1.5km, 2.8km or 3.6km point. The 4km trail ends by the lake, where it's possible to take a 45-minute boat cruise past steaming cliffs.

Highlights include the powder-blue **Inferno Crater Lake**, which fills and emp-

ties every 38 days; **Frying Pan Lake**, the world's largest hot spring; and **Warbrick Terrace**, where the valley's colours are at their most intense. Waimangu (Black Water) refers to the dark water that once shot out of the world's mightiest geyser, reaching heights of up to 400m during its eruptions from 1900 to 1904.

Waimangu is 25 minutes' drive south of Rotorua, 6km off SH5 (towards Taupō) at a marked turn-off.

🟢 ACTIVITIES

Rotorua
Canopy Tours   Adventure Sports

(☑07-343 1001; www.canopytours.co.nz; 147 Fairy Springs Rd, Fairy Springs; Original Tour adult/child $159/129, Ultimate Tour $249/199; ☺8am-8pm Oct-Apr, to 6pm May-Sep) Explore a web of bridges, flying foxes, zip lines and platforms high in a lush native forest canopy 10 minutes out of town. The Original Tour is a 1.2km treetop route, while the new 2.1km Ultimate Tour heads higher and includes a cliff walk. All trips depart from its office opposite the gondola.

Free pick-up from town-centre accommodation available.

Skyline Rotorua
MTB Gravity Park   Mountain Biking

(☑07-347 0027; www.skyline.co.nz; 178 Fairy Springs Rd, Fairy Springs; 1/15/40 gondola uplifts with bike $34/67/128; ☺10am-5pm) Rotorua's status as a world-class mountain-biking destination is in part due to the 12km network of tracks coursing down Mt Ngongotahā. Trails here suit intermediate and crack riders, and access to the top of the park is provided by the **Skyline gondola** (☑07-347 0027; www.skyline.co.nz; 178 Fairy Springs Rd, Fairy Springs; adult/child $34/17; ☺9am-10pm). Bike rental is available at the lower chairlift station from **Mountain Bike Rotorua** (☑07-348 4295; www.mtbrotorua. co.nz; Waipa State Mill Rd, Whakarewarewa; hire 2hr/day from $39/60, ebike 2/4hr $99/129, guided rides from $150; ☺9am-5pm).

Paddle
Board Rotorua
Water Sports

(☑027 669 4410; www.paddleboardrotorua.
com; glowworm paddle $120) Gentle evening
stand-up paddle boarding trips across
Lake Okareka to small caves strung with
glowworms – you'll see constellations of
stars as you paddle on the open lake, and
constellations of glowworms inside the
caves. Also runs daytime SUP trips on
Lake Tarawera ($90). Trips depart from
the Rotorua i-SITE (p97).

Redwoods Treewalk
Walking

(☑027 536 1010; www.treewalk.co.nz; Long
Mile Rd, Whakarewarewa; adult/child $30/20;
☺9am-10.30pm, last entry 10pm) ◢ Billed as
'the world's longest living treewalk', this
elevated walkway extends for 700m, crossing 28 bouncy wooden bridges suspended
between century-old redwood trees. Most
of the pathway is around 6m off the forest
floor, but a high-loop option ascends to
20m. It's most impressive at night when it's
lit by striking wooden lanterns hung from
the trees.

Polynesian Spa
Hot Springs

(☑07-348 1328; www.polynesianspa.co.nz; 1000
Hinemoa St; family pools adult/child $23/10,
pavilion/deluxe pools $32/59, private pools per
30min from $23; ☺8am-11pm) A bathhouse
opened at these Government Gardens
springs in 1882, and people have been
taking to the Poly Pools' waters ever since.
The main pavilion and deluxe mineral pools
(36°C to 41°C) have lake views, making for
a prime sunset soak. The deluxe option
offers even more picturesque rock-lined
lakeside pools and includes a free locker
($5 otherwise) and towel.

Massage, mud and beauty treatments
are also available.

Velocity Valley
Adventure Sports

(☑0800 949 888, 07-357 4747; https://
velocityvalley.co.nz; 1335 Paradise Valley Rd,
Ngongotahā; 1/2/4 rides $55/90/149, bungy
$149; ☺9am-5pm) Velocity Valley provides
a bucolic setting with a buzz, combining

a 43m bungy with the 130km/h Swoop
swing, the Freefall Xtreme skydiving
simulation and the tiny, three-seat Agrojet,
one of NZ's fastest jetboats, which reaches
speeds of up to 100km/h around a very
tight 1km course.

Alongside is the Shweeb, a monorail
velodrome from which you hang in a
clear capsule and pedal yourself along
at speeds of up to 50km/h. You can also
practice your BMX jumps (two hours $35,
BYO bike) on ramps and the Freestyle
Airbag.

Happy Ewe Tours
Cycling

(☑022 622 9252; www.happyewetours.com;
1115 Pukuatua St; adult/child $69/35; ☺10am &
2pm) Saddle up for a three-hour small-
group bike tour of Rotorua, wheeling
past 27 sights around the city. It's all flat
and slow paced, so you don't need to be
at your physical peak (you're on holiday
after all).

⊗ EATING

Rotorua
Night Market
Market $

(www.facebook.com/rotoruanightmarket;
Tutanekai St; ☺5pm-late Thu) Tutanekai St is
closed off on Thursday nights as Rotorua
lays out a world of food. Buskers, coffee
vans and clothing and jewellery makers are
dotted among a couple of dozen food stalls
with global flavours from maple smoked
ribs to vegetarian Palestinian.

Artisan Cafe
Cafe $$

(☑07-348 0057; www.artisancaferotorua.com;
1149 Tutanekai St; mains $11-24; ☺7am-3.30pm
Mon-Fri, from 7.30am Sat & Sun; ☞☑) A spin-
ning wheel and a Mary Poppins–style bicy-
cle lend a folksy feel to Rotorua's best cafe.
But there's nothing old-fashioned about the
town's most creative and tasty breakfast
menu, which includes a vegan mushroom
ragu, chickpea and kumara (sweet potato)
burger, and the Little Miss Bene, an eggs
Benedict on rosti.

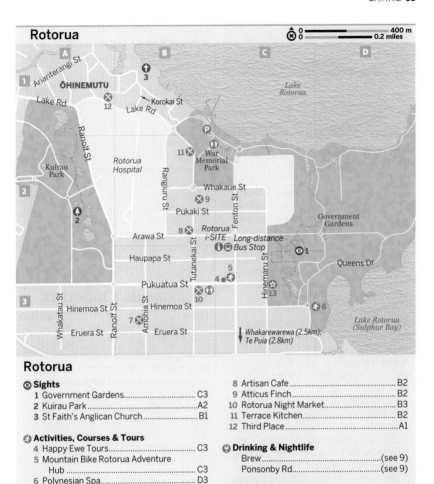

Rotorua

Rotorua

Abracadabra Cafe & Bar
International $$

(☑07-348 3883; www.abracadabracafe.com; 1263 Amohia St; mains $28-37, tapas $11-17; ⊙7.30am-late Tue-Sat, to 3pm Sun; 🛜🅿️👶)
Channelling Mexico and Morocco, sociable Abracadabra is a magical cave of spicy delights, from beef-and-apricot tagine to the grande burrito. There's an attractive front deck and a great beer terrace out the back, with a tepee and play area for kids. Vegan menu available.

Atticus Finch
International $$

(☑07-460 0400; https://atticusfinch.co.nz; Eat Streat, 1106 Tutanekai St; lunch $16-22, shared plates $6-36; ⊙noon-2.30pm & 5pm-late; 👶)
Named after the righteous lawyer in *To Kill a Mockingbird,* the hippest spot on Eat Streat plays to a theme with the Scout Sangria and Radley Sour cocktails, but it's

Hinemoa & Tūtānekai

Hinemoa was a young woman of a *hapū* (subtribe) that lived on the eastern shore of Lake Rotorua, while Tūtānekai was a young man of a Mokoia Island *hapū*. The pair met and fell in love during a regular tribal meeting. While both were of high birth, Tūtānekai was illegitimate, so marriage between the two was forbidden.

Home on Mokoia, the lovesick Tūtānekai played his flute for his love, the wind carrying the melody across the water. Hinemoa heard his declaration, but her people took to tying up the canoes at night to ensure she wouldn't go to him.

Finally, Tūtānekai's music won her over. Hinemoa undressed and swam the long distance from the shore to the island. When she arrived on Mokoia, Hinemoa found herself in a quandary. Having shed her clothing in order to swim, she could hardly walk into Tūtānekai's village naked. She hopped into a hot pool to think about her next move.

Eventually. Tūtānekai found Hinemoa in the pool and secreted her into his hut. Next morning, after a suspiciously long lie-in, a slave reported that someone was in Tūtānekai's bed. The two lovers were rumbled, and when Hinemoa's superhuman efforts to reach Tūtānekai had been revealed, their union was celebrated.

Descendants of Hinemoa and Tūtānekai still live around Rotorua today.

Lake Rotorua
WENDY_PAUL/GETTY IMAGES ©

the extensive menu of around 20 shared plates that makes this place novel in Rotorua. A concise menu of NZ beer and wine imparts a local flavour.

Third Place   Cafe $$
(☎07-349 4852; www.thirdplacecafe.co.nz; 35 Lake Rd, Ōhinemutu; breakfast $13-22, lunch $15-24; ⏰7.30am-4pm Mon-Fri, to 3.30pm Sat & Sun; 🛜) This superfriendly cafe is away from the hubbub, with awesome lake views. All-day breakfasts are headlined by a 'mumble jumble' of roast kumara (sweet potato), fried tomatoes and spicy chorizo, topped with a poached egg and hollandaise sauce, while lunchtime brings fish and chips and variations on a BLT theme. Score a window seat overlooking the steaming shores of Ōhinemutu.

🍷 DRINKING & NIGHTLIFE

Brew   Craft Beer
(☎07-346 0976; www.brewpub.co.nz; Eat Streat, 1103 Tutanekai St; ⏰11.30am-1am) Brew is run by the folks from Croucher Brewing, Rotorua's best microbrewery, It sits in a sunny spot on Eat Street. Thirteen taps showcase the best of Croucher's brews as well as guest beers from NZ and overseas, mopped up by pizzas, burgers and beer snacks such as bratwurst and jalapeño poppers. There's regular live music, and 'Hoppy Hour' every Friday evening.

Ponsonby Rd   Cocktail Bar
(☎021 151 2036; www.facebook.com/ponson byrd; Eat Streat, 1109 Tutanekai St; ⏰4pm-late Tue-Thu, to 3am Fri & Sat; 🛜) What's a lounge bar without chandeliers, a grand piano and red velvet curtains? This place, created by former TV weatherman turned Labour MP Tamati Coffey, is set into a narrow space that seems to remove you from Eat Streat. There's a soulful soundtrack and regular live music (and karaoke). Cocktails are the main focus, and the wine list is mostly faithful to NZ.

Rotorua i-SITE

ℹ️ INFORMATION

Rotorua i-SITE (☏07-348 5179; www.rotorua nz.com; 1167 Fenton St; ⏱7.30am-6pm; 🛜) The hub for travel information and bookings, including DOC walks.

ℹ️ GETTING THERE & AWAY

AIR

Rotorua Airport (ROT; ☏07-345 880; www. rotorua-airport.co.nz; SH30) is around 9km northeast of town.

Air New Zealand (☏0800 737 000; www. airnewzealand.co.nz) flies to/from Auckland, Wellington and Christchurch.

BUSES

All the **long-distance buses** (1167 Fenton St) stop outside the Rotorua i-SITE, where you can arrange bookings.

Daily **InterCity** (☏07-348 0366; www.inter city.co.nz) destinations include Auckland, Taupō, Napier and Wellington.

Skip (☏09-394 9180; https://skip.travel) has coaches to/from Auckland and Wellington daily.

TAUPŌ

In this Chapter

Taupō at a Glance...

Travelling into Taupō on a clear day along the northeastern shores of Lake Taupō is breathtaking: beyond the trout-filled lake (and yes, it's mighty large, the size of Singapore) you can see the snowcapped peaks of Tongariro National Park.

With an abundance of adrenaline-pumping activities, world-famous hikes, thermally heated waters and some wonderful places to eat, Taupō now rivals Rotorua as the North Island's premier resort town. Yet it remains a laid-back sort of place, at ease with itself in the high Central Plateau air.

Two Days in Taupō

Take a boat trip to the **Māori rock carvings** (p110) on Lake Taupō before checking out the excellent **Taupō Museum** (p110) in the afternoon. Have a local Lakeman beer at the **Lakehouse** (p113) – with views of the peaks of Tongariro National Park – to prep yourself for the **Tongariro Alpine Crossing** (p103) the next day, arguably the best day walk in NZ (oh, how they argue...). Celebrate afterwards with a meal at **Bistro** (p112).

Four Days in Taupō

Charge-up with a big breakfast at **Storehouse** (p111), then explore the amazing terraces and geysers at **Orakei Korako** (p110) geothermal area, a half-hour north of town. Alternatively, dangle a line in the lake, and marvel at **Huka Falls** (p110). Back in town, Asian-influenced lunches at **Replete Cafe & Store** (p111) will keep you going, while evenings are cosy at **Vine Eatery & Bar** (p113).

Taupō Map (p112)

Arriving in Taupō

Taxis from **Taupō Airport** (p113) to the centre of town cost between $27 and $30. An **airport shuttle** (p113) is also available.

Air New Zealand (p113) flies to Taupō from Auckland, while **Sounds Air** (p113) flies daily between Wellington and Taupō.

Bus services (p113) stop outside the **Taupō i-SITE** (p107).

Where to Stay

Taupō has plenty of good accommodation – hotels, motels, luxury B&Bs, holiday parks and hostels – all of which is in hot demand during late December and January, and during major sporting events like the Lake Taupō Cycle Challenge (November) and Ironman New Zealand (March); book ahead.

Mt Ngauruhoe

Tongariro National Park

Even before you arrive in Tongariro National Park, its three mighty volcanoes – Ruapehu, Ngauruhoe and Tongariro – steal your breath from the horizon. Get closer via ski fields and along the other-worldly, day-long Tongariro Alpine Crossing.

Great For...

☑ **Don't Miss**

Descending scoria slopes on the Tongariro Alpine Crossing, from the Red Crater to the Blue Lake.

Tongariro National Park – New Zealand's first – was gifted by local Tūwharetoa Māori more than a century ago. Long before it was granted dual Unesco World Heritage status for its volcanic landscape and deep cultural importance, Māori believed that the mountains were strong warriors who fought each other. In the process, they created this landscape that attracts more than 200,000 visitors each year. Visit once and you'll understand why it was worth fighting for.

Volcanoes

At 2797m, **Mt Ruapehu** (www.mtruapehu. com) is the highest mountain in the North Island. It is also one of the world's most active volcanoes. One eruption began in March 1945 and continued for almost a year, spreading lava over Crater Lake

ℹ️ Need to Know

Whakapapa Visitor Centre; ☎07-892 3729; www.doc.govt.nz/tongarirovisitorcentre; SH48; ⊙8am-5.30pm Oct-Apr, to 4.30pm May-Sep

✕ Take a Break

Take in the views with your meals at **Knoll Ridge Chalet** (☎07-892 4000; www.mtruapehu.com/see-and-eat/; Pinnacles breakfast adult/child $25/17.50, lunch $38/27, dinner $59/39; ⊙9am-4pm, dinner from 5.30pm).

★ Top Tip

Sun can soon turn to snow on the Tongariro Alpine Crossing. Be prepared for anything.

and sending huge, dark ash clouds as far away as Wellington. No wonder, then, that the mountain's name translates to 'pit of sound'.

Ruapehu rumbled in 1969, 1973 and most recently in 2007, but its worst disaster was on Christmas Eve 1953, when a crater-lake lip collapsed. An enormous lahar (volcanic mudflow) swept down the mountainside, destroying everything in its path, including a railway bridge. As a result, a crowded train plunged into the river, killing 151 people; it was one of NZ's worst tragedies.

Ongoing rumbles are reminders that the volcanoes in Tongariro National Park are very much in the land of the living. The last major event was in 2012 when **Mt Tongariro** (1967m), the northernmost and lowest peak in the park, gave a couple

of good blasts from its northern craters, causing a nine-month partial closure of the famous Tongariro Alpine Crossing track. (To see video of the 2012 eruptions, visit www. doc.govt.nz/eruption.)

Northeast of Mt Ruapehu is **Mt Ngauruhoe** (2287m), the youngest of Tongariro National Park's three volcanoes. Its first eruptions are thought to have occurred 2500 years ago. Until 1975 Ngauruhoe had erupted at least every nine years, including a 1954 eruption that lasted 11 months and disgorged 6 million cu metres of lava. Its perfectly symmetrical slopes are the reason that it was chosen to star as Mt Doom in Peter Jackson's *The Lord of the Rings* trilogy.

Tongariro Alpine Crossing

This popular **crossing** (www.tongarirocrossing. org.nz) is lauded as one of NZ's finest one-day walks, with more than 100,000 trampers finishing it yearly. It takes between six and eight hours to complete the 19.4km mixed-terrain walk amid steaming vents and springs, stunning rock formations, peculiar moonscape basins, impossible scree slopes and vast views – the most iconic across the Emerald Lakes.

The Crossing starts at Mangatepopo Rd car park, off SH47, and finishes at Ketetahi Rd, off SH46. Since 2017, parking has been restricted to four hours to reduce overcrowding. Organise shuttle transport; your accommodation will likely provide recommendations.

Safety Considerations

This is a fair-weather tramp. In poor conditions it is little more than an arduous up-and-down, with only orange-tipped poles to mark the passing of the day. Strong winds see trampers crawl along the ridge of Red Crater, the high point of the trek, and can blow people off their feet. A sunny day could still be a gusty day, so check in with your nearest information centre.

This is also an alpine crossing, and it needs to be treated with respect. You need a reasonable level of fitness and you should be prepared for all types of weather. Shockingly ill-equipped trampers are legendary on this route – stupid shoes, no rain jackets, blue jeans soaked to the skin – we've seen it all. As well as proper gear, you'll need to stock up on water and snacks. If you're keen to undertake a guided tramp, contact Adrift Tongariro (p111) or Adventure Outdoors (p111).

Mt Ruapehu (p102)

When to Go

The most crowded times on the track are the first nice days after Christmas and Easter, when there can easily be more than 1000 people strung out between the two road ends.

Ski Tongariro

Linked resorts **Whakapapa** (☏07-892 4000; www.mtruapehu.com/whakapapa; Bruce Rd; daily lift pass adult/child $149/89) and **Turoa** (☏06-385 8456; www.mtruapehu.com/turoa; Ōhakune Mountain Rd; daily lift pass adult/child $149/89) straddle either side of Mt Ruapehu and are New Zealand's two largest ski areas. Each offers similar skiing at a similar altitude (around 2300m), with areas to suit every level of experience, from beginners' slopes to black-diamond

runs for the pros. The same lift passes cover both ski areas.

The only accommodation at the Whakapapa ski field is in private lodges (mainly owned by ski clubs), so if not journeying here from Taupō, most visitors stay at Whakapaka or National Park Villages. Turoa is only 16km from Ōhakune, which has the best après-ski scene.

Club-operated **Tukino** (☏06-387 6294, 0800 885 466; www.tukino.org; Tukino Access Rd; day pass adult/child $70/35) is on Mt Ruapehu's east side, 46km from Tūrangi and 35km from Waiouru. It's quite remote, 7km down a gravel road from the sealed Desert Rd (SH1), and you need a 4WD vehicle to get in (or call ahead to book a return shuttle from the 2WD car park, adult/child $20/10). It offers uncrowded, backcountry runs, mostly beginner and intermediate.

Getting There & Away

Passing National Park Village and Ōhakune are buses run by InterCity (p113), and the *Northern Explorer* train run by **KiwiRail Scenic** (☏0800 872 467, 04-495 0775; www.greatjourneysofnz.co.nz) stops at National Park Village.

The main gateway into Tongariro National Park is Whakapapa Village, which also leads to Whakapapa Ski Area on SH48, but the park is also bounded by roads: SH1 (called the Desert Rd) to the east, SH4 to the west, SH46 and SH47 to the north and SH49 to the south.

Ōhakune Mountain Rd leads up to the Turoa Ski Area from Ōhakune. The Desert Rd is regularly closed when the weather is bad; detours will be in force. Likewise, Ōhakune Mountain Rd and Bruce Rd are subject to closures, and access beyond certain points may be restricted to 4WDs or cars with snow chains.

Ask your hotel or call the Tongariro National Park Visitor Centre (p101) in Whakapapa Village if you're uncertain.

JOAO INACIO/GETTY IMAGES ©

NANTWIN MÖLLER/EYEEM/GETTY IMAGES ©

Adventure Sports

Taupō is known as the 'Skydiving Capital of NZ'. Hurl yourself out of a plane if you must, but also on offer here are jetboating, white-water rafting, bungy jumping, parasailing, mountain biking...

Great For...

☑ Don't Miss

The view of Lake Taupō from a *looong* way above it (and getting rapidly closer).

Skydiving

More than 30,000 jumps a year are made over Taupō, which makes it the skydiving capital of the world (not just NZ!). With the deep-blue lake and snowcapped volcanic peaks of Tongariro National Park as a back-drop, it's certainly a picturesque place to do it. Just remember to keep your eyes open. Companies provide free transport to Taupō Airport (p113).

Skydive Taupo   Skydiving
(☎0800 586 766, 07-378 4662; www.
skydivetaupo.co.nz; 1465 Anzac Memorial
Dr; 12,000/15,000/18,500ft jump from
$279/359/499) Packages available and three
altitude options – the 18,500ft (approximately 5600m) skydive includes 75
seconds of free-fall.

CHAMELEONSEYE/SHUTTERSTOCK ©

ⓘ Need to Know

Taupō i-SITE (p113) can help with bookings.

✕ Take a Break

You're going to need some fuel: try Storehouse (p111) cafe.

★ Top Tip

For mega discounts, try booking activities through www.bookme.co.nz or www.grabone.co.nz/rotorua-taupo.

plunge. The 11m Cliffhanger swing is just as terrifying.

Craters MTB Park   Mountain Biking

(www.biketaupo.org.nz; Karapiti Rd; ⊗24hr) **FREE** For 50km of exciting off-road mountain-biking trails for all abilities, head to the Craters MTB Park, around 10 minutes' drive north of Taupō in the Wairakei Forest.

Big Sky Parasail   Adventure Sports

(☏0800 724 4759; www.bigskyparasail.co.nz; berth 20, Taupō Marina, Redoubt St; tandem/solo $99/119; ⊗10am-5pm mid-Oct–Apr) Lofty 12-minute parasailing flights from the lakefront. Choose from 1000ft or 500ft with the option of a free-fall descent when the boat stops.

Taupo Tandem Skydiving   Skydiving

(☏0800 826 336; www.taupotandemskydiving.com; Anzac Memorial Dr; 12,000/15,000ft jump $279/359) Various packages that include DVDs, photos and T-shirts ($418 to $659); **bungy combo** available.

Other Stuff

Taupo Bungy   Bungy Jumping

(☏0800 888 408; www.taupobungy.co.nz; 202 Spa Rd; solo/tandem jump $180/360; ⊗9.30am-5pm Oct-Mar, to 4pm Apr-Sep) On a cliff high above the Waikato River, this picturesque bungy site, now run by AJ Hackett, is the North Island's most popular. The courageous throw themselves off the edge of a platform, jutting 34m out over the cliff, for a heart-stopping 47m

Tongariro River

CHAMELEONSEYE/SHUTTERSTOCK ©

Trout Fishing

Famed around the world, the stellar trout fishing scene around Taupō is also a super-scenic chance for some holiday downtime, knee-deep in Lake Taupō or the mountain-fed rivers of Tongariro National Park.

Early European settlers who wanted to improve New Zealand's farming, hunting and fishing opportunities are responsible for the introduction of such ghastly wreckers as possums and rabbits. But one of their more benign introductions was that of trout – brown and rainbow – released into NZ rivers in the second half of the 19th century.

Today they are prized by sports anglers, who you'll find thigh-deep in limpid rivers and on the edge of deep green pools. Celebrities have also tried their luck in these North Island waters, including ex-US president Jimmy Carter, Michael Keaton, Harrison Ford and Liam Neeson, all of whom have stayed at the exclusive **Tongariro Lodge** (☏07-386 7946; www.tongarirolodge.co.nz; 83 Grace Rd; chalets

Great For...

☑ Don't Miss

Arcing your line across misty-still Lake Taupō before most folks are out of bed.

ⓘ **Need to Know**

Turangi i-SITE (☏0800 288 726, 07-386 8999; www.lovetaupo.com; 1 Ngawaka Pl; ⊙8.30am-4.30pm Nov-May 8am-4pm Jun-Oct; 🛜) is a good stop for information on trout fishing and Tongariro National Park. It issues fishing licences.

✕ **Take a Break**

Recharge with a kickin' coffee from Taupō institution Replete Cafe & Store (p111).

★ **Top Tip**

You'll need a fishing licence before you cast your first fly ($20 per day from outdoors shops).

boat per hour from $125) Just what the name implies! Two decades of experience.

Flyfishtaupo (☏027 445 0223; www.flyfish taupo.com) Tūrangi-based guide Brent Pirie offers a range of fishing excursions.

Fish Cruise Taupo (☏07-378 3444; www. fishcruisetaupo.co.nz; Taupō Marina, 65 Redoubt St; ⊙9am-5pm Oct-Mar, 9.30am-3pm Apr-Sep) Booking office for 13 local fishing boat operators.

from $175, villas from $269-750; 🛜) on the Tongariro River.

Tall tales boast of Taupō trout weighing more than a sack of spuds and measuring the length of a surfboard. Truth be told, more than 28,000 legal trout are bagged annually, by both domestic and international fishing enthusiasts.

Trout fishing is highly regulated, with plenty of rules regarding where and how they're to be fished. Licences are required and can be bought online at www.doc. govt.nz or www.fishandgame.org.nz. Our advice is to seek out a guide. Most are based in Taupō or Tūrangi, and offer flexible trips, with $300 for a half-day a ballpark figure. Operators include the following:

Taupo Troutcatcher (☏0800 876 882; www. taupotroutcatcher.co.nz; Taupō Marina, Ferry Rd;

◎ SIGHTS

Māori Rock Carvings
Historic Site

Accessible only by boat or kayak, these 14m-high carvings were etched into the cliffs near Mine Bay by master carver Matahi Whakataka-Brightwell in the late 1970s. They depict Ngātoro-i-rangi, the Māori navigator who guided the Tūwharetoa and Te Arawa tribes to the Taupō area 1000 years ago.

Orakei Korako
Natural Feature

(☑07-378 3131; www.orakeikorako.co.nz; 494 Orakei Korako Rd; adult/child $39/15; ☺8am-4.30pm Oct-Mar, to 4pm Apr-Sep; ☀) Tucked away from other more popular thermal fields, Orakei Korako is (since the destruction of the Pink and White Terraces, at least) arguably NZ's most spectacular thermal area, with active geysers, stunning terraces, bubbling rainbow lands and one of only two geothermal caves in the world.

Orakei Korako is arguably NZ's most spectacular thermal area

A 2.5km walking track (allow 1½ hours) follows stairs and boardwalks around the colourful silica terraces for which the park is famous. Entry includes the boat ride across the lake.

Taupō Museum
Museum

(☑07-376 0414; www.taupodc.govt.nz; 4 Story Pl; adult/child $5/free; ☺10am-4.30pm) This small but fascinating museum has an excellent Māori gallery and quirky displays, which include a 1960s caravan set up as if the occupants have just popped down to the lake. The centrepiece is an elaborately carved Māori meeting house, Te Aroha o Rongoheikume. Historical displays cover trout fishing, volcanic activity and a scale-model diorama of a sawmill tramway.

Huka Falls
Waterfall

(Huka Falls Rd) The Waikato, NZ's longest river, squeezes through a narrow chasm at Huka Falls, making a dramatic 11m drop into a surging crystal-blue pool at a rate of 220,000L per second. You can see the full force of this torrent that the Māori called Hukanui (Great Body of Spray) from the

Orakei Korako

WESTEND61/GETTY IMAGES ©

footbridge straddling the falls, while walking tracks run along both banks.

ACTIVITIES

Sail Barbary   Boating
(☏07-378 5879; www.sailbarbary.com; berths 9 & 10, Taupō Marina, Redoubt St; adult/child day cruises $49/29, evening $54/54; ☻10.30am, 2pm & 5pm) ✿ Sail to the Māori rock carvings in old-time style with new-time propulsion – a classic 1926 yacht, powered by an emission-free electric motor. The 2½-hour cruises include tea and coffee, and you're welcome to bring your own food and alcohol.

Ernest Kemp Cruises   Boating
(☏07-378 3444; www.ernestkemp.co.nz; berth 2, Taupō Marina, Redoubt St; adult/child $45/15; ☻10.30am & 2pm; 👶🐾) Board the *Ernest Kemp* replica steamboat for a two-hour cruise to view the Māori rock carvings, Hot Water Beach, the lakefront and Acacia Bay. There's lively commentary, and a swim stop if conditions allow. From October to April, a 5pm **cocktail cruise** (adult/child $46/25) includes pizza, wine and beer.

Well-behaved dogs are welcome on board.

Spa Thermal
Park Hot Spring   Hot Springs
(County Ave) FREE The hot thermal waters of the Otumuheke Stream meet the bracing Waikato River at this pleasant spot, redeveloped in 2018, creating a free spa bath with natural nooks. Take care: people have drowned trying to cool off in the fast-moving river. From the car park at the end of County Ave, it's an easy 10-minute walk along the **Huka Falls Walkway** (County Ave) to the stream.

Taupo Kayaking
Adventures   Kayaking
(☏0274 801 231; www.tka.co.nz; 2/876 Acacia Bay Rd, Acacia Bay; tours from adult/child $80/65, 1/2hr hire $20/30) Runs guided kayaking trips from its base in Acacia Bay to the Māori rock carvings, with the return trip

taking around four hours ($110, including refreshments). A range of other trips and walk/bike combos also available, as well as a hire service so you can paddle yourself to the carvings ($55).

Adrift Tongariro   Outdoors
(☏07-892 2751; www.adriftnz.co.nz; 53 Carroll St) Runs guided Tongariro Alpine Crossing walks (from $255), including winter and sunrise trips, as well as Tongariro Northern Circuit hikes (three days, $1195) and walks to Crater Lake on Mt Ruapehu ($295). Other trips on its roster include canoeing the Whanganui River (one/three days $295/1195) and mountain biking the Ōhakune Old Coach Road ($205).

Adventure Outdoors   Outdoors
(☏0800 386 925, 027 242 7209; www.adventure outdoors.co.nz; 60 Carroll St) Guided trips on the Tongariro Alpine Crossing (from $249), including in winter and in time for the summer sunrise – its 4am shuttle can have you first on the track, ahead of the crowds. Also runs paddling tours in inflatable two-person kayaks on the Whakapapa River ($235), and family floats on the Whanganui River ($235). Wetsuits and life jackets provided.

❌ EATING

Storehouse   Cafe $$
(☏07-378 8820; www.storehousetaupo.co.nz; 14 Runanga St; mains $8-26; ☻7am-4pm Mon-Fri, 8am-4pm Sat, to 3pm Sun) Taupō's coolest cafe is just outside the town centre, filling an old plumbing store over two warren-like levels. Indoor plants drape over warehouse beams downstairs, and a couple of old Chinese bikes hang from the walls. The fare is mighty fine, and breakfast dishes aren't afraid to mix genres – take the peanut butter porridge and fried-chicken waffles, for example…

Replete Cafe & Store   Cafe $$
(☏07-377 3011; www.replete.co.nz; 45 Heuheu St; mains $14-20; ☻8am-5pm Mon-Fri, to 4pm Sat & Sun; 📶) Under the same ownership since opening in 1993, this fabulous spot

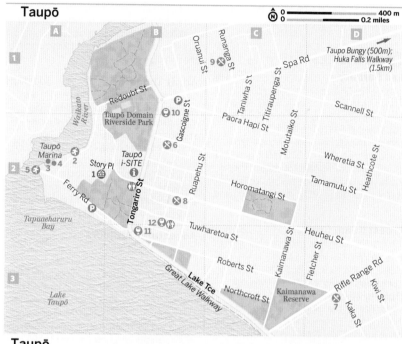

Taupō

Taupō

is one-half cafe and one-half shop selling designer kitchenware, ceramics and souvenirs. The cafe cabinet is as artistic as the neighbouring galleries, while lunch has an Asian flair (Japanese bolognese or kumara and cashew curry, anyone?).

Bistro   Modern NZ **$$**
(☑07-377 3111; www.thebistro.co.nz; 17 Tamamutu St; mains $29-39; ⏱5pm-late) Bistro is in danger of underselling itself with its 'simple but nice' strapline, given its ability to turn local and seasonal produce into creations such as grilled scotch fillet with roasted beets and Parmesan-battered cauliflower. Walnut-brown from ceiling to floor, the restaurant has a dark, wine-bar feel and a small but thoughtful beer-and-wine list.

Brantry   Modern NZ **$$$**
(☑07-378 0484; www.thebrantry.co.nz; 45 Rifle Range Rd; 3-course set menu $65-75; ⏱from 5.30pm) Run by two local sisters and operating out of an unobtrusive 1950s house, the Brantry reigns as arguably the best in the region for well-executed, brilliant-value fine dining. Dinner centres around a three-course set menu, and there's an impressive

wine list. Sit in the covered al fresco dining area (blankets provided) or dine in the cellar.

 DRINKING & NIGHTLIFE

Vine Eatery & Bar   Wine Bar

(📞07-378 5704; www.vineeatery.co.nz; 37 Tuwharetoa St; ⏰11am-midnight) Wineglass chandeliers hang from the sky-high industrial ceiling at this restaurant-cum-wine bar, where you can sit in comfy booths, on raised stools or in leather chairs by the fire. The wine list is global, if predominantly Kiwi, and tapas ($9 to $17) and meaty mains ($36 to $39) assist with the wine consumption. Stepping back out onto workaday Tuwharetoa St feels strangely surreal afterwards.

Crafty Trout Brewing Co   Brewery

(📞07-929 8570; www.craftytrout.co.nz; 133 Tongariro St; ⏰noon-late Wed-Mon; 📶) The beer has only had to journey up the stairs at this brewery-bar with 14 beers – Hefeweizen, pale ales, a porter – and ciders on tap amid faux-Alpine decor, complete with five cuckoo clocks. Try to nab one of the three balcony tables overhanging Tongariro St and dig into a wood-fired pizza ($14 to $28). Brewery tours run at 1pm (book ahead).

Lakehouse   Craft Beer

(📞07-377 1545; www.lakehousetaupo.co.nz; 10 Roberts St; ⏰8am-late) Craft beers in a craftily chosen spot. Nine taps pour a rotating selection of NZ brews, and there's a fridge filled with other hoppy goodness. You can partner your beer with a pizza, burger or stone-grilled steak (mains $22 to $45) and sit outside for fine views of the Tongariro volcanoes. Check the blackboard wall for the rundown of beers.

 INFORMATION

Taupō i-SITE (📞07-376 0027; www.lovetaupo. com; 30 Tongariro St; ⏰8.30am-5pm) Handles bookings for accommodation, transport and activities; dispenses cheerful advice; and stocks Department of Conservation (DOC) maps and town maps.

ℹ GETTING THERE & AWAY

Taupō Airport (📞07-378 7771; www.taupoair port.co.nz; 1105 Anzac Memorial Dr) is 8km south of town. Expect to pay about $27 to $30 for a taxi to the centre of town. **Great Lake Taxis** (📞07-377 8990; www.greatlaketaxis.co.nz) also runs an airport shuttle ($20, two people $30).

Air New Zealand (📞0800 737 000, 09-357 3000; www.airnewzealand.co.nz) flies from Auckland to Taupō two to three times daily (50 minutes), and **Sounds Air** (📞03-520 3080, 0800 505 005; www.soundsair.com) flies daily between Wellington and Taupō (one hour).

InterCity (📞07-348 0366; www.intercity coach.co.nz) and **Skip** (📞09-394 9180; https:// skip.travel) services stop outside the Taupō i-SITE, where bookings can be made.

HAWKE'S BAY

Hawke's Bay at a Glance...

Hawke Bay, the name given to the body of water that stretches from the Mahia Peninsula to Cape Kidnappers, looks like it's been bitten out of the North Island's eastern flank. Add an apostrophe and an 's' and you've got a region that stretches south and inland to encompass the bountiful Hawke's Bay Wine Region. With food, wine and art deco architecture the prevailing obsessions, it's smugly comfortable but thoroughly appealing, and is best viewed through a rosé-tinted wine glass. Napier, Hastings and Havelock North are the happening hubs.

One Day in Hawke's Bay

Check yourself into Napier with breakfast at **Mister D** (p122) (we can't get enough of those dark-rum-and-chocolate doughnuts), then sign up for an art deco architecture tour at the **Art Deco Centre** (p118). Having filled your eyes, fill your belly via a tasting menu at **Bistronomy** (p122). Drinks at hidden-away **Monica Loves** (p122) round out the evening.

Two Days in Hawke's Bay

With an extra day in which to play, after breakfast knock on some cellar doors in the Hawke's Bay Wine Region around Hastings. **On Yer Bike Winery Tours** (p124) offers self-guided cycles past the vines; myriad other outfits run minibus winery tours. Finish up with a show at **MTG Hawke's Bay** (p122) and drinks at **Emporium** (p122).

Previous page: Te Mata Peak (p124)
PHOTOS BRIANSCANTLEBURY/SHUTTERSTOCK ©

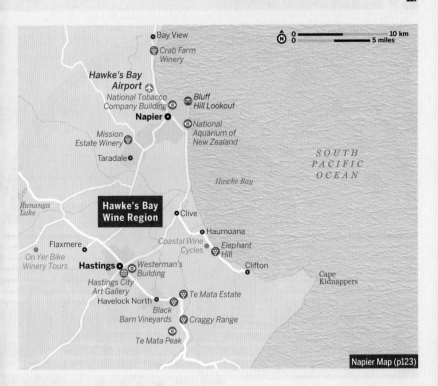

Arriving in Hawke's Bay

Hawke's Bay Airport (p125) lies 8km north of Napier and has flights to/from Auckland, Wellington, Christchurch and Blenheim. Air New Zealand, Jetstar and Sounds Air provide things with wings.

Bus services roll into Napier's **Clive Sq Bus Stop** (p123) from Wellington, Taupō, Rotorua and beyond, continuing to Hastings (or passing through en route), stopping at **Russell St Bus Stop** (p125).

Where to Stay

Unless there's a festival happening, such as the **Art Deco Festival** (p119) in Napier, finding a bed around Hawke's Bay isn't usually a challenge. Expect plenty of good motels, some charismatic hostels and a cache of characterful B&Bs. If you want water views with that, you'll be paying extra.

National Tobacco Company Building

KAREN LEWIS/GETTY IMAGES ©

Art Deco Napier

Napier's claim to fame is undoubtedly its glorious cache of art deco architecture. A close study of these treasures would take days. If you haven't got time for a tour, just hit the streets (particularly Tennyson and Emerson) and remember to look up!

At 10.46am on 3 February 1931, Napier was levelled by a catastrophic earthquake (7.9 on the Richter scale). Fatalities numbered 258. Napier suddenly found itself 40 sq km larger, as the earthquake heaved sections of what was once a lagoon 2m above sea level (Napier airport was once more 'port', less 'air'). A fevered rebuilding program ensued, resulting in one of the world's most uniformly art deco cities.

Great For...

☑ **Don't Miss**

The drop-dead gorgeous National Tobacco Company Building, a little hard to find in Ahuriri.

Deco Tours

Napier's excellent **Art Deco Centre** (☎06-835 0022; www.artdeconapier.com; 7 Tennyson St; ☺9am-5pm) runs daily 1½-hour guided art deco walks ($24) departing the Napier i-SITE (p123) at 10am, plus daily 2½-hour tours ($26) leaving the Art Deco Centre at 2pm. There's also a little shop here, plus

Road sign at the entrance to Napier

EQROY/SHUTTERSTOCK ©

ⓘ Need to Know

Napier's **Art Deco Festival** (www.art deconapier.com; ☉Feb) is a blast from the past, but book your beds well ahead.

✘ Take a Break

Duck into Milk & Honey (p122) cafe in Aruhiri mid-art-deco tour.

★ Top Tip

A little off the tourist trail, Marewa is Napier's art deco suburb, with some marvellous old houses.

National Tobacco Company Building   Architecture

(☎06-834 1911; www.heritage.org.nz/the-list/ details/1170; cnr Bridge & Ossian Sts, Ahuriri; ☉lobby 9am-5pm Mon-Fri) Around the shore at Ahuriri, the National Tobacco Company Building (1932) is arguably the region's deco masterpiece, combining art deco forms with the natural motifs of art nouveau. Roses, raupo (bulrushes) and grapevines frame the elegantly curved entrance.

Hastings

Like Napier, nearby Hastings was devastated by the 1931 earthquake and also boasts some fine art deco and Spanish Mission buildings, which were constructed in the aftermath. Main-street highlights include the **Westerman's Building** (☎06-873 5526; www.heritage.org.nz/the-list/details/178; cnr Russell St & Heretaunga St E, Hastings), arguably the bay's best example of the Spanish Mission style. Hastings i-SITE (p125) stocks the *Art Deco Hastings* brochure.

brochures for the self-guided Art Deco Walk ($10), Art Deco Scenic Drive ($3) and Marewa Meander ($3). Other options include a minibus tour ($45, 1½ hours), vintage car tour ($125, 45 minutes) and the childrens' Art Deco Explorer treasure hunt ($5).

Best Buildings

Daily Telegraph Building   Architecture

(☎06-834 1911; www.heritage.org.nz/the-list/ details/1129; 49 Tennyson St; ☉9am-5pm Mon-Fri) The Daily Telegraph is one of the stars of Napier's art deco show, with superb zigzags, fountain shapes and a ziggurat aesthetic. If the front doors are open, nip inside and ogle the painstakingly restored foyer (it's a real-estate office these days).

Mission Estate Winery

MATTHEW WILLIAMS ELLIS/GETTY IMAGES ©

Hawke's Bay Wine Region

Once upon a time, this district was famous for its orchards. Today, grapevines have top billing, with Hawke's Bay now New Zealand's second-largest wine-producing region (behind Marlborough). Bordeaux-style reds, syrah and chardonnay predominate.

Great For...

☑ Don't Miss

The chardonnay at Black Barn Vineyards – like kissing someone pretty on a summer afternoon.

Visit i-SITE in Napier (p123) or Hastings (p125) for minibus and cycling wine tours.

Best Wineries

Black Barn Vineyards   Winery

(☏06-877 7985; www.blackbarn.com; Black Barn Rd, Havelock North; ⊙cellar door 10am-4pm, restaurant 10am-5pm Sun-Wed, to 9pm Thu-Sat, reduced hours Apr-Oct) This hip, inventive winery has a bistro, a gallery, a farmers market in summer and an amphitheatre for regular concerts and movie screenings. Taste the flagship chardonnay.

Crab Farm Winery   Winery

(☏06-836 6678; www.crabfarmwinery.co.nz; 511 Main North Rd, Bay View; ⊙10am-5pm Thu, Sat & Sun, to 9pm Fri) Decent, reasonably priced wines, and a great cafe with regular live

❶ Need to Know

Find the *Hawke's Bay Winery Guide* at local i-SITEs, or download it from www.winehawkesbay.co.nz.

✕ Take a Break

Eat at a winery restaurant, or try Opera Kitchen (p125) in Hastings.

★ Top Tip

Wine tasting by bike? Pick up the *Hawke's Bay Trails* cycling map, or download it from www.winehawkesbay.co.nz.

troubadours and relaxed, rustic vibes. Good for lunch, a glass of rosé or both.

Craggy Range   Winery

(☏06-873 7126; www.craggyrange.com; 253 Waimarama Rd, Havelock North; ☺10am-6pm) Definitely one of Hawke's Bay's flashiest wineries – wonderful wines, excellent restaurant.

Mission Estate Winery   Winery

(☏06-845 9354; www.missionestate.co.nz; 198 Church Rd, Taradale; ☺9am-5pm Mon-Sat, 10am-4.30pm Sun) New Zealand's oldest winery (1851). Follow the long tree-lined driveway up the hill to the restaurant (serving lunch and dinner, mains $30 to $40) and cellar door.

Te Mata Estate   Winery

(☏06-877 4399; www.temata.co.nz; 349 Te Mata Rd, Havelock North; ☺10am-5pm Mon-Sat, 11am-4pm Sun) ✍ The legendary Coleraine red at this unpretentious, old-school, family-run winery is worth the trip.

Wining & Dining

Elephant Hill   Winery

(☏06-872 6073; www.elephanthill.co.nz; 86 Clifton Rd, Te Awanga; ☺11am-5pm Sep-May, to 4pm Jun-Aug) ✍ Huge picture windows provide unencumbered views of Cape Kidnappers and vineyards, and Elephant Hill's award-winning wines partner supremely with seasonal dishes. Exquisite.

Paper Mulberry Café   Cafe $

(☏06-856 8688; www.papermulberrycafe.co.nz; 89 SH2, Pukehou; snacks $5-10, lunch mains $13-22; ☺7am-4pm) Halfway between Waipawa and Hastings, this retro cafe-gallery in a 100-year-old, aquamarine-coloured church serves excellent coffee, smoothies and homespun food (try the chubby lamb pie). Well worth a stop for a chomp, a browse through the local crafts on the side tables and to warm your buns by the wood heater in winter.

Napier

◎ SIGHTS

MTG Hawke's Bay   Museum
(Museum Theatre Gallery; ☏06-835 7781; www.
mtghawkesbay.com; 1 Tennyson St; ◎9.30am-
5pm) **FREE** The beating cultural heart of
Napier is the smart-looking MTG – a
gleaming-white museum-theatre-gallery
space by the water. The MTG showcases
live performances, film screenings and
regularly changing gallery and museum
displays (earthquake gallery, Māori heritage, social history), along with touring and
local exhibitions. Napier's rather lovely
public **library** (www.napierlibrary.co.nz) is
here too (free wi-fi).

National Aquarium of
New Zealand   Aquarium
(☏06-834 1404; www.nationalaquarium.
co.nz; 546 Marine Pde; adult/child/family
$23/11.50/62; ◎9am-5pm, last entry 4.30pm)
Inside this modern complex with its sting-
ray-inspired roof are piranhas, terrapins,
eels, kiwi, tuatara and a whole lotta fish.
Snorkellers can swim with sharks ($100),
or sign up for a Little Penguin Close Encounter ($70). The penguins get a feed at
9.30am, 1.30pm and 3.30pm, the reef fish
at 10am and the sharks at 2pm.

Bluff Hill Lookout   Viewpoint
(Lighthouse Rd) The convoluted route to the
top of Bluff Hill (102m) goes up and down
like an elevator on speed (best to drive),
but rewards intrepid mountaineers with
expansive views across the busy port. Bring
a picnic or some fish and chips.

✖ EATING & DRINKING

Bistronomy   Bistro $$$
(☏06-834 4309; www.bistronomy.co.nz; 40
Hastings St; lunch mains $22-35, dinner 6/9
courses $80/110; ◎5pm-late Wed & Thu,
noon-late Fri & Sat; ♪) ✿ Bistronomy is
proof that NZ's regional restaurants can
create high-end cuisine just as well as
the spiffy eateries in Auckland, Welling-

ton and Christchurch. Finely judged
seasonal menus might include lamb loin
with sage custard and charred leek, or a
blue-cheese omelette with truffle oil and
polenta fries. Wines from Argentina to the
Esk Valley; interior design from the big-
city playbook.

Mister D   Modern NZ $$
(☏06-835 5022; www.misterd.co.nz; 47
Tennyson St; mains breakfast $15-24, lunch &
dinner $27-38; ◎7.30am-4pm Sun-Wed, to late
Thu-Sat) This long, floorboarded room with
its green-tiled bar is the pride and joy of the
Napier foodie scene. Hip and slick but not
grossly unaffordable, with quick-fire service
delivering the likes of chestnut flan with
mushrooms or roast-duck risotto. Addictive
doughnuts are served with syringes full of
chocolate, jam or custard (DIY injecting...
adult versions infused with booze). Bookings essential.

Milk & Honey   Cafe $$
(☏06-833 6099; www.themilkandhoney.co.nz;
19 Hardinge Rd, Ahuriri; mains breakfast $9-21,
lunch $14-25, dinner $29-35; ◎7am-9pm) One
of Ahuriri's top options, Milk & Honey
combines ocean and boardwalk views with
versatile day-to-night menus. Hawke's Bay
beers and wines do their thing alongside the likes of a vegan Bircher muesli
breakfast bowl, chicken and lemongrass
broth for lunch, or tamarind beef cheeks for
dinner – all amid polished concrete, wicker
and ambient tunes.

Monica Loves   Bar
(☏06-650 0240; www.monicaloves.co.nz; 39
Tennyson St; ◎3pm-late Wed-Sat) Big-city
laneway style comes to Napier at this bar
tucked away off Tennyson St. Look for the
big neon sign proclaiming 'Who shot the
barman?' and you're in the right place
for cool cocktails, regular surprises in the
beer taps and a Hawke's Bay–centric wine
list. We love the black wine barrels and
Pollock-goes-graffiti mural too, Monica.

Emporium   Bar
(☏06-835 0013; www.emporiumbar.co.nz; Art
Deco Masonic Hotel, cnr Tennyson St & Marine

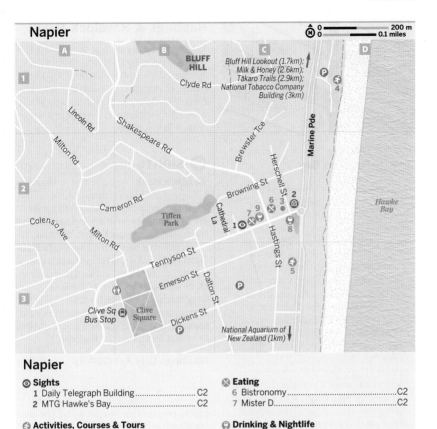

Napier

Sights
1 Daily Telegraph Building	C2
2 MTG Hawke's Bay	C2

Activities, Courses & Tours
3 Art Deco Centre	C2
4 Fishbike	D1
5 Napier City Bike Hire	C3

Eating
6 Bistronomy	C2
7 Mister D	C2

Drinking & Nightlife
8 Emporium	C2
9 Monica Loves	C2

Pde; ⊙7am-late; 🛜) Napier's most civilised venue, Emporium is super atmospheric, with its marble-topped bar, fab art deco details and old-fashioned relics strewn about. Brisk staff, creative cocktails, good coffee, NZ wines, bistro fare (plates $15 to $39) and a prime location seal the deal. On a warm night the windows fold open to the sea air.

ℹ️ INFORMATION

Napier i-SITE (📞06-834 1911; www.napiernz. com; 100 Marine Pde; ⊙9am-5pm, extended

hours Dec-Feb; 🛜) Central, helpful and right by the bay.

ℹ️ GETTING THERE & AWAY

Air New Zealand (www.airnewzealand.co.nz) flies direct to/from Auckland, Wellington and Christchurch.

It is possible to book **InterCity** (www. intercity.co.nz) buses online or at the i-SITE (p123), with services departing from **Clive Sq bus stop**.

Cycling Hawke's Bay

The 200km network of Hawke's Bay Trails (www.nzcycletrail.com/hawkes-bay-trails) – part of the national Ngā Haerenga, New Zealand Cycle Trails project – offers cycling opportunities from short, city scoots to hilly, single-track shenanigans. Dedicated cycle tracks encircle Napier, Hastings and the coastline, with landscape, water and wine themes. Pick up the *Hawke's Bay Trails* brochure from the Napier i-SITE (p123) or online.

Fishbike (06-835 6979; www.fishbike.co.nz; Pacific Surf Club, 22 Marine Pde; bike hire per half-/full day from $30/40, tandems per hour $40; ◷9am-5.30pm) rents comfortable bikes – including tandems. **Napier City Bike Hire** (0800 245 344; www.bikehirenapier.co.nz; 117 Marine Pde; bike hire adult/child half-day from $30/40, full day from $35/50; ◷9am-5pm) is another option. Numerous cycle companies pedal fully geared-up tours around the bay, with winery visits near-mandatory. Operators include the following:

Coastal Wine Cycles (06-875 0302; www.winecycles.co.nz; 41 East Rd, Te Awanga; tours adult/child $40/20; ◷10am-6pm)

On Yer Bike Winery Tours (021 292 8080; www.onyerbikehb.co.nz; 2543 SH50, Roy's Hill; full-day tours from $55; ◷10am-4pm)

Tākaro Trails (06-835 9030; www.takarotrails.co.nz; 9 Nelson Quay, Ahuriri; mountain bike hire per half-/full day $75/110; ◷9am-5.30pm)

D. PIMBOROUGH/SHUTTERSTOCK ©

Hastings & Havelock North

Positioned at the centre of the Hawke's Bay Wine Region, busy Hastings is a commercial hub 20km south of Napier. A few kilometres of vines and orchards still separate it from Havelock North, with its prosperous village atmosphere and the towering backdrop of Te Mata Peak.

◉ SIGHTS

Te Mata Peak   Mountain

(027 945 6970; www.tematapark.co.nz; off Te Mata Rd, Havelock North; ◷daylight hours) Rising dramatically from the Heretaunga Plains 16km south of Havelock North, Te Mata Peak (399m) is part of the 1-sq-km **Te Mata Trust Park**. The summit road passes sheep tracks, rickety fences and vertigo-inducing stone escarpments, cowled in a bleak, lunar-landscape-meets-Scottish-Highlands atmosphere. On a clear day, views from the **lookout** fall away to Hawke's Bay, the Mahia Peninsula and distant Mt Ruapehu.

Hastings City Art Gallery   Gallery

(HCAG; 06-871 5095; www.hastingscityartgallery.co.nz; 201 Eastbourne St E, Hastings; ◷10am-4.30pm) **FREE** The city's neat little gallery presents contemporary NZ (including Māori) and international art in a bright, purpose-built space. Expect some wacky stuff. On the lawns out the front is *Ngā Pou o Heretuanga* – 19 fantastic Māori totems, each carved by reps from a regional *marae*.

✦ EATING & DRINKING

Maina   Cafe $$

(06-877 1714; www.maina.co.nz; 11 Havelock Rd, Havelock North; mains breakfast & lunch $10-24, dinner $29-36; ◷7am-11pm Mon-Fri, 8am-11pm Sat, 9am-3pm Sun; ✎) ✦ Blur the lines between breakfast, lunch and dinner at Havelock North's best cafe, inside a former post office infused with stylish retro Kiwiana decor. Highlights include creamy Te Mata mushrooms on organic sourdough, and roast pork belly with pumpkin puree. Pizzas and an ever-evolving salad selection are safe bets, while superior home-style baking includes perfect midmorning coffee and doughnuts.

Common Room
Bar

(📞06-211 2446; www.facebook.com/common roomhb; 227 Heretaunga St E, Hastings; ⊙3pm-late Tue-Thu & Sat, noon-late Fri & Sun) There's pretty much nothing wrong with this hip little bar in central Hastings: cheery staff, bar snacks, craft beer, local wines, zany retro interior, garden bar, Persian rugs, live music and a tune-scape ranging from jazz to alt-country to indie – all the good stuff!

GodsOwn Brewery
Craft Beer

(📞027 931 1042; www.godsownbrewery.co.nz; 3672 SH50, Maraekakaho; ⊙noon-10pm Mon & Sat, 3-10pm Fri, noon-8pm Sun) 🍺 This low-key, earthy microbrewery 22km east of Hastings operates out of a safari tent and a 1973 caravan. Bucolic aromas, hop vines, laid-back tunes, outdoor tables, a smouldering fire pit...it's a uniquely NZ scene. Trad European beers like French *biere de garde* and German pilsner emerge from the taps. Spent brewing grains are used in zesty wood-fired flatbreads ($10 to $22).

Opera Kitchen
Cafe $$

(📞06-870 6020; www.eatdrinksharehb.co.nz; 306 Eastbourne St E, Hastings; mains $15-26; ⊙7.30am-4pm Mon-Fri, 9am-3pm Sat & Sun; 🍴) Occupying a high-ceilinged heritage building – formerly the HB Electric Power Board – our favourite Hastings cafe serves up sophisticated breakfasts and lunches

with international accents. Spend a few hours browsing design mags and feasting on all-day omelettes or porcini mushroom risotto with thyme and hazelnuts. Heavenly pastries, great coffee and efficient staff. A 'morning medicine' Bloody Mary will right your rudder.

ℹ️ INFORMATION

Hastings i-SITE (📞06-873 5526; www.hawkes baynz.com; Westermans Bldg, cnr Russell St & Heretaunga St E; ⊙9am-5pm Mon-Fri, to 3pm Sat, 10am-1.45pm Sun) offers maps, brochures and bookings.

Havelock North i-SITE (📞06-877 9600; www. havelocknorthnz.com; 1 Te Aute Rd, Havelock North; ⊙10am-5pm Mon-Fri, to 3pm Sat, to 1.45pm Sun) provides local info in a cute little booth.

ℹ️ GETTING THERE & AWAY

Napier's **Hawke's Bay Airport** (📞06-834 0742; www.hawkesbay-airport.co.nz; cnr SH2 & Watchman Rd) is a 20-minute drive from Hastings. **Air New Zealand** (www.airnewzealand.co.nz) flies direct to/from Auckland, Wellington and Christchurch. **Jetstar** (www.jetstar.com) also flies to Napier from Auckland, while **Sounds Air** (www.soundsair.com) has direct flights to/from Blenheim a few times a week.

InterCity (www.intercity.co.nz) buses stop at the **Russell St bus stop**.

WELLINGTON

Wellington at a Glance...

On a sunny, windless day, Wellington is up there with the best of them. It's lovely to behold, sitting on a hook-shaped harbour ringed with ranges that wear a snowy cloak in winter. The compact downtown area gives 'Welly' a bigger-city buzz and, being the capital, it's endowed with museums, theatres, galleries and arts organisations. Wellingtonians are rightly proud of their caffeine and craft-beer scenes, and there's no shortage of artsy types doing interesting things in old warehouses across town.

Sadly, windless days are not the norm for Wellington. In New Zealand the city is infamous for two things: its frequent tremors and the umbrella-shredding gales that barrel through with regularity. Wellington: terrible for hairstyles, brilliant for kites.

Two Days in Wellington

First up, drive to **Mt Victoria Lookout** (p138) to see an overview of the city. Shop and lunch on boho-hipster **Cuba St**, then catch some Kiwi culture at **Te Papa** (p130) or the **Wellington Museum** (p131). Wash off the day at **Golding's Free Dive** (p132). The next day, reconstitute at **Fidel's** (p142), then visit **Zealandia** (p138) to learn about NZ conservation. Grab dinner at **Logan Brown** (p143).

Four Days in Wellington

Break the fast at **Husk** (p144), then tour **Parliament** (p139; is Jacinda in the house?). The **Wellington Botanic Gardens** (p138) are wander-ful; take the **Wellington Cable Car** (p141) to the top (killer views), then meander downhill. Make dinner reservations at **Noble Rot** (p143), and then finally drinks beckon: hit rooftop **Dirty Little Secret** (p144) and bookish **Library** (p144) for craft beer and cocktails. On day four, take a **Wellington Movie Tour** (p135) and then grab dinner at **Ortega** (p143) before a movie at the **Embassy Theatre** (p134).

Previous page:
TUPUNGATO/SHUTTERSTOCK ©

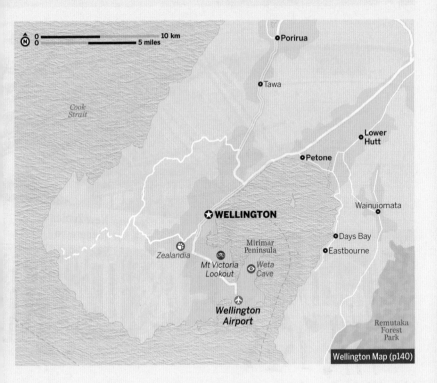

Arriving in Wellington

Wellington Airport (p145) Wellington's airport is 6km southeast of the city. Shuttles cost $20 (15 minutes). Airport Flyer buses run 7am to 9pm ($9); a taxi costs about $30.

Ferry To/from Picton on the South Island (3½ hours). **Bluebridge Ferries** (p146) and **Interislander** (p146) are the operators.

Buses InterCity (p146) and **Skip** (p146) depart for North Island destinations.

Trains Depart for Auckland and Palmerston North.

Where to Stay

Accommodation in Wellington is more expensive than in regional areas, but there are plenty of options close to the city centre. Free parking spots are a rarity – ask in advance. Wellington's budget accommodation largely takes the form of multistorey hostel megaliths. Motels dot the city fringes. Self-contained apartments are popular, and often offer bargain weekend rates. Book well in advance.

Te Papa

GEORGECLERK/GETTY IMAGES ©

Wellington's Museums & Galleries

Wellington is an arty, learned kinda town – expect quality gallery experiences and some truly fab museums (...particularly useful on those rainy, hurricane-swept Wellington afternoons).

Great For...

☑ Don't Miss

The chance to visit a Māori *marae* (meeting house) at Te Papa.

Te Papa

New Zealand's national museum, **Te Papa** (☎04-381 7000; www.tepapa.govt.nz; 55 Cable St; ⊙10am-6pm; 🖐) 🖋 **FREE** is hard to miss, taking up a sizeable chunk of the Wellington waterfront. 'Te Papa Tongarewa' loosely translates as 'treasure box': the riches inside include an amazing collection of Māori artefacts and the museum's own colourful *marae* (meeting house); natural history and environment exhibitions; Pacific and NZ history galleries; and themed hands-on 'discovery centres' for children. Toi Art, a revitalised home for the National Art Collection, also opened here in 2018. General admission is free, but there is an admission fee for big-name temporary exhibitions.

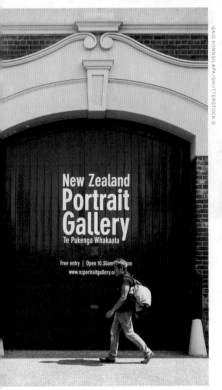

GAID KORNSILAPA/SHUTTERSTOCK ©

New Zealand
**Portrait
Gallery**
Te Pukenga Whakaata

Free entry | Open 10.30am—4.30pm
www.nzportraitgallery.or

❶ Need to Know

The museums and galleries listed here are within walking distance of one another – make a day of it!

✖ Take a Break

Near Te Papa, **Field & Green** (📞04-384 4992; www.fieldandgreen.co.nz; 262 Wakefield St; mains $15-36; ⏱8.30am-2.30pm & 5.30-9.30pm Wed-Fri, 9.30am-9.30pm Sat, 9.30am-2.30pm Sun) serves classy 'European soul food'.

★ Top Tip

Guided tours of Te Papa are free; at Wellington Museum you'll pay from $29/21 per adult/child.

City Gallery Wellington

Housed in the monumental old library in Civic Sq, Wellington's much-loved **City Gallery** (📞04-913 9032; www.citygallery.org.nz; Civic Sq; ⏱10am-5pm) FREE does a cracking job of securing acclaimed contemporary international exhibitions, as well as unearthing up-and-comers and supporting those at the forefront of the NZ scene. Charges may apply for major exhibits.

New Zealand Portrait Gallery

Housed in a heritage red-brick warehouse on the waterfront, this excellent **gallery** (📞04-472 2298; www.nzportraitgallery.org.nz; Shed 11, Customhouse Quay; ⏱10.30am-4.30pm) FREE presents a diverse range of NZ portraiture and caricature from its own collection, plus frequently changing guest exhibitions.

Wellington Museum

For an imaginative, interactive experience of Wellington's social and maritime history, head to this beguiling little **museum** (📞04-472 8904; www.museumswellington.org.nz; 3 Jervois Quay, Queens Wharf; ⏱10am-5pm; 👶) FREE, housed in an 1892 Bond Store on the wharf. Highlights include a moving documentary on the *Wahine*, the interisland ferry that sank in the harbour in 1968 with the loss of 51 lives. Māori legends are dramatically told using tiny holographic actors and special effects.

The Attic has eclectic exhibits including a whiz-bang time machine and a suitably kooky display on Wellington vampire flick *What We Do in the Shadows*.

Garage Project Taproom

KRISTA ROSSOW/ALAMY STOCK PHOTO ©

Craft Beer

Fuelled by a heady mix of musos, web developers and filmmakers, Wellington sustains the best craft-beer scene in the southern hemisphere. It's also a compact scene, easily explored on foot.

Great For...

☑ Don't Miss

Garage Project's Dirty Boots Mosh Pit APA – dank hoppy deliverance.

Bars

Golding's Free Dive
Craft Beer

(☏04-381 3616; www.goldingsfreedive.co.nz; 14 Leeds St; ⏰noon-midnight; ⛺) Hidden down a busy little back alley near Cuba St, gloriously garish Golding's is a bijou craft-beer bar with far too many merits to mention. We'll single out ex-casino swivel chairs, a ravishing Reuben sandwich and Zappa and Bowie across the airways.

Fortune Favours
Craft Beer

(☏04-595 4092; www.fortunefavours.beer; 7 Leeds St; ⏰11am-11pm Sun-Thu, to midnight Fri & Sat) The bold and the beautiful head to the rooftop of this old furniture factory to sup on beer brewed in the shiny vats downstairs. Along with seven of its own concoctions it serves guest brews, wine and cocktails.

● Need to Know
Visit www.craftbeercapital.com for
beery propaganda.

✕ Take a Break
Cuba St's Loretta (p143) is a relaxed
bistro near some of Wellington's best
craft-beer bars.

★ Top Tip
Wellington's annual **Beervana** (www.
beervana.co.nz) festival chases away the
August chills.

Microbreweries

Garage Project Taproom   Craft Beer
(☑04-802 5324; www.garageproject.co.nz; 91
Aro St, Aro Valley; ☺3-10pm Mon-Fri, noon-
10pm Sat & Sun) The actual microbrewery
occupies a former petrol station just down
the road (68 Aro St), serving craft beer
by the litre, petrol-pump style. If you'd
rather consume your brew in less industrial
quantities, head to this narrow, graffiti-lined
bar. Order a tasting flight or chance your
arm on the Pernicious Weed or Venusian
Pale Ale.

Hashigo Zake   Craft Beer
(☑04-384 7300; www.hashigozake.co.nz; 25
Taranaki St; ☺noon-late; 🛜) This bricky
bunker is the HQ for a zealous beer-import
business, splicing big-flavoured international brews into a smartly selected NZ
range. Hopheads squeeze into the sweet
little side-lounge on live-music nights.

Fork & Brewer   Craft Beer
(☑04-472 0033; www.forkandbrewer.co.nz; 20a
Bond St; ☺11.30am-11pm) Aiming to improve
on the post-beer kebab experience, F&B
offers excellent burgers, pizzas, pies, share
plates and meaty mains to go along with
its crafty brews (of which there are dozens
– the Low Blow IPA comes highly recommended). Oh, and there are dark-beer
doughnuts for dessert!

Little Beer Quarter   Craft Beer
(☑04-803 3304; www.littlebeerquarter.co.nz;
6 Edward St; ☺3.30pm-late Mon, noon-late
Tue-Sat, 3pm-late Sun) Buried in a back lane,
lovely LBQ is warm, inviting and moodily
lit in all the right places. Well-curated taps
and a broad selection of bottled beer pack
a hoppy punch.

Weta Workshop

Wellywood

In recent years Wellington has stamped its name firmly on the world map as the home of New Zealand's booming film industry and off-piste Hollywood big-screen production, earning itself the nickname Wellywood.

Acclaimed director Sir Peter Jackson still calls Wellington home; the success of his *The Lord of the Rings* films and subsequent productions such as *King Kong, The Adventures of Tintin* and *The Hobbit* have made him a powerful Hollywood player, and have bolstered Wellington's reputation.

Canadian director James Cameron is also in on the action; shooting has commenced for his four *Avatar* sequels, the first of which is due for a 2021 release. Cameron and his family are NZ residents, with land-holding in rural Wairarapa. They have that in common with Jackson, who also has a property there.

Great For...

☑ Don't Miss

Winter's **New Zealand International Film Festival** (www.nzff.co.nz; ⊙Jul-Aug), a roving two-week indie film fest.

Cinemas

Embassy Theatre
Cinema

(☎04-384 7657; www.embassytheatre.co.nz; 10 Kent Tce; tickets adult/child $18/12; ⊙10am-

Embassy Theatre

FILEDIMAGE/GETTY IMAGES ©

ⓘ Need to Know

Movie times are listed in the daily *Dominion Post* and at www.flicks.co.nz.

✕ Take a Break

Close to the Embassy Theatre, Ortega (p143) is a top seafood eatery.

★ Top Tip

Most of Wellington's mainstream cinemas offer cheap tickets on Tuesdays (aka Cheap-arse Tuesdays).

Tours

Weta Workshop   Workshop

(☏04-909 4035; www.wetaworkshop.com; 1 Weka St, Miramar; single tour adult/child $28/13, both tours $48/22; ⊗9am-5.30pm) Academy Award–winning special-effects and props company Weta Workshop has been responsible for bringing the likes of *The Lord of the Rings, The Hobbit, King Kong, District 9* and *Thor: Ragnarok* to life. Learn how they do it on entertaining 45-minute guided tours, starting every half-hour; bookings recommended. Weta Workshop is 8km east of the city centre: drive, catch bus 31 or book transport ($40 return) with your admission.

Wellington Movie Tours   Tours

(☏027 419 3077; www.adventuresafari.co.nz; tours from $60) Half- and full-day tours with more props, clips, and Middle-earth film locations than you can shake a staff at.

late) Wellywood's cinema mother ship is an art-deco darling, built in the 1920s. Today she screens mainly mainstream films with state-of-the-art sound and vision. Be sure to check out the glamorous Black Sparrow cocktail bar out the back.

Light House Cinema   Cinema

(☏04-385 3337; www.lighthousecinema.co.nz; 29 Wigan St; tickets adult/child $17.50/13.50; ⊗10am-late; 🛜) Tucked away near the top end of Cuba St, this small, stylish cinema throws a range of mainstream, art-house and foreign films up onto the screens in three small theatres. High-quality snacks. Tuesday tickets $11.50.

City Sculpture Tour

Wellington takes street art to sophisticated, sculptural levels. Here's our hit list of the weirdest, most engaging and actually rather moving installations around the city.

Start Post Office Sq
Distance 2.8km
Duration One hour

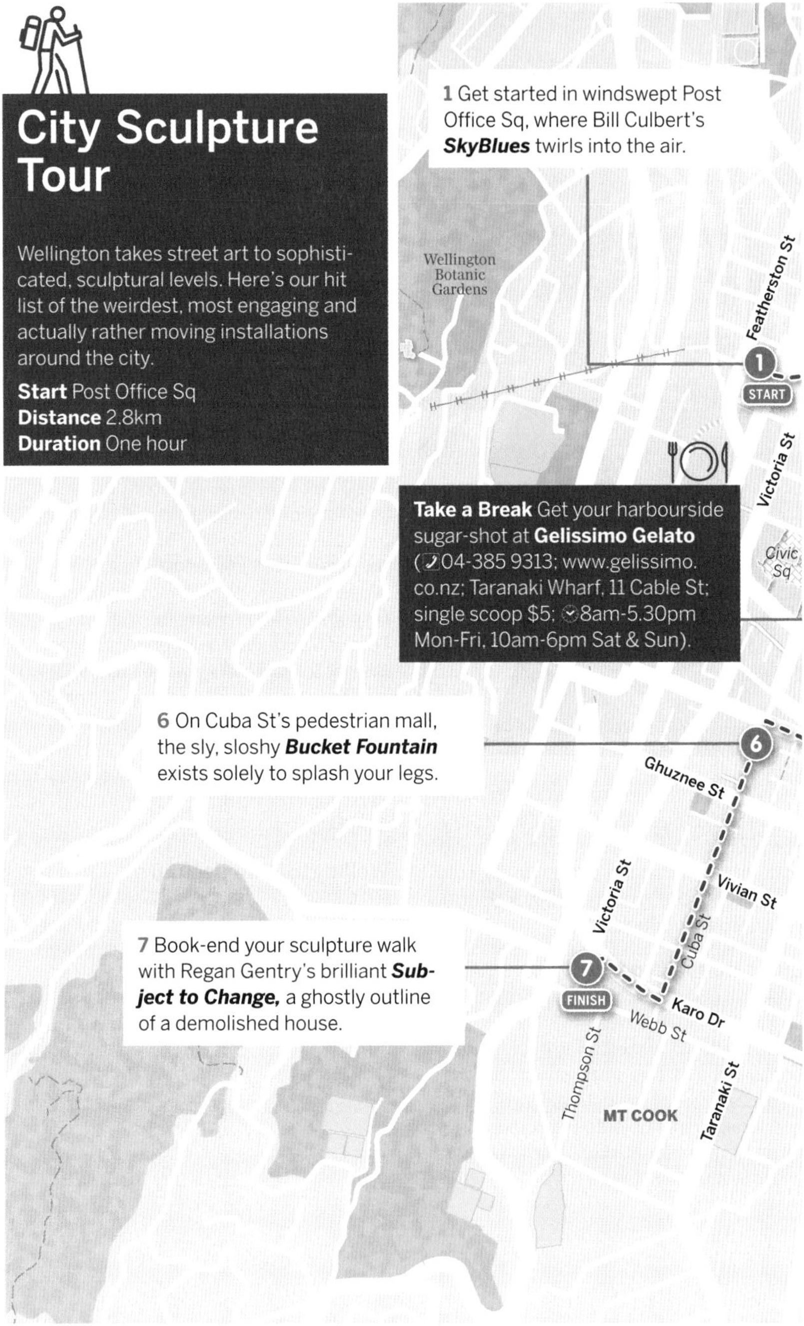

1 Get started in windswept Post Office Sq, where Bill Culbert's *SkyBlues* twirls into the air.

Take a Break Get your harbourside sugar-shot at **Gelissimo Gelato** (☏04-385 9313; www.gelissimo. co.nz; Taranaki Wharf, 11 Cable St; single scoop $5; ☷8am-5.30pm Mon-Fri, 10am-6pm Sat & Sun).

6 On Cuba St's pedestrian mall, the sly, sloshy *Bucket Fountain* exists solely to splash your legs.

7 Book-end your sculpture walk with Regan Gentry's brilliant *Subject to Change,* a ghostly outline of a demolished house.

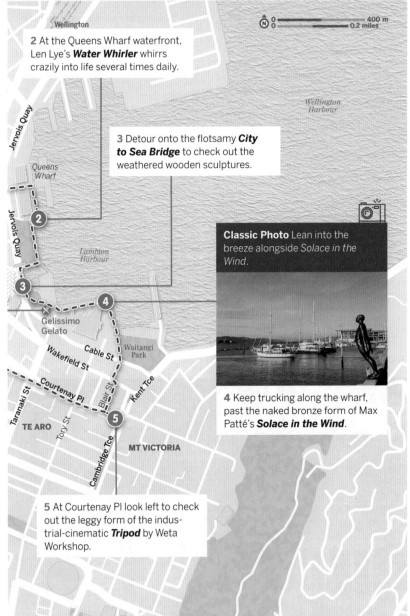

Wellington

Wellington Harbour

Jervois Quay

2 At the Queens Wharf waterfront, Len Lye's **Water Whirler** whirrs crazily into life several times daily.

Queens Wharf

Jervois Quay

2

3 Detour onto the flotsamy **City to Sea Bridge** to check out the weathered wooden sculptures.

Lambton Harbour

3

4

Gelissimo Gelato

Cable St

Wakefield St

Waitangi Park

Courtenay Pl

Taranaki St

Tory St

Blair St

Kent Tce

5

TE ARO

Cambridge Tce

MT VICTORIA

Classic Photo Lean into the breeze alongside *Solace in the Wind*.

4 Keep trucking along the wharf, past the naked bronze form of Max Patté's **Solace in the Wind**.

5 At Courtenay Pl look left to check out the leggy form of the indus-trial-cinematic **Tripod** by Weta Workshop.

4 JOEYCHEUNG/SHUTTERSTOCK ©

⊙ SIGHTS

Mt Victoria Lookout   Viewpoint
(Lookout Rd; ⊙24hr) The city's most impressive viewpoint is atop 196m-high Mt
Victoria (Matairangi), east of the city centre. You can take bus 20 most of the way
up, but the rite of passage is to sweat it out
on the walk (ask a local for directions or
just follow your nose). If you've got wheels,
take Oriental Pde along the waterfront and
then scoot up Carlton Gore Rd. Aside from
the views there are some interesting info
panels to ogle.

Wellington
Botanic Gardens   Gardens
(⊉04-499 1400; www.wellingtongardens.nz; 101
Glenmore St, Thorndon; ⊙daylight hours) **FREE**
These hilly, 25-hectare botanic gardens can
be effortlessly visited via the Wellington
Cable Car (p141) (nice bit of planning, eh?),
although there are several other entrances

> *The gardens boast a tract of*
> *original native forest*

hidden in the hillsides. The gardens boast
a tract of original native forest, the beaut
Lady Norwood Rose Garden, 25,000 spring
tulips and various international plant
collections. Add in fountains, a playground,
sculptures, a duck pond, cafe, the Space
Place (p139) observatory and the small-
but-nifty Cable Car Museum (p141) and
you've a busy day out.

Zealandia   Wildlife Reserve
(⊉04-920 9213; www.visitzealandia.com; 53
Waiapu Rd, Karori; admission only adult/child/
family $21/10/49, with tour $55/27.50/110;
⊙9am-5pm; 🚻) ⊘ This groundbreaking eco-
sanctuary is nooked into a valley in the hills
about 2km west of downtown Wellington.
Living wild within the fenced, predator-free habitat are more than 30 native
bird species, including rare little spotted
kiwi, takahe, saddleback, hihi and kaka,
as well as NZ's little dinosaur, the tuatara.
An excellent exhibition relays NZ's natural
history and world-renowned conservation
story. Buses 2 and 21 stop nearby, or see
the Zealandia website for info on the free
shuttle.

Duck Pond, Wellington Botanic Gardens

NATALIA RAMIREZ ROMAN/SHUTTERSTOCK ©

More than 30km of tracks can be explored independently, or on regular guided tours. Twilight and night tours provide an opportunity to spot nocturnal creatures including kiwi, frogs and glowworms (adult/child $85/40).

Space Place
Observatory

(☎04-910 3140; www.museumswellington.org.nz; 40 Salamanca Rd, Kelburn; adult/child/family $14/9/45; ⏰4-11pm Tue & Fri, 10am-11pm Sat, 10am-5.30pm Sun) Inside the Carter Observatory at the top of the Botanic Gardens (p138), this full-dome planetarium offers space-themed multimedia shows and stargazing sessions through the historic Thomas Cooke telescope. Check the website for show times. Open daily during school holidays.

New Zealand Parliament
Historic Building

(☎04-817 9503; www.parliament.nz; Molesworth St; ⏰tours hourly 10am-4pm) **FREE** New Zealand might be a young country but it has one of the oldest continuously functioning parliaments in the world and has chalked up more than its share of firsts, including being the first to give women the vote (in 1893) and the first to include an openly transgender Member of Parliament (in 1999). You can learn all about NZ's unique version of democracy on a free guided tour.

Hour-long tours usually depart on the hour, with half-hour highlights tours squeezed in between, but check the website for details (arrive 15 minutes early to allow for security and coat check).

Tours start with a 12-minute film screened in the visitor centre in the foyer of the Beehive (1980), a distinctive modernist building designed by British architect Sir Basil Spence. Looking like it sounds, this squat but oddly charming building contains the offices of government ministers, including the Prime Minister on the 9th floor and the (infamously hot) cabinet room on the top. Tours then cross the bridge into Wellington's austere grey-and-cream Parliament House (1922),

Days Bay & Matiu/ Somes Island

Wellingtonians have been taking trips across the harbour to **Days Bay** since the 1880s. At the bay there's a beach, a park and a cafe, and a boatshed with kayaks and bikes for hire. A 10-minute walk from Days Bay leads to Eastbourne, a beachy township with cafes, a cute 'gastrobar', a summer swimming pool and a playground.

The sweet little **East by West Ferry** (☎04-499 1282; www.eastbywest.co.nz; Queens Wharf; return adult/child $24/12) plies the 20- to 30-minute route 16 times a day each way Monday to Friday and five to eight times on weekends. Several of the daily ferries also stop at Matiu/Somes Island in the middle of the harbour, a DOC-managed predator-free reserve that is home to weta, tuatara, kakariki and little blue penguins, among other critters. The island has a chequered history: it was once a prisoner-of-war camp and quarantine station. Take a picnic lunch, or even stay overnight in the basic campsite (adult/child $15/7.50) or at one of three DOC cottages (sole-occupancy $105 to $200): book online at www.doc.govt.nz.

Eastbourne harbour
BOWEN JIA/SHUTTERSTOCK ©

where you'll visit the Debating Chamber, Banquet Hall and one of the committee rooms. The longer tours also include the Grand Hall, Legislative Council Chamber and the neo-Gothic Parliamentary Library (1899) next door.

Wellington

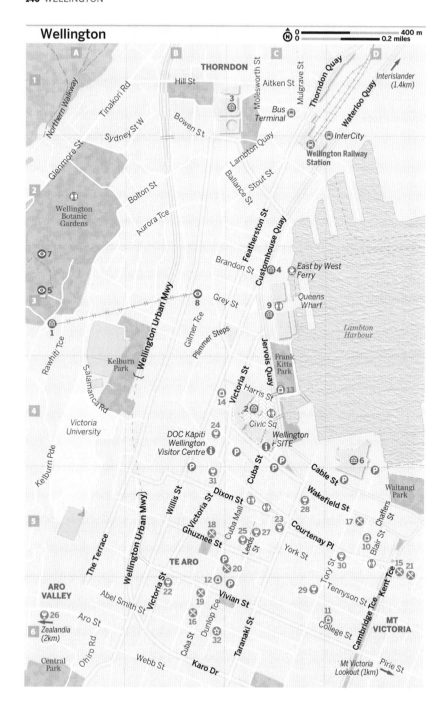

N

0 — 400 m
0 — 0.2 miles

THORNDON

Northern Walkway

Tinakori Rd

Hill St

Molesworth St

Aitken St

Mulgrave St

Thorndon Quay

Waterloo Quay

Interislander
(1.4km)

3

Sydney St W

Bowen St

Bus
Terminal

InterCity

Glenmore St

Bolton St

Lambton Quay

Wellington Railway
Station

Wellington
Botanic
Gardens

Aurora Tce

Ballance St

Stout St

Featherston St

Customhouse Quay

7

Brandon St

4

East by West
Ferry

5

Grey St

9

Queens
Wharf

Wellington Urban Mwy

8

Gilmer Tce

Plummer Steps

Jervois Quay

Lambton
Harbour

1

Rawhiti Tce

Salamanca Rd

Kelburn
Park

Frank
Kitts
Park

13

Victoria St

Harris St

Victoria
University

14

2

Civic Sq

Wellington
i-SITE

6

Kelburn Pde

DOC Kāpiti
Wellington
Visitor Centre

24

31

Cable St

Waitangi
Park

The Terrace

Willis St

Victoria St

Dixon St

Cuba St

Wakefield St

28

17

Chaffers St

Wellington Urban Mwy

Ghuznee St

Cuba Mall

18

23

25

27

Courtenay Pl

10

Blair St

TE ARO

Leeds
St

York St

30

15

21

**ARO
VALLEY**

26

Zealandia
(2km)

Aro St

Abel Smith St

Victoria St

22

12

20

Vivian St

Tory St

29

Tennyson Tce

Cambridge Tce

Kent Tce

**MT
VICTORIA**

Dunlop Tce

19

16

32

Cuba St

Taranaki St

11

College St

Mt Victoria
Lookout (1km)

Pirie St

Central
Park

Ohiro Rd

Webb St

Karo Dr

Wellington

Parliament usually sits from Tuesday to Thursday for around 30 weeks of the year. If you're keen to see the elected members duelling it out, you can watch from the public galleries.

Wellington Cable Car
Cable Car

(☏04-472 2199; www.wellingtoncablecar. co.nz; Cable Car Lane, rear 280 Lambton Quay; adult/child one way $5/2.50, return $9/4.50; ⏱departs every 10min, 7am-10pm Mon-Fri, 8.30am-10pm Sat, 8.30am-9pm Sun; 🚻) One of Wellington's big-ticket attractions is the little red cable car that clanks up the slope from Lambton Quay to Kelburn. At the top you'll find the Wellington Botanic Gardens (p138), Space Place (p139) as well as the small but nifty **Cable Car Museum** (☏04-475 3578; www.museumswellington.org.nz; 1a Upland Rd, Kelburn; ⏱9.30am-5pm) FREE. The last of these attractions evocatively depicts the cable car's story since it was built in 1902 to open up hilly Kelburn for settlement. Ride the cable car back down the hill, or wander down on foot through the gardens. It's an essential Wellington experience.

🟢 ACTIVITIES

Wellington's harbour offers plenty of opportunities to get active: kayaking, paddle boarding, sailing, windsurfing... (Wellington is windy: might as well make the most of it!). Back on dry land there's rock climbing, cycling and high-wire walking to keep you off the streets. Pick up the *Wellington City Cycle Map* for bike-trail info.

🟢 TOURS

Flat Earth
Driving

(☏04-472 9635; www.flatearth.co.nz; half-day tours from $95) An array of themed small-group guided tours: city highlights, *The Lord of the Rings* filming locations and arts and culture. Pricier full-day Martinborough wine tours also available.

🔒 SHOPPING

Kura
Art

(☏04-802 4934; www.kuragallery.co.nz; 19 Allen St; ⏱10am-6pm Mon-Fri, 11am-5pm Sat & Sun) Contemporary, edgy and progressive Māori and NZ art: paintings, carvings, ceramics, jewellery and sculpture. A gorgeous

From left: Underground Market; Fidel's; Slow Boat Records

gallery – come for a look even if you're not buying.

Slow Boat Records   Music
(☑04-385 1330; www.slowboatrecords.co.nz; 183 Cuba St; ⊙9.30am-5.30pm Mon-Thu, to 7.30pm Fri, 10am-5pm Sat & Sun) Country, folk, pop, indie, metal, blues, soul, rock, Hawaiian nose-flute music – it's all here at Slow Boat, Wellington's long-running music shop and Cuba St mainstay.

Unity Books   Books
(☑04-499 4245; www.unitybooks.co.nz; 57 Willis St; ⊙9am-6pm Mon-Thu, to 7pm Fri, 10am-6pm Sat, to 5pm Sun) Sets the standard for every bookshop in the land, with dedicated NZ tables piled high, plus regular book launches, author readings and literary events. We could stay all day.

Underground Market   Market
(www.undergroundmarket.co.nz; under Frank Kitts Park, Jervois Quay; ⊙10am-4pm Sat) On Saturday mornings (and the occasional Sunday) the car park under Frank Kitts Park is filled with stalls selling interesting craft, artsy gifts, clothes by up-and-coming

designers, and nibbles – plus the inevitable dreamcatchers and tie-dye T-shirts. It's somewhere between hippie and mainstream.

Moore Wilson's   Food & Drinks
(☑04-384 9906; www.moorewilsons.co.nz; 36 College St; ⊙7.30am-7pm Mon-Fri, to 6pm Sat, 8.30am-6pm Sun) A call-out to self-caterers: this positively swoon-inducing grocer is one of NZ's most committed supporters of independently produced and artisanal produce. If you want to chew on the best of Wellington and NZ, here's your chance. Head upstairs for dry goods, wine and beer.

🍴 EATING

Fidel's   Cafe $$
(☑04-801 6868; www.fidelscafe.com; 234 Cuba St; mains $10-20; ⊙7.30am-11pm Mon-Fri, 8am-11pm Sat, 9am-11pm Sun; 🖤) A Cuba St institution for caffeine-craving rebels, Fidel's cranks out eggs any which way, pizzas, panini and egg salads, along with the city's best milkshakes. Revolutionary memorabilia adorns the walls of the low-lit interior,

KRISTA ROSSOW/ALAMY STOCK PHOTO ©

and there's a weathered outdoor area beneath a huge Cuban flag. The comrades in the kitchen cope with the chaos admirably. Pizzas from noon.

Loretta
Cafe $$

(04-384 2213; www.loretta.net.nz; 181 Cuba St; mains $14-34; ⊙9am-9.30pm Tue, 7am-9.30pm Wed & Thu, 7am-10pm Fri, 8am-10pm Sat, 8am-8.30pm Sun; ⚡) Italian? Fusion? Wine bar? Loretta is a hard gal to categorise, but she's won leagues of fans with her classy, well-proportioned offerings served in bright, airy surrounds. Split a wood-fired chicken, sausage and fennel pizza and a grain-filled salad between two, with a couple of juniper negronis. Bookings for lunch only.

Noble Rot
European $$$

(04-385 6671; www.noblerot.co.nz; 6 Swan La; mains $29-41; ⊙4pm-late) This warmly lit, atmospheric wine bar serves some of Wellington's best food. Euro influences pervade the menu, featuring the likes of charcuterie plates, duck-liver parfait, ricotta gnocchi and Spanish pork *pastirma* (cured beef). Prop yourself on a tall bentwood stool and

survey the wine list: 400 bottles, with 80 by the glass. Cancel your other plans.

Logan Brown
Bistro $$$

(04-801 5114; www.loganbrown.co.nz; 192 Cuba St; mains $39-48, 5-/7-course degustation menu $115/145, with wine $165/215; ⊙noon-2pm Wed-Sat & 5pm-late Tue-Sun; ☎) 🍴 Deservedly ranked among Wellington's best restaurants, Logan Brown oozes class without being overly formal. Its 1920s banking-chamber dining room is a neoclassical stunner – a fitting complement to the produce-driven modern NZ cuisine. The three-course bistro menu ($50) won't hurt your wallet too badly, but the epic wine list and Saturday-night degustation menu might force a blow-out.

Ortega
Seafood $$$

(04-382 9559; www.ortega.co.nz; 16 Majoribanks St, Mt Victoria; mains $36-40, set menus from $69; ⊙5.30pm-late) Mounted trout, salty portraits, marine-blue walls and Egyptian floor tiles cast a Mediterranean spell over Ortega – a magical spot for a seafood dinner. Fish comes many ways (including as zingy sashimi), while desserts

 History of the Harbour

Māori tradition has it that the explorer Kupe was first to discover Wellington Harbour. Wellington's original Māori name was Te Whanganui-a-Tara (great harbour of Tara), named after the son of a chief named Whatonga who had settled on the Hawke's Bay coast. Whatonga's followers moved to the Wellington area and founded the Ngāi Tara tribe.

On 22 January 1840 the first European settlers arrived in the New Zealand Company's ship *Aurora,* expecting to take possession of land that the local Māori denied selling. The Treaty of Waitangi was signed a few weeks later, and in the years that followed the Land Claims Commission was established to sort out the mess. By 1850 Wellington was a thriving settlement of around 5500 people, despite a shortage of flat land. Originally the waterfront was along Lambton Quay, but reclamation of parts of the harbour began in 1852.

In 1855 a significant earthquake raized many parts of Wellington. In 1865 the seat of government was moved from Auckland to Wellington, although it took until the turn of the century for the city to really flourish. In the early 1900s the port prospered, with export boards and banks springing up in its surrounds.

ACQUES VAN DINTEREN/GETTY IMAGES ©

continue the Mediterranean vibes with Catalan orange crêpes and one of Welly's best cheeseboards.

Husk Cafe

(☑04-282 0583; www.huskbar.co.nz; 62 Ghuznee St; ☺ 8am-late Mon-Fri, 9am-late Sat & Sun) Follow the throbbing basslines down the twinkling alley into Husk, where punky leather guys and laptop-wielding students convene for pork-shoulder tacos, chilli eggs and 'dirty' chips with beef brisket, house-smoked cheddar and red chimichurri. In true Wellington form, Husk is a brewery too: the Superunknown APA is appropriately rockin', while the Power of Voodoo white stout is irrefutably magical.

🍷 DRINKING & NIGHTLIFE

Library Bar

(☑04-382 8593; www.thelibrary.co.nz; Level 1, 53 Courtenay Pl; ☺5pm-late Mon-Thu, 4pm-late Fri-Sun) Into books, much? You'll find yourself in the right kind of bind at moody Library, with its velveteen booths, board games and swish cocktails. An excellent all-round drink selection is complemented by a highly shareable menu of sweet and savoury stuff. Killer cocktails, and live music every now and then.

Dirty Little Secret Rooftop Bar

(☑021 0824 0298; https://dirtylittlesecret. co.nz; Level 8, 7-8 Dixon St; ☺3pm-late Mon-Sun; ☜) While it's not strictly a secret (it's packed to the gills on balmy evenings) this hip bar atop the historic Hope Gibbons Ltd building plays hard to get, with a nondescript entrance on Taranaki St. Expect some beaut craft beers, slugged-together cocktails, loud indie music and plastic awnings straining to keep the elements at bay.

Counter Culture Bar

(☑04-891 2345; www.counterculture.co.nz; 211 Victoria St; 3hr of games $5; ☺noon-10pm Mon-Thu, to 11pm Fri, 11am-11pm Sat, to 10pm Sun; ☜🧒) Who doesn't secretly love a board game? Assume an ironic stance if you must, but here's the chance to embrace your inner games nerd in public. There are almost 600 games to choose from (Battleships! They have Battleships!) plus

Library bar

Fortune Favours craft beers and cocktails to take the edge off your ugly competitive streak.

Hawthorn Lounge Cocktail Bar

(04-890 3724; www.hawthornlounge.co.nz; Level 1, 82 Tory St; ⊙5pm-3am Mon-Sat) This classy cocktail bar has a 1920s speakeasy feel, suited-up in waistcoats and wide-brimmed fedoras. Sip a whisky sour and play poker, or watch the behind-the-bar theatrics from the house mixologists, twisting the classics into modern-day masterpieces. Open till the wee smalls; don't dress lazy.

☻ ENTERTAINMENT

Wellington has a simmering theatre scene and is the home of large national companies such as the Royal NZ Ballet and the NZ Symphony Orchestra. Most shows can be booked via **Ticketek** (www.ticketek.co.nz), **Ticketmaster** (www.ticketmaster.co.nz) and **Ticket Rocket** (www.ticketrocket. co.nz). Discounted same-day tickets for productions are sometimes available at the i-SITE.

❶ INFORMATION

DOC Kāpiti Wellington Visitor Centre (04-384 7770; www.doc.govt.nz; 18 Manners St; ⊙9.30am-5pm Mon-Fri, 10am-3.30pm Sat) Maps, bookings, passes and information for local and national walks (including Great Walks), parks, huts, camping and Kāpiti Island.

Wellington i-SITE (04-802 4860; www. wellingtonnz.com; 111 Wakefield St; ⊙8.30am-5pm Mon-Fri, 9am-5pm Sat & Sun;) Staff book almost everything here, and cheerfully distribute Wellington's *Official Visitor Guide,* along with other maps and helpful pamphlets.

❶ GETTING THERE & AWAY

AIR

Wellington is an international gateway to NZ. **Wellington Airport** (WLG; 04-385 5100; www. wellingtonairport.co.nz; Stewart Duff Dr, Rongotai) has the usual slew of airport accoutrements:

ALEXANDRA/ALAMY STOCK PHOTO ©

Interislander ferry

info kiosks, currency exchange, ATMs, car-rental desks, shops, espresso... If you're in transit or have an early flight, note that you can't linger overnight inside the terminal (it closes between 1.30am and 3.30am).

The following service domestic destinations:

Air New Zealand (0800 737 000; www.air newzealand.co.nz) Auckland, Hamilton, Tauranga, Rotorua, Gisborne, Napier, New Plymouth, Palmerston North, Nelson, Blenheim, Christchurch, Timaru, Queenstown, Dunedin and Invercargill.

Golden Bay Air (www.goldenbayair.co.nz) Takaka.

Jetstar (www.jetstar.com) Auckland, Christchurch and Queenstown.

Sounds Air (0800 505 005; www.soundsair. com) Taupō, Blenheim, Picton, Nelson and Westport.

BOAT

Bluebridge Ferries (04-471 6188; www. bluebridge.co.nz; 50 Waterloo Quay, Pipitea; adult/child/car/campervan/motorbike from $50/26/120/185/54;) Up to four sailings between Wellington and Picton daily (3½ hours).

Interislander (04-498 3302; www. interislander.co.nz; Aotea Quay, Pipitea; adult/child/car/campervan/motorbike from $56/28/123/188/56) Up to five sailings between Wellington and Picton daily; crossings take 3¼ to 3½ hours.

BUS

Wellington is a major terminus for North Island bus services.

InterCity (04-385 0520; www.intercity. co.nz) coaches depart several times daily from Platform 9 at Wellington Railway Station. Destinations include Auckland (from $30, 11¼ hours), Rotorua (from $29, 7½ hours), Taupō (from $33, six hours), Napier (from $23, 5¼ hours), Palmerston North (from $18, 2¼ hours) and New Plymouth (from $29, seven hours).

Also departing from Platform 9, **Skip** (09-394 9180; www.skip.travel) is a budget service running between Wellington and Auckland ($16, 11½ hours) via Taupō ($12, 6¼ hours), Rotorua ($13, 5¾ hours) and Hamilton ($15, 9½ hours). Connections to Tauranga and Whangarei also available.

TRAIN

Regular **Metlink** (0800 801 700; www.
metlink.org.nz) commuter trains head as far as
Paekākāriki ($10.50, 46 minutes), Paraparaumu
($12, 55 minutes), Waikanae ($13, one hour) and
Masterton ($19, 1¾ hours).

Three days a week the **Northern Explorer**
(www.greatjourneysofnz.co.nz) heads to/from
Palmerston North (from $69, two hours), Ōhakune
(from $109, five hours), National Park Village (from
$109, 5¼ hours), Hamilton (from $179, 8½ hours)
and Auckland (from $179, 11 hours).

Run by the same folks (Great Journeys), the
weekday morning **Capital Connection** heads
to Wellington from Palmerston North ($35,
two hours), Waikanae ($14.50, one hour) and
Paraparaumu ($13.50, 50 minutes), returning in
the evening.

ℹ️ GETTING AROUND

Metlink is the one-stop shop for Wellington's
regional bus, train and harbour ferry networks;
there's a handy journey planner on its website.
You can pay by cash or use **Snapper** (www.
snapper.co.nz), an integrated prepaid smart
card. The Snapper fares are cheaper ($1.71 for a
one-zone trip as opposed to $2.50) but the card
costs $10, so it's probably not worth purchasing
for a short stay.

Frequent and efficient Metlink buses cover
the whole Wellington region, running between
approximately 6am and 11.30pm. The main
bus terminal (Lambton Quay) is near the Wellington Railway Station; there's another hub on
Courtenay Pl near the Cambridge Tce intersec-
tion. Pick up route maps and timetables from
the i-SITE (p145) and convenience stores, or
online.

Metlink also runs **After Midnight** buses,
departing from two city stops (Courtenay Pl
and Manners St) between midnight and 4.30am
Saturday and Sunday, following a number of
routes to the outer suburbs. There's a set $7 fare
for most trips.

MARLBOROUGH

Marlborough at a Glance...

Sunny Marlborough is a region of two main enticements: the astonishingly gorgeous Marlborough Sounds, where you can hike, bike and kayak to your heart's content; and the world-trumping Marlborough Wine Region, home to grapes that, with a bit of New Zealand know-how, become the cool-climate wines that grace the world's best restaurants.

Local produce, including hops, wild game, seafood and summer fruits, is also a highlight, best enjoyed in hip local cafes and classy vine-side eateries.

Two Days in Marlborough

Picturesque little **Picton** (p160) is much more than just a drive-thru ferry hub – fuel up at Gusto before spending a day tackling some of its lovely local walks. On day two hit the Marlborough Wine Region. Standout vineyards include **Saint Clair Estate** (p157) and **Framingham** (p157), while in little Renwick near Blenheim, **Arbour** (p164) delivers the best of Marlborough produce in seamlessly elegant surrounds.

Four Days in Marlborough

For days three and four rev up the energy levels by exploring the photogenic Marlborough Sounds along the **Queen Charlotte Track** (p152). This convoluted 70km waterside trail is one of NZ's Great Rides, but you can hike it or (with a little help from water taxis) kayak sections of it too.

Previous page: Picton (p160)
YAN CAZABAN/SHUTTERSTOCK ©

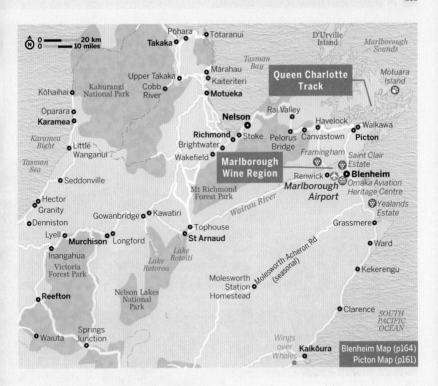

Arriving in Marlborough

Picton Ferry Terminal (p161) Terminus for vehicle ferries from Wellington. Buses and shuttles from Christchurch, Kaikōura, Nelson and beyond arrive here or at the nearby **i-SITE** (p160).

Marlborough Airport (p165) The airport is 6km west of Blenheim, with flights to/from Wellington, Auckland, Napier and Kaikōura.

Where to Stay

As a popular holiday destination for domestic and international travellers alike (these are NZ's sunniest latitudes!), Marlborough delivers a plethora of accommodation options across all budgets. The broadest selection can be found in and around Blenheim in the Marlborough Wine Region, plus pretty little Picton and Kaikōura.

CHRISNOE/SHUTTERSTOCK ©

Queen Charlotte Track

One of New Zealand's classic walks – and now one of its Great Rides, too – the meandering, 70km Queen Charlotte Track offers gorgeous coastal scenery through the hushed, tranquil Marlborough Sounds.

Great For...

☑ **Don't Miss**

Cooling off with a swim in a mirror-flat, isolated cove along the track.

The track runs from historic Ship Cove to Anakiwa, passing through a mixture of privately owned land and DOC reserves. Access depends on the cooperation of local landowners; respect their property by utilising designated campsites and toilets, and carrying out your rubbish. Your purchase of the **Track Pass** ($10 to $18), available from the Picton i-SITE (p160) and track-related businesses, provides the co-op with the means to maintain and enhance the experience for all. The i-SITE also handles bookings for transport and accommodation. See also the Queen Charlotte Track website (www.qctrack.co.nz) and the Queen Charlotte Track Land Cooperative website (www.qctlc.com).

❶ Need to Know

For all things track-related, including sleeping and eating options, see www.qctrack.co.nz.

✕ Take a Break

The in-house restaurant at the stylish **Bay of Many Coves Resort** (☏03-579 9771; www.bayofmanycoves.co.nz; Arthurs Bay; apt from $1345; 🛜🐕) is the best QCT eating option.

★ Top Tip

Unless you're camping, book your accommodation well in advance, especially in summer.

Hiking & Biking

Queen Charlotte is a well-defined track, suitable for people of average fitness. Numerous boat and tour operators service the track, allowing you to tramp the whole three- to five-day journey, or to start and finish where you like, on foot or by kayak or bike. We're talking mountain biking here, and a whole lot of fun for fit, competent off-roaders. Part of the track is off-limits to cyclists from 1 December to the end of February, but there is still good riding to be had during this time.

Ship Cove is the usual (and recommended) starting point – mainly because it's easier to arrange a boat from Picton to Ship Cove than vice versa – but the track can also be started from Anakiwa. There's a public phone at Anakiwa but not at Ship Cove.

Sleeping

There are lots of great day-trip options, allowing you to base yourself in Picton; but there's also plenty of accommodation spaced along the way. Boat operators will transport your luggage along the track.

There are six DOC campsites, all with toilets and a water supply but no cooking facilities, and a variety of resorts, lodges, backpackers and guesthouses. Unless you're camping, book your accommodation way in advance, especially in summer.

Getting There & Away

Picton water taxis can drop you off and pick you up at numerous locations along the track.

Marlborough Wine Region

Languidly exploring the wineries of the Marlborough Wine Region is a quintessential NZ experience. Dining among the vines on a sunny southern hemisphere afternoon is also an absolute highlight.

Great For...

ⓘ **Need to Know**

Pick up a copy of the *Marlborough Wine Trail* map from Blenheim i-SITE (p165), also available online at www. wine-marlborough.co.nz.

★ **Top Tip**

If you don't have time to visit the wineries, **Wino's** (☏03-578 4196; www.winos.co.nz; 49 Grove Rd; ☉10am-7pm Sun-Thu, to 8pm Fri & Sat) in Blenheim stocks some mighty fine local bottles.

ADAM JAN JONES/SHUTTERSTOCK ©

Marlborough is NZ's vinous colossus, producing around three-quarters of the country's wine. At last count, there were 244 sq km of vines planted – that's more than 28,000 rugby pitches! Sunny days and cool nights create the perfect conditions for cool-climate grapes: world-famous sauvignon blanc, top-notch pinot noir, and notable chardonnay, riesling, gewürztraminer, pinot gris and bubbly. Drifting between tasting rooms and dining among the vines is a divine way to spend a day on the South Island.

Wine Tastings

Around 35 wineries are open to the public. Our picks of the bunch provide a range of high-quality cellar-door experiences, with most being open from around 10.30am till 4.30pm (some scale back operations in winter). Wineries may charge a small fee for tasting, normally refunded if you purchase a bottle.

Allan Scott Family Winemakers (03-572 9054; www.allanscott.com; 229 Jacksons Rd, Rapaura; tastings $3, free with purchase or lunch; 9am-4.30pm)

Bladen (03-572 9417; www.bladen.co.nz; 83 Conders Bend Rd, Renwick; 11am-4.30pm Nov-Apr)

Brancott Estate (03-520 6975; www.brancottestate.com; 180 Brancott Rd, Fairhall; tastings $5-15, free with purchase; 10am-4.30pm)

Clos Henri Vineyard (03-572 7293; www.clos-henri.com; 639 State Hwy 63, Waihopai Valley; 10am-4pm Mon-Sat Oct-Apr)

Cloudy Bay (03-520 9147; www.cloudybay.co.nz; 230 Jacksons Rd, Rapaura; tastings $10-25; 10am-4pm)

Clos Henri Vineyard

Forrest (☏03-572 9084; www.forrest.
co.nz; 19 Blicks Rd, Renwick; tastings free-$10;
🕑10am-4.30pm)
Framingham (☏03-572 8884; www.framing
ham.co.nz; 19 Conders Bend Rd, Renwick; tastings
$5, free with purchase; 🕑10.30am-4.30pm) ✔
Huia (☏03-572 8326; www.huiavineyards.com;
22 Boyces Rd, Rapaura; 🕑10.30am-4.30pm
Nov-Mar) ✔
Saint Clair Estate (☏03-570 5280; www.
saintclair.co.nz; 13 Selmes Rd, Rapaura; tastings
$5-10, free with meal or purchase; 🕑9am-5pm
Nov-Apr, 11am-4pm May-Oct)
Spy Valley Wines (☏03-572 6207; www.
spyvalleywine.co.nz; 37 Lake Timara Rd West,

Waihopai Valley; tastings $5-10, free with pur-
chase; 🕑10.30am-4.30pm daily Nov-Apr, Mon-Fri
May-Oct) ✔
Wither Hills (☏03-520 8284; www.witherhills.
co.nz; 211 New Renwick Rd, Burleigh; tastings $5,
free with purchase; 🕑10am-4.30pm)
Yealands Estate (☏03-575 7618; www.
yealands.co.nz; cnr Seaview & Reserve Rds,
Seddon; 🕑10am-4.30pm) ✔ **FREE**

Wining & Dining

With wine there must be food, and here are
our recommendations for dining among
the vines. Opening hours are for summer,
when bookings are recommended.

Arbour (p164)
Wairau River Restaurant (p164)
Rock Ferry (p163)
Wither Hills

Wine Tours

Wine tours are generally conducted in a
minibus (or on a bike!), last between four
and seven hours, take in four to seven
wineries and range in price from $65 to
$95 (with a few grand tours up to around
$200 for the day, including a winery lunch).
Recommended operators:

Bike2Wine (☏03-572 8458; www.bike2wine.
co.nz; 9 Wilson St, Renwick; standard/tandem
per day $30/60, pick-ups within 15km $10;
🕑10am-5.30pm)
Bubbly Grape Wine Tours (☏027 672 2195;
www.bubblygrape.co.nz; tours $100-195)
Highlight Wine Tours (☏03-577 9046; www.
highlightwinetours.co.nz; tours $90-130)

> ✕ **Take a Break**
>
> For a fortifying brunch before a wine-
> soaked afternoon, try Rock Ferry (p163)
> in Blenheim.

ROBIN SMITH/GETTY IMAGES ©

> ☑ **Don't Miss**
>
> For extra pizzazz, don't miss February's
> **Marlborough Wine & Food Festival**
> (www.wine-marlborough-festival.co.nz).

Humpback whale

KONRAD MOSTERT/SHUTTERSTOCK ©

Wildlife-Watching in Kaikōura

Around 129km southeast of Blenheim (or 180km north of Christchurch) is pretty Kaikōura – one of the best places on the planet to spy whales, dolphins, NZ fur seals, penguins, shearwaters, petrels and several species of albatross.

Great For...

☑ Don't Miss

Snorkelling with curious NZ fur seal pups as they swoop and dive around you.

Marine animals are abundant here due to ocean-current and continental-shelf conditions: the seabed gradually slopes away from the land before plunging to more than 800m, where the southerly current hits the continental shelf. This creates an upwelling of nutrients from the ocean floor into the feeding zone.

Whale-watching tours are offered by boat, plane or helicopter. Aerial options are shorter and pricier, but allow you to see the whole whale, as opposed to just a tail, flipper or spout.

Whale Watch Kaikōura
Whale Watching

(☏03-319 6767; www.whalewatch.co.nz; Whaleway Station Rd; tours adult/child $150/60) ✍ With knowledgable guides and fascinating on-board animation, Kaikōura's biggest

Ruffled yellow-eyed penguin

NATALIA KHALAMAN/SHUTTERSTOCK ©

ⓘ Need to Know

Kaikōura i-SITE (✆03-319 5641; www.kaikoura.co.nz; West End; ⊙9am-5pm, extended hours Dec-Mar)

✕ Take a Break

Green Dolphin (✆03-319 6666; www.greendolphin.co.nz; 12 Avoca St; mains $28-39; ⊙5pm-late Tue-Sat) is Kaikōura's consistent top-ender, dishing up high-quality local seafood, beef, lamb and venison.

★ Top Tip

Sometimes whale-watching boat trips are cancelled due to poor weather: allow some leeway in your schedule.

operator heads out on boat trips in search of the big fellas (success rate: 95%).

Albatross Encounter   Birdwatching

(✆03-319 6777; www.albatrossencounter.co.nz; 96 Esplanade; adult/child $130/65; ⊙tours 9am & 1pm year-round, plus 6am Nov-Apr) ✿ A close encounter with various albatross species, plus shearwaters, shags, mollymawks and petrels.

Dolphin Encounter   Wildlife

(✆03-319 6777; www.encounterkaikoura.co.nz; 96 Esplanade; adult/child swim $180/165, observation $95/55; ⊙tours 8.30am & 12.30pm year-round, plus 5.30am Nov-Apr) ✿ Claiming NZ's highest success rate (over 90%) for locating dolphins, this operator runs DOC-permitted three-hour tours, which often encounter sizeable pods of sociable duskies. Note that while concerns over the

impact of swimming tours on the bottlenose dolphins in the Bay of Islands have caused such tours to be banned, they are currently still allowed here.

Seal Swim Kaikōura   Wildlife

(✆03-319 6182; www.sealswimkaikoura.co.nz; 58 West End; adult/child $120/80, viewing $60/40; ⊙Nov-Apr) ✿ Take a warmly wet-suited swim with Kaikōura's healthy population of playful seals – including very cute pups – on guided snorkelling tours (by boat).

Wings over Whales   Whale Watching

(✆03-319 6580; www.whales.co.nz; Kaikōura South Rd, Peketa; 30min flights adult/child $195/100; ⊙8am-5pm) Light-plane flights departing from Kaikōura Airport, 8km south of town on SH1. Whale-spotting success rate: 95%.

South Pacific Helicopters   Whale Watching

(✆03-319 5548; www.southpacificwhales.co.nz; 72 West End; per person $275-950) Offers a wide range of whale-watching and flightseeing trips by helicopter.

Picton

Half asleep in winter, but hyperactive in summer (with up to eight fully laden ferry arrivals per day), boaty Picton clusters around a deep and beautiful gulch at the head of Queen Charlotte Sound. It's a major entry point for the South Island, and the best base for tackling the Marlborough Sounds and Queen Charlotte Track. Over the last few years this little town has really bloomed, and offers visitors plenty of reasons to linger even after the obvious attractions are knocked off the list.

SIGHTS

Edwin Fox
Maritime Museum
Museum

(☑03-573 6868; www.edwinfoxsociety.com; Dunbar Wharf; adult/child $15/5; ☺9am-3pm) Built near Calcutta and launched in 1853, the *Edwin Fox* is purportedly the world's ninth-oldest surviving ship. During its chequered career it carried troops to the Crimean War, booze to India and immigrants to NZ. Most notably, it's the last remaining ship to have transported convicts to Australia. Displays relate its fascinating story but the real thrill is walking around the ship itself, moored in a dry dock next door.

ACTIVITIES

The town has some very pleasant walks. A free i-SITE map details many of these, including an easy 1km track to **Bob's Bay**. The **Snout Track** (three hours return) continues along the ridge offering superb water views. Climbing a hill behind the town, the **Tirohanga Track** is a two-hour leg-stretching loop offering the best view in the house.

The **Link Pathway** (www.linkpathway. nz) is a new 42km walking and cycling track connecting Picton to Havelock, with a spur heading to the Queen Charlotte Track trailhead at Anakiwa. When fully completed it will all be off road.

Escape to Marlborough
Bus

(☑03-573 5573; www.escapetomarlborough. co.nz; day ticket $75; ☺8am-6pm) Hop-on/ hop-off bus services linking Picton and Blenheim, and then stopping at 13 key attractions including vineyards and breweries. Bespoke wine tours are also offered. Check the website for the service timetables.

EATING

Picton Village Bakkerij
Bakery $

(☑03-573 7082; www.facebook.com/Picton VillageBakery; 46 Auckland St; items $3-8.50; ☺6am-4pm Mon-Sat; ☑) Dutch owners bake trays of European and Kiwi goodies here, including interesting breads, filled rolls, cakes, tarts and savoury pies. It's an excellent place to stock up for a packed lunch.

Gusto
Cafe $$

(☑03-573 7171; 33 High St; mains $8-22; ☺7am-2.30pm Sun-Fri) With only a handful of tables and a bench by the window, this friendly joint does beaut cooked breakfasts including a warming porridge in winter. Lunch options include homemade savoury pies, local mussels, curry and pasta.

Cockles
Pub Food $$

(☑03-573 6086; www.facebook.com/cockles kitchen/; 7 Auckland St; mains $16-35; ☺11am-late;) Don't be put off by the sports-bar vibe, this place adjacent to the train station serves very tasty dishes including a delicious spaghetti with massive local clams and mussels. Other options include sandwiches, burgers, fish and chips, and seafood chowder.

ℹ INFORMATION

Picton i-SITE (☑03-520 3113; www.marl boroughnz.com; Auckland St; ☺8.30am-6pm Dec-Feb, 9am-4pm Mar-Nov; ☺) All vital tourist guff including maps, Queen Charlotte Track information, lockers and transport bookings. Dedicated DOC counter.

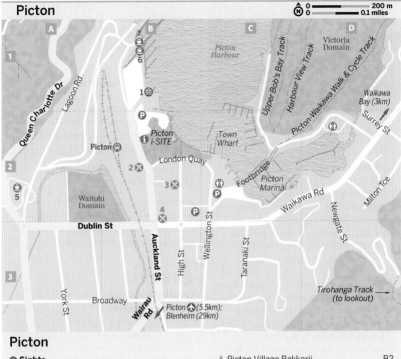

Picton

ℹ GETTING THERE & AWAY

The main transport hub (with car-rental depots) is at the Interislander ferry terminal, which also has a cafe and internet facilities. Most buses also depart from here or at the nearby i-SITE.

AIR

Sounds Air (☏03-520 3080, 0800 505 005; www.soundsair.co.nz; 10 London Quay; ⊙7.30am-5.30pm Mon-Thu & Sat, to 7pm Fri, 9am-7pm Sun) flies between Picton and Wellington; a shuttle bus to/from the airstrip at Koromiko is available ($10).

BOAT

Ferries depart and arrive at **Picton Ferry Terminal** (Auckland St). There are two operators crossing Cook Strait between Picton and Wellington, and although all ferries leave from more or less the same place, each has its own terminal. Crossing the strait take around 3½ hours.

Bluebridge (☏04-471 6188; www.bluebridge. co.nz; Lagoon Rd; adult/child/motorbike/car/ campervan from $50/26/54/120/150; ☏) operates four sailings in each direction daily.

Interislander (☏04-498 3302; www.great journeysofnz.co.nz; Auckland St; adult/

 European Visitors

Abel Tasman sheltered on the east coast of D'Urville Island in 1642, more than 100 years before James Cook blew through in 1770. It was Cook who named Queen Charlotte Sound (in Māori it's Tōtaranui); his reports made the area the best-known sheltered anchorage in the southern hemisphere. In 1827 French navigator Jules Dumont d'Urville discovered the narrow strait now known as French Pass. His officers named the island just to the north in his honour. In the same year a whaling station was established at Te Awaiti in Tory Channel, which brought about the first permanent European settlement in the district.

French Pass
PHOTOSTYLER/SHUTTERSTOCK ©

child/motorbike/car/campervan from $56/26/43/111/132) has five sailings in each direction daily.

Picton is also the hub for water taxis and cruises along Queen Charlotte Sound.

BUS

InterCity (03-365 1113; www.intercity.co.nz; outside Interislander Ferry Terminal, Auckland St) has two coaches a day to/from Christchurch (from $37, six hours) via Blenheim (from $10, 30 minutes) and Kaikōura (from $25, 2½ hours); and one or two daily to Nelson ($23, 2¼ hours) via Blenheim and Havelock ($14, one hour).

Escape to Marlborough (p160) has three morning departures to Blenheim ($19), with two returning in the afternoon as part of their hop-on/hop-off bus service.

TRAIN

KiwiRail's scenic **Coastal Pacific** (04-495 0775; www.greatjourneysofnz.co.nz) service operates daily from October to April, heading to/from Christchurch (from $99, 6¼ hours) via Blenheim (from $39, 26 minutes) and Kaikōura (from $59, three hours).

Blenheim

Blenheim is a good base from which to explore the Marlborough Wine Region, with a couple of interesting museums and an increasingly lively food scene.

◎ SIGHTS

Omaka Aviation Heritage Centre   Museum

(03-579 1305; www.omaka.org.nz; 79 Aerodrome Rd, Omaka; adult/child WWI $25/12, WWII $20/10, both $39/16; ⊙10am-5pm) When Sir Peter Jackson has a passion for something, there are no half measures. That's abundantly clear in the Knights of the Sky exhibition, which features the movie director's personal collection of WWI aircraft and memorabilia, brought to life in a series of life-sized dioramas that depict dramatic wartime scenes such as the death of the Red Baron. The other half of the centre, WWII-themed Dangerous Skies, is the work of local aviation enthusiasts.

The latter may not be as slick as Sir Peter's section – the backgrounds are hand painted and there are fewer of the hyper-realistic mannequins produced by the Oscar-winning Weta Workshop – but all of these aircraft have been restored and are airworthy, and it includes an eight-minute immersive Stalingrad Experience.

Marlborough Museum   Museum

(03-578 1712; www.marlboroughmuseum.org.nz; 26 Arthur Baker Pl; adult/child $10/5;

Omaka Aviation Heritage Centre

⊙10am-4pm) The history of NZ's wine industry is celebrated here, along with fascinating displays devoted to finds from Wairau Bar, the site of the country's earliest known settlement. Look out for the *karetao*, a traditional wooden puppet covered in *moko* (tattoos) and designed to perform a *haka* (ceremonial dance). The museum is situated within the **Bradshaw Heritage Park**, a collection of transported Victorian buildings that includes a miniature railway and a farm-machinery museum.

Omaka Classic Cars   Museum
(☑03-577 9419; www.omakaclassiccars.co.nz; Aerodrome Rd, Omaka; adult/child $15/free; ⊙noon-4pm daily Oct-May, Fri-Sun Jun-Sep) Opposite the Aviation Heritage Centre is this collection of more than 100 restored cars dating from the 1950s to the '80s.

🜚 ACTIVITIES
Driftwood Eco-Tours   Ecotour
(☑03-577 7651; www.driftwoodecotours.co.nz; tours from $180) ⚑ Tour through private

farmland to the ecologically and historically significant Wairau Lagoon, 10 minutes' drive from Blenheim. Alternatively book one of the specialist-led themed day or multiday tours to learn about the flora and fauna.

🜚 EATING
The Burleigh   Pies $
(☑03-579 2531; www.facebook.com/the burleighnz; 72 New Renwick Rd, Burleigh; pies $6-9; ⊙7.30am-3pm Tue-Fri, to 1.30pm Sat) The humble pie rises to stratospheric heights at this fabulous bakery-deli on Blenheim's rural fringes. Try the pork-belly or steak and blue cheese, or perhaps both. Freshly filled baguettes, local sausage, French cheeses and great coffee also make tempting appearances. Avoid the lunchtime rush.

Rock Ferry   Bistro $$
(☑03-579 6430; www.rockferry.co.nz; 80 Hammerichs Rd; mains $28-30, tastings $5, free with purchase or meal; ⊙cafe 11.30am-3pm,

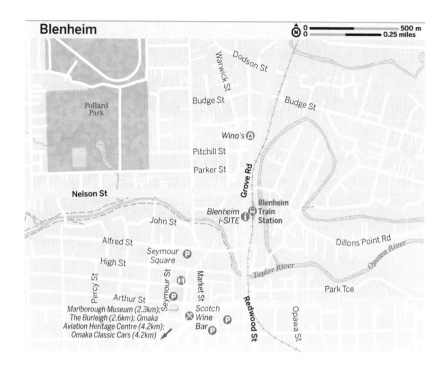

Blenheim

Pollard Park

Warwick St

Dodson St

Budge St

Budge St

Wino's

Pitchill St

Parker St

Grove Rd

Nelson St

Blenheim
i-SITE

Blenheim
Train
Station

John St

Alfred St

Dillons Point Rd

Opawa River

Seymour
Square

High St

Taylor River

Percy St

Park Tce

Arthur St

Market St

Seymour St

Marlborough Museum (2.3km);
The Burleigh (2.6km); Omaka
Aviation Heritage Centre (4.2km);
Omaka Classic Cars (4.2km)

Scotch
Wine
Bar

Redwood St

Opawa St

cellar door 10am-4.30pm) 🥐 Although it calls itself a cafe, that doesn't really cover the sophisticated but concise modern NZ menu on offer here (for example, monkfish, steak and a delicious crusted baked salmon served on pearl barley). A very pleasant environment, inside and out.

Scotch Wine Bar — Tapas $$

(☑03-579 1176; www.scotchbar.co.nz; 24-26 Maxwell Rd; dishes $7-28, tasting menu $45; ☺4pm-late Mon-Fri) A versatile and sociable spot in central Blenheim, Scotch offers local wines, craft beer on tap and delicious sharing plates in a range of sizes. The southern fried chicken with chilli mayo is a crispy and filling crowd-pleaser but, if you're feeling adventurous, we'd recommend the raw hangar steak with juniper, pine needles and sorrel.

Wairau River — International $$

(☑03-572 9800; www.wairauriverwines.com; 11 Rapaura Rd, Rapaura; mains $27-30, tastings

$5, free with purchase or meal; ☺noon-3pm; 🛜) This modish, mud-brick cellar door and bistro has a wide veranda and beautiful gardens with plenty of shade. The adventurous cuisine-straddling menu may include the likes of *togarashi* (Japanese spice mix) prawns with miso mayo, Marlborough mussel chowder, braised beef cheeks with sambal (Malaysian chilli paste), hot-smoked salmon salad or tandoori chicken burger.

Arbour — International $$$

(☑03-572 7989; www.arbour.co.nz; 36 Godfrey Rd, Renwick; set menu $89-109; ☺5.30-11pm Tue-Sat Aug-Jun) Located in the thick of Renwick wine country, Marlborough's most lauded restaurant focuses on local produce fashioned into top-notch contemporary dishes. Settle in for a multiple-course degustation, either with or without suggested matches from the mesmerising wine list.

ℹ️ INFORMATION

Blenheim i-SITE (📞03-577 8080; www.marlbor
oughnz.com; Train Station, 8 Sinclair St; ⏰9am-
4pm Mon-Fri, 10am-3pm Sat & Sun) Information
on Marlborough and beyond. Wine-trail maps
and bookings for everything under the sun.

ℹ️ GETTING THERE & AWAY

AIR

Marlborough Airport (📞03-572 8651; www.
marlboroughairport.co.nz; 1 Tancred Cres, Wood-
bourne) is 6km west of town. **Blenheim Shuttles**
(📞03-577 5277; www.blenheimshut
tles.co.nz) provides door-to-door services
between the airport and the town centre, as does
Marlborough Taxis (📞03-577 5511); expect to
pay around $20.

Air New Zealand (📞0800 737 000; www.
airnewzealand.co.nz) has direct flights to/from
Wellington and Auckland.

Sounds Air (p161) flies to Wellington, Kāpiti
Coast and Christchurch.

BUS

InterCity (📞03-365 1113; www.intercity.co.nz)
buses depart from the Blenheim i-SITE. Destinations include Picton (from $10, 30 minutes),
Kaikōura (from $19, 1¾ hours) and Christchurch
(from $37, 5½ hours).

 **Motuara
Island**

DOC-managed, predator-free **Motuara
Island reserve** (www.doc.govt.nz) 🏝️, at
the entrance to Queen Charlotte Sound,
is chock-full of rare NZ birds including
the Ōkārito brown kiwi (rowi), wood
pigeon (kererū), saddleback (tīeke) and
king shag. You can get here by water taxi
and on tours from Picton.

Saddleback bird
CMH IMAGES/ALAMY STOCK PHOTO ©

TRAIN

KiwiRail's scenic Coastal Pacific (p162) service
operates daily from October to April, heading to/
from Picton, Kaikōura and Christchurch.

Abel Tasman National Park

Sea kayaking, boating and tramping are the best ways to experience the beautiful beaches and forested coves of this national park on the South Island's northwestern tip.

Great For...

ℹ Need to Know

www.doc.govt.nz/abeltasmantrack

ROBERT CHG/SHUTTERSTOCK ®

★ **Top Tip**

Tour companies usually offer free Motueka pick-up/drop-off, with Nelson pick-up available at an extra cost.

Abel Tasman Coast Track

The Abel Tasman Coast Track is arguably NZ's most beautiful Great Walk – 60km of sparkling seas, golden sand, quintessential coastal forest, and hidden surprises such as Cleopatra's Pool. Such pulling power attracts more than 37,000 hikers and kayakers per year. Across easy terrain, it's almost impossible to get lost here and you can hike the track in sneakers.

The Route

Leaving the boots behind is a bonus, as you'll probably get your feet wet – indeed, you'll probably want to get your feet wet. This track features long stretches of beach walking and crazy tides. In fact, the tidal ranges in the park are among the greatest in the country – up to a staggering 6m. At

Torrent and Bark Bays, it's much easier and more fun to cross the soggy sands than take the high-tide track. At Awaroa Bay you have no choice but to plan on crossing close to low tide. Daylight tide times are published on the DOC website (www.doc.govt.nz), and also displayed at regional i-SITEs.

The entire hike takes three to five days, although with water-taxi transport you can tackle it in myriad ways, particularly if you combine it with a kayak leg. A rewarding short option (with beaches, seals and coastal scenery) is to loop through the northern end of the park, hiking the Coast Track from Tōtaranui, passing Anapai Bay and Mutton Cove, overnighting at Whari-wharangi Hut, then returning to Tōtaranui via the Gibbs Hill Track.

Bookings

The track operates on DOC's Great Walks Pass. Book online (www.doc.govt.nz) or in person at the Nelson, Motueka or Takaka i-SITES or DOC offices, where staff can offer suggestions to tailor the track to your needs and organise transport at each end. Book well in advance, especially between December and March.

Accommodation

Along the Abel Tasman Coast Track are four Great Walk huts with bunks, heating, flush toilets and limited lighting, but no cooking facilities. There are also 18 designated Great Walk campsites. An interesting

> **☑ Don't Miss**
>
> A swim at one golden-sand bay along the Coast Track, regardless of season.

alternative is **Aqua Packers** (☑027 430 7400; www.aquapackers.co.nz; Anchorage; dm/r $110/265; ☺Oct-Easter), a catamaran moored permanently in Anchorage Bay.

Paddling the Abel Tasman

The Abel Tasman Coast Track has long been hiking territory, but its coastal beauty makes it an equally seductive spot for sea kayaking, which can easily be combined with walking and camping. Options include either guided tours or freedom trips (unguided, but often requiring a minimum of two people). Recommended operators include the following (shop around):

Kahu Kayaks (☑03-527 8300; www.kahukay aks.co.nz; 325 Sandy Bay-Mārahau Rd, Mārahau; guided tours from $100, full-day rental $85)

R&R Kayaks (☑03-527 8197; www.rrkayaks. co.nz; 279 Sandy Bay-Mārahau Rd, Mārahau; tours from $150, full-day rental $85)

Wilsons (☑03-528 2027; www.abeltasman. co.nz; 409 High St, Motueka; walks, cruises $38-89, tours $79-185)

Getting There & Around

The closest big town to Abel Tasman is Motueka. Mārahau is the southern gateway; Tōtaranui is the usual finishing point. **ScenicNZ Abel Tasman** (☑03-548 0285; www.scenicnzabeltasman.co.nz) and **Golden Bay Coachlines** (☑03-525 8352; www.golden baycoachlines.co.nz) service these towns.

Water taxis can shunt you to/from any point on the track. Operators include **Abel Tasman Aqua Taxi** (☑03-527 8083; www. aquataxi.co.nz; 275 Sandy Bay-Mārahau Rd, Mārahau) and **Marahau Water Taxis** (☑03-527 8176; www.marahauwatertaxis.co.nz; 229 Sandy Bay-Mārahau Rd, Mārahau) ✆.

> **✕ Take a Break**
>
> Food is available at Mārahau and Kaiteriteri; within the park it's self-catering all the way.

GURTY PHOTOGRAPHY/SHUTTERSTOCK ©

CHRISTCHURCH

Christchurch at a Glance...

Today Christchurch is in the midst of an epic rebuild that has completely reconstructed the city centre, where over 80% of buildings needed to be demolished after the quakes. Scaffolding and road cones will be part of Christchurch's landscape for a while yet, but don't be deterred; exciting new buildings are opening at an astonishing pace, and sights are open for business. Curious travellers will revel in this chaotic, crazy and colourful mix, full of surprises and inspiring in ways you can't even imagine.

Two Days in Christchurch

After breakfast at **C1 Espresso** (p183), visit **Quake City** (p175) and wander through **Cathedral Square** (p182), at the heart of rebuilding efforts. Visit **Christchurch Art Gallery** (p178) then explore the Victoria St restaurant strip. Start day two at **Addington Coffee Co-op** (p183) and then head up Mt Cavendish on the **gondola** (p182) for views and a walk at the top. **Pomeroy's Old Brewery Inn** (p185) awaits with beers, followed by **Smash Palace** (p185) with burgers.

Four Days in Christchurch

Gather picnic supplies at **Riverside Market** (p183) and head to the lovely **Botanic Gardens** (p178). After lunch, visit the excellent **Canterbury Museum** (p179), before dinner at **Twenty Seven Steps** (p184). On day four, soak up the nautical vibes in soulful **Lyttelton** (p176), Christchurch's port town, before finishing with dinner at **Earl** (p184).

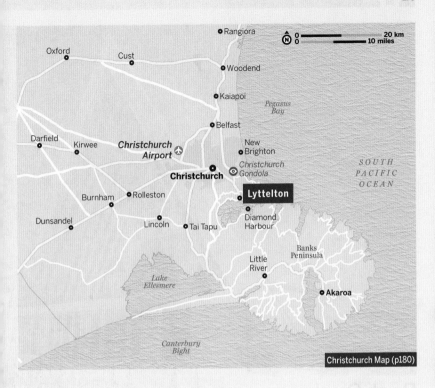

Christchurch Map (p180)

Arriving in Christchurch

Christchurch Airport (p187) is located 10km from the city centre. A taxi into town costs around $60. Public buses (www.metroinfo.co.nz) also run to the airport. Shuttle services cost around $25 per person. Local and some long-distance services arrive at the inner-city **Bus Interchange** (p187) on the corner of Lichfield and Colombo Sts.

Where to Stay

Sleepy? Christchurch has a wide variety of accommodation available, from luxury hotels to a plethora of backpacker beds. As the city's rebuild progresses, more and more beds are becoming available in the city centre and its inner fringes. Merivale, Riccarton and around Colombo St offer good motels, while the heritage suburb of Fendalton has boutique B&Bs.

Cardboard Cathedral

Post-Quake Christchurch

Resilience and creativity have defined the people of Christchurch since the lethal 6.3-magnitude 2011 earthquake, and while the planned rebuild slowly progresses, quirky initiatives are also inspiring NZ's second biggest city.

Great For...

☑ Don't Miss

Hearing harrowing earthquake survival stories at Quake City (p175).

Following the Christchurch earthquake of 22 February 2011, diverse creativity and DIY entrepreneurship have emerged as the city works through the painstaking process of a 20-year rebuild that's been estimated to cost up to $50 billion. Around 80% of the buildings within the city centre's famed four avenues have been or are due to be demolished. Amid the doomed, the saved and the shiny new builds are countless construction sites and empty plots still strewn with rubble... but a compact new low-rise city centre with parks and cycleways along the Avon River is slowly taking shape. Meanwhile, Christchurch locals are getting on with making the city a more interesting and rewarding place to live.

Quake City

GAID KORNSILAPA/SHUTTERSTOCK ©

❶ Need to Know

See www.facebook.com/rebuild christchurch for an independent point of view on the progress of the city's rebuild.

✕ Take a Break

Much more than just a food hall, **Little High Eatery** (p184) is a stylish pan-planet eating option.

★ Top Tip

See www.neatplaces.co.nz to find out about newly opened shops, bars and restaurants in ever-changing Christchurch.

5pm Apr-Oct, to 7pm Nov-Mar) due to the 98 cardboard tubes used in its construction, this interesting structure serves as both the city's temporary Anglican cathedral and as a concert venue. Designed by Japanese 'disaster architect' Shigeru Ban, the entire building was constructed in 11 months.

Gap Filler

Starting from the ground up after the earthquakes, the Gap Filler folks fill the city's empty spaces with creativity and colour. Projects range from temporary art installations, performance spaces and gardens, to a minigolf course scattered through empty building sites, to the world's first giant outdoor arcade game. Gaps open up and get filled, so check out the Gap Map on the website (www.gapfiller.org.nz), or simply wander the streets and see what you can find.

Quake City

A must-visit for anyone interested in understanding the impact of the Canterbury earthquakes, compact **Quake City** (☎03-366 5000; www.canterburymuseum.com/quake-city; 299 Durham St N; adult $20, child accompanied/unaccompanied free/$8; ⊗10am-5pm) tells stories through photography, video footage and various artefacts, including the remnants of ChristChurch Cathedral's celebrated rose window and other similarly moving debris. There are exhibits aimed at engaging both adults and children. Most affecting of all is the film featuring survivors recounting their own experiences.

Transitional Cathedral

Universally known as the **Cardboard Cathedral** (www.cardboardcathedral.org.nz; 234 Hereford St; entry by donation; ⊗9am-

Lyttelton marina

Lyttelton

Christchurch's port, little Lyttelton is a raffish, artsy harbour town – like Fremantle in Western Australia or Valparaíso in Chile – where the world washes in on the tide and washes out again, leaving the locals buzzing with global zeitgeist. It's a funky enclave with sea-salty soul to burn.

Christchurch's first European settlers landed at Lyttelton in 1850 to embark on their historic trek over the hills. These days a 2km road tunnel makes the journey considerably quicker.

Lyttelton was badly damaged during the 2010 and 2011 earthquakes and, sadly, many of the town's heritage buildings along London St were subsequently demolished. Today, however, Lyttelton has re-emerged as one of Christchurch's most interesting communities. The town's arty, independent and bohemian vibe is stronger than ever, and it is once again a hub for great bars, cafes and shops. It's well worth catching the bus from Christchurch and getting immersed in the local scene.

Great For...

☑ Don't Miss

A visit on Saturday morning when the farmers market is buzzing.

❶ Need to Know

Contact the **Lyttelton Visitor Information Centre** (☑03-328 9093; www.lytteltoninfocentre.nz; 20 Oxford St; ⏰10am-4pm Oct-Apr, 10.30am-2.30pm May-Sep) for the local low-down.

✖ Take a Break

Craft beer aficionados can quench their thirst at Eruption Brewing (p177).

★ Top Tip

Nowhere expresses Lyttelton's bohemian soul better than Wunderbar (p177) – stop in for the decor alone.

Eating & Drinking

Lyttelton Farmers Market   Market $

(www.lyttelton.net.nz; London St; ⏰10am-1pm Sat; 🖉🚼) 🍃 Every Saturday morning food stalls take the place of cars on Lyttelton's main street. Stock up alongside locals on fresh bread, baked goods, flowers, cheeses, local produce and good coffee.

Lyttelton Coffee Company   Cafe $$

(☑03-328 8096; www.facebook.com/lyttelton coffeecompany; 29 London St; mains $13-20; ⏰7am-4pm Mon-Fri, 8am-4pm Sat & Sun; 🖉🚼) 🍃 Local institution Lyttelton Coffee Company has risen from the rubble and continues its role as a stalwart of the London St foodie scene, serving consistently great coffee and wholesome food in its cavernous, exposed-brick warehouse space.

Wunderbar   Bar

(☑03-328 8818; www.wunderbar.co.nz; 19 London St; ⏰5pm-late Mon-Fri, 1pm-3am Sat & Sun) Wunderbar is a top spot to get down, with regular live music covering all spectra, and clientele to match. The kooky decor and decapitated dolls' heads alone are worth the trip. Enter via the stairs in the rear car park.

Eruption Brewing   Microbrewery

(☑03-355 5632; www.eruptionbrewing.com; 26 London St; ⏰4-9pm Wed & Thu, to 11pm Fri, 10am-11pm Sat, to 8pm Sun) Every heritage port town needs a decent craft brewery and Eruption Brewing doesn't disappoint. It's a firm local favourite, especially on Friday and Saturday nights when the vintage 1970s furniture hosts punters enjoying decent brews like the Eruption IPA packed with citrusy NZ hops. Dining options include pizza, platters and gourmet burgers. Ask what other interesting seasonal beers are on offer.

⊙ SIGHTS

Botanic Gardens   Gardens

(www.ccc.govt.nz; Rolleston Ave; ⊘7am-9pm
Nov-Feb, to 8.30pm Mar & Oct, to 6.30pm Apr-
Sep) **FREE** Strolling through these 30 blissful
riverside hectares of arboreal and floral
splendour is a consummate Christchurch
experience. Gorgeous at any time of the
year, the gardens are particularly impressive in spring when the rhododendrons,
azaleas and daffodil woodland are in
riotous bloom. There are thematic gardens
to explore, lawns to sprawl on, and a playground adjacent to the **Botanic Gardens
Visitor Centre** (☑03-941 7590; ⊘9am-4pm),
which also contains a lovely cafe and gift
shop.

Christchurch Art Gallery   Gallery

(Te Puna o Waiwhetū; ☑03-941 7300; www.
christchurchartgallery.org.nz; cnr Montreal St &
Worcester Blvd; ⊘10am-5pm Thu-Tue, to 9pm

*Gorgeous at any time of year,
the gardens are particularly
impressive in spring*

Wed; **P**) **FREE** Damaged in the earthquakes,
Christchurch's fantastic art gallery has
reopened brighter and bolder, presenting
a stimulating mix of local and international
exhibitions. Collection items range from
the traditional to the startlingly contemporary – think light installations and
interactive sculptures. Highlights from New
Zealand painters capturing the country's
bold landscapes include works by Rita
Angus and Colin McCahon. Free one-hour
guided tours take place at 11am and 2pm
daily.

Arts Centre   Historic Building

(www.artscentre.org.nz; 2 Worcester Blvd;
⊘10am-5pm) **FREE** Dating from 1877, this
enclave of Gothic Revival buildings was
originally Canterbury College, the forerun-
ner of Canterbury University. The buildings
are now reopening to the public after extensive restoration work due to quake damage.
Inside you'll find the visitor information
centre i-SITE (p187), as well as shops,
cafes, museums and galleries. Exhibition spaces play host to regular concerts,
rehearsals, markets and events. Of the cen-

Botanic Gardens

JOSHUA SMALL-PHOTOGRAPHER/SHUTTERSTOCK ©

tre's 23 buildings, 21 are listed by Heritage New Zealand as category 1 Historic Place structures.

If there's nothing on during your visit, you can still wander in and check out the North Quad and Great Hall in all their restored heritage splendour.

Watch This Space
Cultural

(www.watchthisspace.org.nz) With works enlivening post-earthquake derelict spaces and buildings, Christchurch is one of the world's best cities for street art, especially around the High St precinct. Check out this excellent website showcasing Christchurch street art, including a comprehensive map, photos and details of relevant artists. Guided tours of the city's street art scene are available by appointment ($30 per person).

See the website for details. Tours usually leave at 10am from outside the Canterbury Museum. Interviews with urban artists, reviews of new sites and previews of upcoming events are listed under Blogs on the website.

Te Papa Ōtākaro/ Avon River Precinct
Public Art

(www.otakaroltd.co.nz) One of the city's key post-earthquake redevelopment projects is reinvigorating the area around the Avon (Ōtākaro) River. Running along the river as a self-guided walk, Ngā Whāriki Manaaki (Woven Mats of Welcome) is a series of 13 paved artworks welcoming visitors to the city. Look for them as you stroll along the riverside from the **Canterbury Earthquake National Memorial** (Oi Manawa; www.canterburyearthquakememorial.co.nz; Oxford Tce) to the Margaret Mahy Family Playground (p183).

Canterbury Museum
Museum

(☑03-366 5000; www.canterburymuseum.com; Rolleston Ave; ☉9am-5.30pm Oct-Mar, to 5pm Apr-Sep; ☑) FREE Yes, there's a mummy and dinosaur bones, but the highlights of this museum are more local and more recent. The Māori galleries contain some beautiful *pounamu* (greenstone) pieces, while Christchurch Street is an atmospheric walk

⚠ The Christchurch Earthquakes

Christchurch's seismic nightmare began at 4.35am on 4 September 2010. Centred 40km west of the city, a 40-second, 7.1-magnitude earthquake caused wide-spread damage to older buildings in the central city. There were no fatalities, and many Christchurch residents felt that the city had dodged a bullet.

Fast forward to 12.51pm on 22 February 2011, when central Christchurch was busy with shoppers and workers enjoying their lunch break. This time the 6.3-magnitude quake was much closer, centred just 10km southeast of the city and only 5km deep. The tremor was significantly greater, and many locals report being flung violently and almost vertically into the air.

When the dust settled after 24 traumatic seconds, NZ's second-largest city had changed forever. The towering spire of the iconic ChristChurch Cathedral lay in ruins; walls and verandas had cascaded down on shopping strips; and two multistorey buildings had pancaked. Elsewhere, the historic port town of Lyttelton was badly damaged; roads and bridges were crumpled; and residential suburbs in the east were inundated by oozy silt.

The earthquakes resulted in 185 deaths across 20 nationalities. In the months that followed, hundreds of aftershocks rattled the city's traumatised residents (and claimed one more life).

Christchurch Cathedral
ROBERT CHG/SHUTTERSTOCK ©

Christchurch

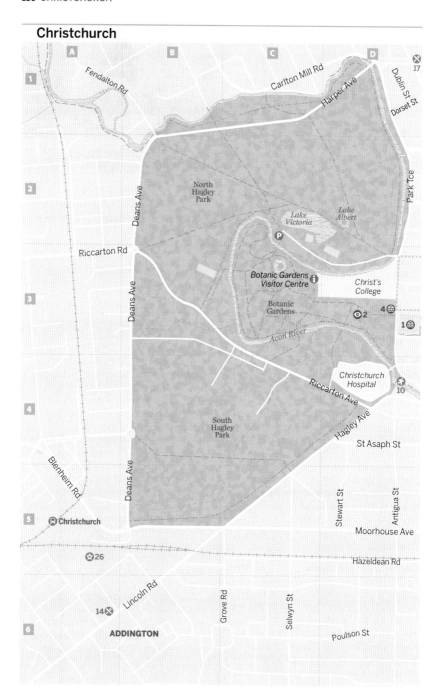

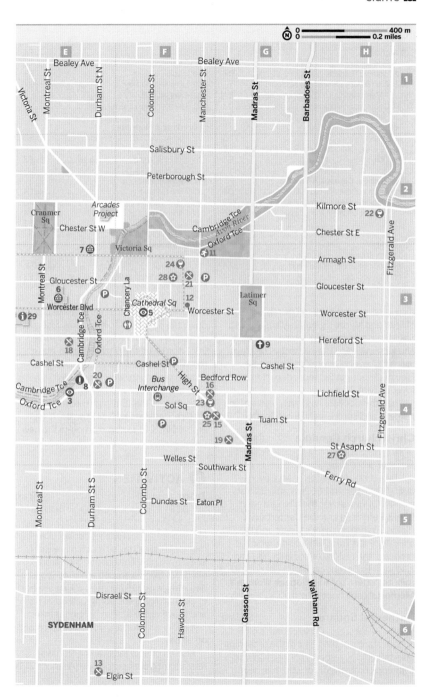

Christchurch

through the colonial past. The reproduction of Fred and Myrtle's gloriously kitsch Paua Shell House embraces Kiwiana at its best, and kids will enjoy the interactive displays in the Discovery Centre (admission $2). Free one-hour guided tours depart from the foyer daily at 2pm.

The 4th-floor cafe has lovely views of the gardens and surprisingly decent coffee.

Christchurch Gondola　Cable Car

(www.christchurchattractions.nz; 10 Bridle Path Rd; return adult/child $30/15; ⊙10am-5pm; P) Take a ride to the top of Mt Cavendish (500m) on this 862m cable car for wonderful views over the city, Lyttelton, Banks Peninsula and the Canterbury Plains. At the top there's a cafe and the child-focused Time Tunnel ride, which recounts the history of the area. You can also walk to Cavendish Bluff Lookout (30 minutes return) or the **Pioneer Women's Memorial** (one hour return).

Cathedral Square　Square

(www.reinstate.org.nz) Christchurch's city square stands at the heart of the rebuilding efforts, with the remains of ChristChurch Cathedral emblematic of what has been

lost. The February 2011 earthquake brought down the 63m-high spire, while subsequent earthquakes in June 2011 and December 2011 destroyed the prized stained-glass rose window. Other heritage buildings around the square were also badly damaged, but one modern landmark left unscathed is the 18m-high metal sculpture *Chalice*, designed by Neil Dawson. It was erected in 2001 to commemorate the new millennium.

⚙ ACTIVITIES

Tram　Tram

(☏03-366 7830; www.christchurchattractions. co.nz; adult/child $25/free; ⊙9am-6pm Oct-Apr, 10am-5pm May-Sep) Excellent driver commentary makes this so much more than just a tram ride. The beautifully restored old dears trundle around a 17-stop loop, departing every 15 minutes, taking in a host of city highlights, including Cathedral Sq and New Regent St. The full circuit takes just under an hour, and you can hop on and off all day.

Also on offer is the evening Tramway Restaurant (four courses with/without wine matches $139/109) taking a leisurely two to three hours.

Punting on the Avon Boating

(www.punting.co.nz; 2 Cambridge Tce; adult/child $30/15; ⊙9am-6pm Oct-Mar, 10am-4pm Apr-Sep; 📷) ✿ If rowing your own boat down the Avon sounds a bit too much like hard work, why not relax in a flat-bottomed punt while a strapping lad in Edwardian clobber glides you peaceably through the Botanic Gardens? Tours depart year-round from the **Antigua Boat Sheds** (✆03-366 5885; www.boatsheds.co.nz; 2 Cambridge Tce; ⊙9am-5pm; 📷) ✿; during the warmer months alternative trips run from sites at Mona Vale and Worcester Bridge.

Margaret Mahy
Family Playground Playground

(cnr Manchester & Armagh Sts) Named after beloved Kiwi children's author Margaret Mahy, this magical playground has four separate themed zones – peninsula, forest, wetlands and plains. From a splash park to a giant spiral slide, you'll find plenty to keep the kids (and kids at heart) entertained.

Amiki Local Tours Food & Drink

(✆027 532 7248; www.hiddengemsnz.com; per person $65-225) Join passionate and in-the-know locals on walking tours combining the history and culture of the city – including indigenous Māori elements – with the best of eating and drinking around central Christchurch. Options include the one-hour Ōtautahi Hikoi culture walk, the two-hour food-focused City Meander, and the three-hour after-dark Kai Safari (Kai translates to 'food' in Māori).

ⓐ SHOPPING

Tannery Shopping Centre

(www.thetannery.co.nz; 3 Garlands Rd, Woolston; ⊙10am-5pm) In a city mourning the loss of its heritage, this post-earthquake conversion of a 19th-century tannery couldn't be more welcome. The Victorian buildings have been beautifully restored, and are crammed with all manner of delightful boutiques selling everything from surfboards to vintage clothing to exquisite homewares.

When you're tired of shopping, stop by the **Brewery** (https://cassels.nz; 3 Garlands Rd, Woolston; ⊙8am-late) for an afternoon pick-me-up. There are also several cafes, an art-house cinema and live music at **Blue Smoke** (✆03-288 0543; www.bluesmoke.co.nz; The Tannery, 3 Garlands Rd; variable; ⊙hours vary by event).

ⓧ EATING

Riverside Market Market $

(www.riverside.nz; 96 Oxford Tce; meals $10-20; ⊙9am-6pm Mon-Wed, to 9pm Thu-Sat, 10am-6pm Sun; 📷) ✿ Central Christchurch's new essential destination for travelling foodies is this superb multi-level market combining fresh produce stalls with opportunities for eating and drinking. Many of Christchurch's most popular food trucks are represented, making the market a good one-stop option for great coffee, Greek souvlaki, Argentinean barbecue and Japanese ramen noodles. There's also a craft beer filling station and bar.

Addington Coffee Co-op Cafe $

(✆03-943 1662; www.addingtoncoffee.org.nz; 297 Lincoln Rd, Addington; mains $9-29; ⊙7.30am-4pm Mon-Fri, from 9am Sat & Sun; 📶🍴) You will find one of Christchurch's biggest and best cafes packed to the rafters most days. A compact shop selling fair-trade gifts jostles for attention with delicious cakes, gourmet pies, legendary breakfasts (until 2pm) and, of course, excellent coffee. An on-site laundry completes the deal for busy travellers.

C1 Espresso Cafe $

(www.c1espresso.co.nz; 185 High St; mains $10-22; ⊙7am-10pm; 📶) ✿ C1 sits pretty in a grand former post office that somehow escaped the cataclysm. Recycled materials fill the interior (Victorian oak panelling, bulbous 1970s light fixtures) and tables spill onto a little square. Excellent coffee, eggy brekkies and bagels are available all day,

Christchurch Combo Tickets

Christchurch Attractions (www.christchurchattractions.nz) is the company that runs the punting (p183), tram (p182) and gondola (p182). A baffling array of combo tickets are available, which will save you some money if you're considering doing more than one activity. All of the attractions above are included on the five-hour **Grand Tour** (adult/child $129/69).

Punting on the Avon River
CK TRAVELS/SHUTTERSTOCK ©

beers from Christchurch's Three Boys Brewery, while the pomegranate-glazed lamb shoulder partners with vegetables enlivened by hummus, garlic and feta. A serious approach to cocktails also makes 5th Street ideal for a drink and snacks.

Twenty Seven Steps
Modern NZ $$$

(☑03-366 2727; www.twentysevensteps.co.nz; 16 New Regent St; mains $33-42; ☺5pm-late) ☞ Overlooking the pastel-coloured New Regent St strip, this elegant restaurant showcases locally sourced seasonal ingredients. Mainstays include modern renditions of lamb, beef, venison and seafood, as well as outstanding risotto. Delectable desserts and friendly waitstaff seal the deal; reservations are advised.

Inati
Bistro $$$

(☑03-390 1580; www.inati.nz; 48 Hereford St; shared plates $16-22, 4/6/8-course tasting menus $59/79/99; ☺noon-2pm & 5pm-late Tue-Fri, from 5.30pm Sat; ☑) ☞ Shared plates enjoyed around an elegantly curved bar are divided into Earth, Land and Sea and include innovative and playful dishes harnessing ingredients like smoked mutton tartare, citrus-cured fish with fennel, and kiwifruit sorbet. Four- to eight-course tasting menus are a good way to explore the Inati ethos, and one of Christchurch's best wine lists featuring many South Island varietals.

Gatherings
Modern NZ $$$

(☑021 0293 5641; www.gatherings.co.nz; 2 Papanui Rd, Merivale; dinner 5-course tasting menu $65-80, with matched wines $120-135; ☺6-11pm Wed-Sat; ☑) ☞ Thoughtful, seasonal vegetarian dishes are the focus at this petite restaurant on the edge of the Papanui Rd dining strip. The set five-course tasting menu changes regularly, with a focus on sustainable, local produce and unique flavour combinations.

Little High Eatery
Food Hall $$

(www.littlehigh.co.nz; 255 St Asaph St; dishes $10-20; ☺7.30am-10pm Mon-Wed, to midnight Thu & Fri, 8.30am-late Sat & Sun; ☑⚘) Can't

while sliders (delivered via retro pneumatic tubes!) and burgers combine with craft beer later in the day.

Earl
Bistro $$

(☑03-365 1147; www.earl.co.nz; 128 Lichfield St; mains $22-34; ☺noon-late Tue-Sun; ☑) ☞ Mediterranean flavours are presented with flair in Earl's spacious dining room. Combine slow-cooked lamb and smoked yoghurt with a quinoa salad or mix it up from the shared plates menu including charcuterie, grilled octopus or fish crudo. The Eat like an Earl option ($60) presents the chef's favourites, while the concise wine list highlights a few different local producers each week.

5th Street
Bistro $$

(☑03-365 9667; www.5thstreet.co.nz; 5 Elgin St, Sydenham; shared plates $18-24; ☺4.30-11pm; ☑) Global influences punctuate the shared plates menu at this recent opening south of the city centre. The honey- and chipotle-fired chicken goes well with

decide whether you want sushi, pizza or Thai for dinner? At Little High, you won't have to choose – this stylish and energetic food hall is home to eight different gourmet businesses, offering everything from dumplings to burgers. Stop in for your morning coffee or swing by for a late-night mojito in the beautifully outfitted space.

🅾 DRINKING & NIGHTLIFE

Pomeroy's Old Brewery Inn   Pub

(☏03-365 1523; www.pomspub.co.nz; 292 Kilmore St; ☺3pm-late Tue-Thu, from noon Fri-Sun) With more than 30 taps featuring the best NZ craft beers, Pomeroy's is an essential Christchurch destination. Among this cosy British-style pub's other endearing features are regular live music, a snug and sunny courtyard and **Victoria's Kitchen**, serving comforting pub food (mains $25 to $34). Also onsite, pretty **Little Pom's** cafe serves excellent brunch fare ($11 to $25) until mid-afternoon.

Smash Palace   Bar

(☏03-366 5369; www.thesmashpalace.co.nz; 172 High St; ☺3pm-late Mon-Thu, from noon Fri-Sun) Epitomising the spirit of transience, tenacity and resourcefulness that Christchurch is now known for, this deliberately downcycled and ramshackle beer garden is an intoxicating mix of grease-monkey garage, trailer-trash park and proto-hipster hang-out, complete with a psychedelic school bus, edible garden and blooming roses. There's craft beer, chips, Cheerios, and burgers made from scratch ($11 to $15).

The Last Word   Cocktail Bar

(☏022 094 7445; www.facebook.com/thelastword.nz; 31 New Regent St; ☺4pm-late Mon-Fri, 2pm-late Sat & Sun) This cosy spot amid the heritage Spanish Mission facades of New Regent St is a fine option any time of the evening. One of the city's best selections of whisky partners with good cocktails

also on offer are special whisky and chocolate pairing menus

The Last Word

FILEDIMAGE/SHUTTERSTOCK ©

Isaac Theatre Royal

from opera and ballet to contemporary theatre and rock concerts

and a well-curated beer menu. Moreish bar snacks include platters and grilled-cheese sandwiches, and also on offer are special whisky and chocolate pairing menus.

ENTERTAINMENT

Isaac Theatre Royal   Theatre
(☎03-366 6326; www.isaactheatreroyal.co.nz; 145 Gloucester St; ⏰box office 10am-5pm Mon-Fri) This century-old dear survived the quakes and emerged restored to full glory in 2014. Its heritage features are enjoyed by patrons venturing inside for everything from opera and ballet to contemporary theatre and rock concerts.

Alice Cinema   Cinema
(☎03-365 0615; www.alice.co.nz; 209 Tuam St; adult/child $17/12) This delightful two-screen art-house cinema can be found within the long-standing and excellent Alice In Video-land DVD library.

Court Theatre   Theatre
(☎03-963 0870; www.courttheatre.org.nz; Bernard St, Addington; ⏰box office 9am-8.15pm Mon-Thu, to 10.15pm Fri, 10am-10.15pm Sat) Christchurch's original Court Theatre was an integral part of the city's Arts Centre, but it was forced to relocate to this warehouse after the earthquakes. The new premises are much more spacious; it's a great venue to see popular international plays and works by NZ playwrights.

Darkroom   Live Music
(www.darkroom.bar; 336 St Asaph St; ⏰7pm-late Thu-Sat) A hip combination of live-music venue and bar, Darkroom has lots of Kiwi beers and great cocktails. Live gigs are frequent – and frequently free.

ℹ INFORMATION

Airport i-SITE (☎03-741 3980; www. christchurchnz.com; International Arrivals Hall; ⏰8am-6pm)

Christchurch i-SITE (☏03-379 9629; www.
christchurchnz.com; Arts Centre, 28 Worcester
Blvd; ⊙8.30am-5pm)

DOC Visitor Centre (☏03-379 4082; www.doc.
govt.nz; Arts Centre, 28 Worcester Blvd; ⊙9am-
4.45pm) Information on South Island national
parks, including walk and hut bookings; located
within the Christchurch i-SITE.

❶ GETTING THERE & AWAY

Christchurch Airport (CHC; ☏03-358 5029;
www.christchurchairport.co.nz; 30 Durey Rd)
is located 10km from the city centre. A taxi
into town costs $50 to $65. Alternatively, the
airport is well served by public buses (www.
metroinfo.co.nz). The Purple Line bus heads
through Riccarton (20 minutes) to the central
Bus Interchange (30 minutes) and on to Sumner
(1¼ hours). Bus 29 heads through Fendalton (10
minutes) to the Bus Interchange (30 minutes).
Both services cost $8.50 (pay the driver) and
run every 30 minutes from approximately

7am to 11pm. Shuttle services are available for
around $25 per person.

Ride-share services Uber, Ola and Zoomy all
leave from the airport's Rideshare Pick-up Zone
located outside of the main terminal behind the
purple Express Car Park.

❶ GETTING AROUND

Christchurch's **Metro bus network** (☏03-366
8855; www.metroinfo.co.nz) is inexpensive, efficient and comprehensive. Most buses run from
the inner-city **Bus Interchange** (cnr Lichfield &
Colombo Sts).

Pick up timetables from the i-SITE or the
Interchange. Tickets (adult/child $4.20/2.40)
can be purchased on board and include one free
transfer within two hours. Alternatively, Metro-
cards allow unlimited zone one travel for two
hours/one day/one week for $2.65/5.30/26.50.
Cards are available from the Interchange; they
cost $10 and must be loaded with a minimum of
$10 additional credit.

THE WEST COAST

The West Coast at a Glance...

With colossal mountains, forests and glaciers, Westland Tai Poutini National Park clobbers visitors with its mind-bending proportions. Reaching from the West Coast to the razor peaks of the Southern Alps, the park's supreme attractions are twin glaciers Franz Josef and Fox: nowhere else at this latitude do glaciers descend so close to the ocean.

Just 23km apart, the towns bearing the glaciers' names are geared up for visitors, with plenty of good places to eat, drink and sleep. Not far away, the far-flung seaside hubs of Hokitika and Ōkārito deliver typically quirky West Coast experiences.

One Day in the West Coast

Only have one day on the West Coast? Don't muck around: head straight to **Franz Josef Glacier** (p192) and get a good look at this monstrous icy beast, either via a helihike or scenic flight. Repair to the **SnakeBite Brewery** (p195) for dinner, with further imbibing at **Monsoon** (p195).

Three Days in the West Coast

Fox Glacier (p196) is bigger and longer than Franz Josef, which often makes for a less crowded ice encounter. Once you're all iced-out, head to **Lake Matheson** (p197) for a hike, **Hokitika** (p201) for history and Māori culture, or **Ōkārito** (p198) for some wetland wildlife.

Previous page: Lake Matheson (p197)
SODA_02/SHUTTERSTOCK ©

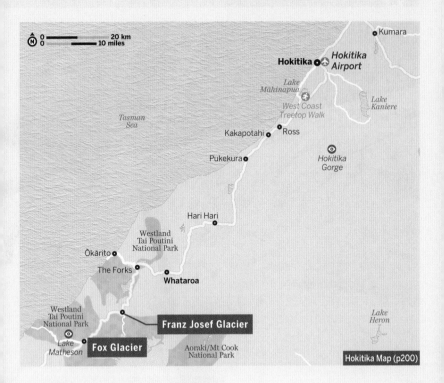

Franz Josef Glacier

Fox Glacier

Hokitika Map (p200)

Arriving in the West Coast

Hokitika Airport (p203) is 1.5km east of the town centre. Air New Zealand (www.airnewzealand.com) has two flights most days to/from Christchurch.

InterCity (p307) bus routes service Franz Josef Glacier and Fox Glacier villages, with onward connections.

Where to Stay

A big, all-budgets accommodation scene has sprung up to meet tourist demand in both glacier towns. Franz Josef has the biggest range (and the most luxurious options) while Fox is filled with motels and campgrounds. Booking ahead is recommended, particularly between November and March. Hokitika and its surrounds have some of the West Coast's most charming accommodation, and there's plenty of it for all budget levels.

MATTHEW MICAH WRIGHT/GETTY IMAGES ©

Franz Josef Glacier

Franz Josef's cloak of ice once flowed from the mountains right to the sea. Following millennia of gradual retreat, the glacier is now 19km inland and accessible only by helicopter.

Swarms of small aircraft take off from Franz Josef village, 5km north of the glacier, lifting visitors to views of sparkling ice and toothy mountains. Many land on the glacier to lead groups into blue-tinged caves and crevasses. A glacier experience is the crowning moment for thousands of annual visitors, but walking trails, hot pools and adventure sports, from quad-biking to clay target shooting, keep the adrenaline pulsing.

Geologist Julius von Haast led the first European expedition here in 1865, and named the glacier after the Austrian emperor. The dismal forecast of a rainier, warmer future spells more shrinkage for Franz Josef, whose trimlines (strips of vegetation on the valley walls) mark out decades of dramatic glacial retreat.

Great For...

☑ Don't Miss

Landing on the ice at the head of the great glacier – pricey but priceless.

Ōkārito ● The Forks

Tasman Sea   Whataroa ●

◉ **Franz Josef Glacier**

Fox Glacier ●   Westland Tai Poutini National Park

❶ Need to Know

Check out www.glaciercountry.co.nz for the low-down on both Franz Josef and Fox glaciers and to book activities; or visit the Franz Josef i-SITE (63 Cron St).

✖ Take a Break

Warm up at the **Glacier Hot Pools** (☎03-752 0099; www.glacierhotpools.co.nz; 63 Cron St; adult/child $29/25; ⊙11am-9pm) in a private pool.

★ Top Tip

Enjoy a change of pace with a guided SUP or kayak trip on Lake Mapourika.

Independent Walks

A series of walks start from the glacier car park, 5km from the village. **Sentinel Rock** (20 minutes return) reveals either impressive views of the glacier valley or a mysterious panorama swallowed by mist and cloud. The **Franz Josef Glacier/Kā Roimata o Hine Hukatere Walk** (1½ hours return) is the main glacier valley walk and leads you to the best permissible view of the terminal face.

Other walks include the **Douglas Walk** (one hour return), off the Glacier Access Rd, which passes moraine piled up by the glacier's advance in 1750, and **Peters Pool**, a small kettle lake. The **Terrace Track** (15 minutes return) is an easy amble over bushy terraces behind the village, with Waiho River views. Two good rainforest walks, **Callery Gorge Walk** and **Tatare**

Tunnels (both around 1½ hours return), start from Cowan St – bring a torch for the latter.

Much more challenging walks, such as the five-hour **Roberts Point Track** and eight-hour **Alex Knob Track**, are detailed, along with all the others, in DOC's excellent *Glacier Region Walks* booklet ($2), which provides maps and illuminating background reading.

A rewarding alternative to driving to the glacier car park is the richly rainforested **Te Ara a Waiau Walkway/Cycleway**, starting from near the fire station at the south end of town. It's a one-hour walk (each way) or half that by bicycle. Ask in the **i-SITE** (☎0800 354 748; www.glaciercountry.co.nz; 63 Cron St; ⊙8.30am-5pm) for the latest.

Guided Walks & Helihikes

Franz Josef Glacier Guides (☎03-752 0763; www.franzjosefglacier.com; 63 Cron St) runs small group walks with experienced guides (boots, jackets and equipment supplied).

With dazzling blue ice, photo ops in ice caves, and helicopter rides to and from the ice, these might be one of your most memorable experiences in NZ. A standard trip involves taking a helicopter ride to the ice and then experiencing two hours on the glacier exploring dazzling blue ice caves ($485). The daring can seize an ice pick for a four-hour ice climb ($609) or even camp on the glacier overnight ($999). Three-hour guided valley walks are also available (adult/child $82/67). **Glacier Valley Eco Tours** (0800 925 586; www.glaciervalley. co.nz; 20 Main Rd; adult/child $80/40) offers conservation-focused walking tours that unlock the geological and wildlife secrets of Glacier Country. Three- to four-hour tours explore either Franz Josef, Fox Glacier, Ōkārito or Lake Matheson, with the Franz Josef tour getting closer to the terminal face than is otherwise permitted. Full-day tours immerse you in local flora and fauna over seven hours of hiking (adult/child $180/90).

Aerial Sightseeing

Forget sandflies and mozzies, the buzzing you're hearing is a swarm of small aircraft. The most affordable scenic flights involve 10 or 12 minutes in the air above Franz Josef Glacier (around $120 to $165) but it's worth paying for 20 minutes or more to get a snow landing or to view both Franz Josef and Fox glaciers (from $245). Pricier, 40-minute flights (around $370 to $460) enjoy the most eye-popping views, swooping around Aoraki/Mt Cook. Fares for children under 12 years usually cost around 70% of the adult price. Shop around: most operators are situated on the main road.

Franz Josef on the Move

A town built on top of a fault line can't just up and leave. Or can it? A fault line slices right through Franz Josef, and fears of future earthquake damage and flooding from the ever-rising Waiho River have prompted regional council members to consider a lift and shift: moving the township 10km north. Building an earthquake-resistant town next to Lake Mapourika has its appeal, though the price-tag – an estimated $600m – has sent town planners scrambling for alternatives.

> ### ★ Did You Know?
>
> The early Māori knew Franz Josef as Kā Roimata o Hine Hukatere (Tears of the Avalanche Girl). Legends tell of a woman persuading her lover to join her in the mountains only for him to die in a fall; her flood of tears froze into the glacier.

KERRY KISSANE/GETTY IMAGES ©

West Coast Wildlife Centre

The purpose of this feel-good **attraction** (☎03-752 0600; www.wildkiwi.co.nz; cnr Cron & Cowan Sts; adult/child $39/20, incl backstage pass $59/35; ◷8am-5.30pm) ✈ is breeding two of the world's rarest kiwi – the rowi and the Haast tokoeka. The entry fee is well worth the price by the time you've viewed the conservation, glacier and heritage displays, hung out with kiwi in their ferny enclosure, and met the five resident tuatara (native reptiles). The backstage pass into the incubating and rearing area is a rare opportunity to learn how a species can be brought back from the brink of extinction.

Eating & Drinking

SnakeBite Brewery   Asian $$

(☎03-752 0234; www.snakebite.co.nz; 28 Main Rd; mains $16-29; ◷7.30am-10.30pm) Snake Bite's motley Asian meals awaken tastebuds after their long slumber through the West Coast's lamb-and-whitebait menus. Choices include nasi goreng (fried rice), Thai- and Malaysian-style curries and salads of calamari and carrot that zing with fresh lime. Try the mussel fritters with wasabi mayo. Between courses, glug craft beers on tap or 'snakebite' (a mix of cider and beer).

Monsoon   Pub Food $$

(☎03-752 0101; www.monsoonbar.co.nz; 46 Cron St; mains $16-39; ◷4.30pm-late) Sip drinks in the sunshine or within the cosy, chalet-style bar of the **Rainforest Retreat** (☎03-752 0220; www.rainforest.nz; 46 Cron St; sites $48, dm/r/units from $37/100/195; 🅿🛜), usually packed to the rafters with a sociable crowd of travellers. Bar snacks, burgers and posh pizzas (with toppings like chorizo and prawn) ensure you needn't move from your comfy spot by the fire.

> ### ★ Top Tip
>
> The well-maintained outdoor Glacier Hot Pools (p193) are perfect for après-hike or on a rainy day.

Fox Glacier

Impassable Fox Glacier seems to flow ominously towards the town below, but this 12km glacier (named for former New Zealand PM Sir William Fox) has been steadily retreating over the past century. Surrounded by farmland, the township's cafes and tour operators are strung along the main road.

Great For...

☑ Don't Miss

Pray the weather gods deliver the picture-perfect reflection of Aoraki/Mt Cook on Lake Matheson.

Glacier Walks & Helihikes

The only way on to the ice is by taking a helihiking trip, run by the superb **Fox Glacier Guiding** (☏03-751 0825; www.foxguides. co.nz; 44 Main Rd). Independent walks offer a chance to explore the valley and get as close to the glacier's terminal face as safety allows (also a good option when unstable weather grounds the helicopters).

It's 1.5km from Fox village to the glacier turn-off, and a further 2km to the car park, which you can reach under your own steam via **Te Weheka Walkway/Cycleway**, a pleasant rainforest trail starting just south of the Bella Vista motel. It's 2½ hours return on foot, or an hour by bike (leave your bikes at the car park – you can't cycle on the glacier walkways). Hire bikes from **Fox Glacier Lodge** (☏0800 369 800, 03-751 0888; www. foxglacierlodge.com; 41 Sullivan Rd; unpowered/

MARCO SIMONI/GETTY IMAGES ©

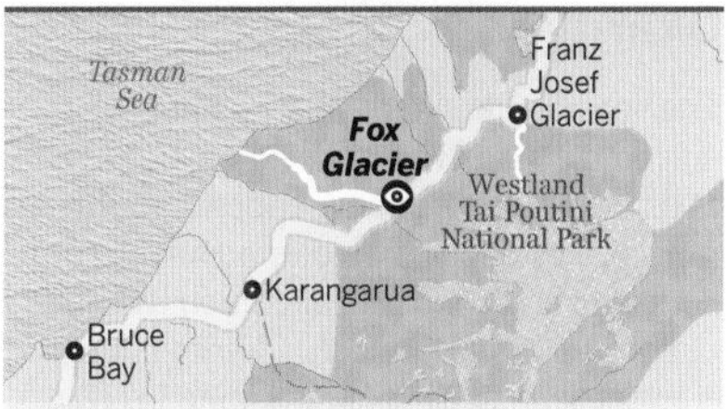

Need to Know

There's no ATM in Fox (there's one in Franz Josef). If you're heading south, Fox has the last fuel before Haast, 120km away.

Take a Break

Lake Matheson Cafe (p197) does everything right: sharp architecture, strong coffee and mountain views.

★ Top Tip

Fox Glacier is brimming with midrange accommodation options, but book ahead from November to March.

powered sites $30/40, d $175-235;) (per hour/half-day $5/15).

From the car park, the terminal-face view point is around 40 minutes' walk, depending on conditions. Obey all signs: this place is dangerously dynamic.

Short return walks near the glacier include the half-hour **Moraine Walk** (over a major 18th-century advance) and 20-minute **Minnehaha Walk**. The fully accessible **River Walk Lookout Track** (20 minutes return) starts from the Glacier View Rd car park.

Pick up a copy of DOC's excellent *Glacier Region Walks* booklet ($2), which provides maps and illuminating background reading.

Skydiving & Aerial Sightseeing

Short heliflights (10 to 20 minutes) offer a spectacular vantage point over Fox Glacier with a snow landing up top. On a longer flight (30 to 50 minutes) you can also enjoy sky-high sightseeing over Franz Josef Glacier and Aoraki/Mt Cook. Ten-minute joy flights cost from around $120, but we recommend 20 minutes or more in the air (from $245). Shop around: most operators are situated on the main road in Fox Glacier village.

What's Nearby

The famous 'mirror lake', **Lake Matheson** (Lake Matheson Rd) can be found 6km down Cook Flat Rd. Wandering slowly (as you should), it will take 1½ hours to complete the circuit. The best time to visit is early morning, or when the sun is low in the late afternoon, although the presence of the **Lake Matheson Cafe** (03-751 0878; www.lakematheson.com; Lake Matheson Rd; breakfast & lunch $13-22, dinner $25-39; 8am-late Nov-Mar, to 3pm Apr-Oct;) makes any time a good time.

Ōkārito

The seaside hamlet of Ōkārito has a magnificent setting, with a pounding surf beach at its doorstep, the snow-capped Southern Alps as a backdrop, forest-clad hills on one flank and an expansive lagoon on the other.

Barely 10km from SH6, Ōkārito Lagoon is the largest unmodified wetland in NZ. More than 76 bird species preen and glide among its waterways, including the kōtuku (white heron). Hiding out in the forest are rowi kiwi, the rarest species of NZ's iconic land-bird.

Ōkārito has no shops, limited visitor facilities and patchy phone reception, so stock up and book before you arrive. It's hard to believe that during the height of the gold rush, 4000 people lived here.

✪ ACTIVITIES

From a car park on the Strand you can begin the easy **Wetland Walk** (20 minutes), which leads into the 10km-long **Three Mile Pack Track** (3½ hours; the coastal return route is tide dependent, so check in with the locals for tide times). Otherwise, branch off on the **Ōkārito Trig Walk** (1½ hours return), where a jolly good puff to the top is rewarded with spectacular Southern Alps and Ōkārito Lagoon views (weather contingent).

Okarito Kiwi Tours   Birdwatching

(☏03-753 4330; www.okaritokiwitours.co.nz; 53 The Strand; 3-5hr tours $75) ✆ Spotting the rare kiwi in Ōkārito's tangle of native forest isn't easy, but bird-whisperer Ian has a 98% success rate for his small-group evening tours. Patience, tiptoeing and fine weather are essential. If you have your heart set on a kiwi encounter, book ahead and be within reach of Ōkārito for a couple of nights, in case of poor weather.

Okarito Kayaks   Kayaking

(☏0800 652 748; www.okarito.co.nz; 1 The Strand; 2hr/3hr tours $110/130, half-/full-day rental $70/80; ☉hours vary) This hands-on operator hires out kayaks for paddles across Ōkārito's shallow lagoon in the company of strutting waterfowl and beneath a breathtaking mountainscape.

Ōkārito wetlands

STEVE TODD/SHUTTERSTOCK ©

Honest advice is offered on weather, tides and paddling routes. Personalised guided kayaking trips are ideal for getting to know the landscape. It also serves homemade ice cream and cake, and surprisingly good coffee.

Okarito Boat
Eco Tours
Birdwatching

(☑03-753 4223; www.okaritoboattours.co.nz; 31 Wharf St; ☺late Oct–May) Runs bird-spotting lagoon tours, the most fruitful of which is the 80-minute Early Bird (adult/child $85/40, 7.30am). The popular two-hour Eco Tour offers deeper insights into this remarkable natural area ($95/45, 9am and 11.30am), or there's a 90-minute afternoon Wetlands Tour' ($75/35, 2.30pm) if you aren't a morning person. Book at least 24 hours in advance.

 GETTING THERE & AWAY

Ōkārito is 10km north off SH6 between Franz Josef and Whataroa. You'll need your own wheels to get there.

There are no buses but **Glacier Shuttles & Charters** (☑027 205 5922; www.glaciershuttlescharters.co.nz; 20 Main Rd) runs scheduled shuttles to and from Franz Josef ($30 return, two daily).

Hokitika

Hokitika is the archetypal West Coast town, positioned between a surf-battered beach and the snow-capped Southern Alps. Of the coast's three major towns (the others being Greymouth and Westport), Hokitika is by far the most appealing. There are some good places to eat, and a thriving community of local artisans selling their wares in shops scattered around the compact town centre. The town's artsy credentials have been buoyed further by its starring role in Eleanor Catton's 2013 book *The Luminaries*. There are just enough grand buildings from Hokitika's golden days dotted about to capture the imagination of fans of the

West Coast Wilderness Trail

One of the 22 Great Rides that together form the Ngā Haerenga NZ Cycle Trail, this easy (Grade 2) 133km route stretches from Ross to Greymouth via Hokitika and Kumara, following gold-rush tracks, reservoirs, old tramways and railway lines. The trail reveals dense rainforest, glacial rivers, lakes and wetlands, and views to the Southern Alps and wild Tasman Sea.

The trail can be ridden in either direction and is gently graded most of the way. Although the full shebang takes a good four days by bike, it can easily be sliced up into sections of various lengths, catering to every ability and area of interest. Novice riders can tackle the relatively flat *Ross Railway* section between Ross and Hokitika (33km, three to five hours). Another goodie is the 49km *Majestic Forests & Lake Ride* from the Kawhaka Intake to Hokitika via Lake Kaniere, which takes in major highlights over seven hours, or a 45km ride following Kumara's gold trails (four hours).

Bike hire, transport and advice are available from the major setting-off points. In Hokitika, contact **Cycle Journeys** (☑021 263 3299; www.cyclejourneys.co.nz; 23 Hamilton St; bike hire per day from $55, shuttles $20-55) or **Hokitika Cycles & Sports World** (☑03-755 8662; www.hokitikasportsworld.co.nz; 33 Tancred St; bike rental per day $55; ☺9am-5pm Mon-Sat Oct-Mar, 9am-5pm Mon-Fri, to 1pm Sat Apr-Sep).

Hokitika River
ALEX CIMBAL/SHUTTERSTOCK ©

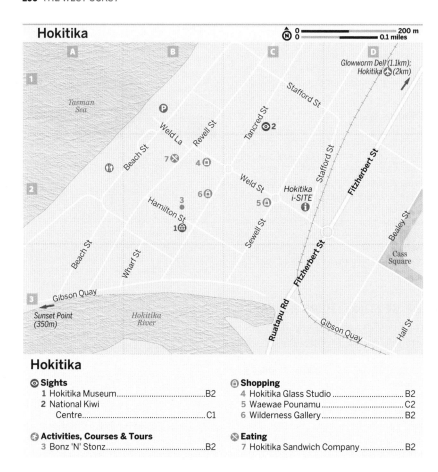

Hokitika

Hokitika

◉ **Sights**
1 Hokitika Museum..B2
2 National Kiwi
  Centre...C1

◉ **Activities, Courses & Tours**
3 Bonz 'N' Stonz..B2

◉ **Shopping**
4 Hokitika Glass Studio B2
5 Waewae Pounamu C2
6 Wilderness Gallery B2

◉ **Eating**
7 Hokitika Sandwich Company B2

Man Booker–winning novel, set during the 1860s gold rush.

Radiant sunsets and a glowworm dell add extra sparkle to this coastal idyll, though many visitors prefer to work up a sweat on the West Coast Wilderness Trail (p199) and the scenic tracks at lakes Kaniere and Māhinapua.

◉ SIGHTS

Hokitika Gorge   Gorge
(www.doc.govt.nz; Whitcombe Valley Rd) Water this turquoise doesn't come easily. Half a million years of glacial movement sculpted

Hokitika's ravine; the rock 'flour' ground over millennia intensifies the water's hue. The gorge is a scenic 32km drive south of Hokitika, well signposted from Stafford St (past the dairy factory). From the car park it's a 150m walk to a viewing platform, then a further 300m to a swing bridge and 200m to a point where you can access the river.

En route, you will pass a poignant monument in **Kōwhitirangi**, the site of one of NZ's deadliest mass murders (immortalised in the 1982 classic film *Bad Blood*). Visitors can peer towards the farmstead site through a shaft bored through the stone.

Glowworm Dell
Natural Feature

(Kumara Junction Hwy) At nightfall, bring a
torch (or grope your way) into this grotto
on the northern edge of town, signposted
off SH6. The dell is an easy opportunity
to glimpse legions of glowworms (aka
fungus gnat larvae), which emit an other-worldly blue light. An information panel
at the entrance will further illuminate
your way.

Lake Kaniere
Lake

(www.doc.govt.nz; Lake Kaniere Rd) Lying at
the heart of a 7000-hectare scenic reserve,
18km southeast of Hokitika, beautiful Lake
Kaniere is 8km long, 2km wide, up to 195m
deep, and freezing cold (as you'll discover if
you swim). You can camp or picnic at **Hans
Bay**, peer at **Dorothy Falls** (4km south of
the campground), or undertake one of numerous walks, ranging from the 15-minute
Canoe Cove Walk to the seven-hour return
gut-buster up **Mt Tuhua**.

The historic **Kaniere Water Race Walkway** (3½ hours one-way) forms part of the
West Coast Wilderness Trail (p199).

Lake Māhinapua
Lake

(www.doc.govt.nz; Shanghai Rd, Ruatapu) Se-
rene Lake Māhinapua lies 10km southwest
of Hokitika, screened from SH6 by its
surrounding forest. The scenic reserve,
gazetted in 1907, has a picnic area and DOC
campsite that bask in mountain views, and
the shallow water is warm enough for a
paddle. There are several short walks (an
hour return or less) signposted along the
shore.

The starting point of the Mahinapua
Walkway is on SH6, 8km south of Hokitika.
It's an easy four- to five-hour return walk
(6km each way) following an old logging
tramway to Woodstock Rimu Rd, with a
short spur track connecting to the lake.

Sunset Point
Viewpoint

(Gibson Quay) A visit to Sunset Point is a
quintessential Hokitika experience: watch
the day's light fade away, observe white-
baiters casting nets, munch fish and chips,

or stroll around the quayside shipwreck
memorial.

Hokitika Museum
Museum

(☑03-755 6898; www.hokitikamuseum.co.nz;
17 Hamilton St; ⏰10am-5pm Nov-Mar, to 2pm
Apr-Oct) FREE Housed in the gorgeous,
recently strengthened Carnegie Building (1908), this museum has displays
on greenstone, gold mining, history and
whitebait fishing.

National Kiwi Centre
Nature Centre

(☑03-755 5251; www.thenationalkiwicentre.
co.nz; 64 Tancred St; adult/child $26/15; ⏰9am-
5pm; 👶) Tiptoe through the darkened kiwi
house to watch the birds rummage for
tasty insects, or stare a tuatara – a reptile
unchanged for 150 million years – in its
beady eyes. There's also a pond where you
can catch-and-return crayfish and a large
tank full of giant eels, the oldest of which is
thought to be over 120 years old.

Time your visit for eel feeding time
(10am, noon and 3pm) when you can
hold out scraps of meat for these slithery
critters to grab from a pair of tongs (or your
bare hands, if you dare).

⊕ ACTIVITIES

Hokitika is a great base for walking and
cycling. Download DOC's *Walks in the Hokitika Area,* and visit Hokitika Cycles & Sports
World (p199) for bike rental, repairs and
advice on tracks, including the West Coast
Wilderness Trail (p199).

Bonz 'N' Stonz
Arts & Crafts

(☑03-755 6504; www.bonz-n-stonz.co.nz; 16
Hamilton St; carving per hour $35) Design,
carve and polish your own *pounamu*
(greenstone/jade, $190), bone ($100)
or paua-shell ($100) masterpiece, with
tutelage from Steve Gwaliasi. Bookings
recommended, and 'laughter therapy'
included in the price. There's also a good
range of Steve's accomplished carvings to
purchase.

From left: Dorothy Falls (p201); West Coast Treetop Walk; National Kiwi Centre (p201)

West Coast
Treetop Walk   Outdoors

(✆03-755 5052; www.treetopsnz.com; 1128 Woodstock-Rimu Rd, Ruatapu; adult/child $32/16; ⏲9am-3.15pm) Visitors strolling along this wobbly but wheelchair-friendly steel walkway, 450m long and 20m off the ground, can enjoy an unusual perspective on the canopy of native trees (allow 45 minutes). The highlight is the 47m-high tower, from which views extend to the Southern Alps and the Tasman Sea. It's 17km south of Hokitika, near the southern shore of Lake Māhinapua

🔒 SHOPPING

Hokitika has a buzzing arts and crafts scene centred on carving and polishing *pounamu* (greenstone/jade) into ornaments and jewellery. Be aware that some galleries sell jade imported from Europe and Asia, so ask before you buy. Along for the ride are woodworkers, textile weavers and glass-blowers, all represented at classy boutiques in the centre of town.

Waewae Pounamu   Arts & Crafts
(✆03-755 8304; www.waewaepounamu.co.nz; 39 Weld St; ⏲8.30am-6.30pm Nov-Mar, 8.30am-5pm Mon-Fri, 10am-4pm Sat & Sun Apr-Oct) Linked to Ngāti Waewae, a local *hapū* (sub-tribe) of the broader Ngāi Tahu tribe, this stronghold of *pounamu* carving displays traditional and contemporary designs in its main-road gallery-boutique. Watch the carvers at work before deciding on a piece to purchase.

Hokitika Glass Studio   Arts & Crafts
(✆03-755 7775; www.hokitikaglass.co.nz; 9 Weld St; ⏲8.30am-4.30pm Mon-Fri, 10am-3pm Sat & Sun) Call in on weekdays to watch the blowers at work at the furnace producing glistening glass birds, multicoloured bowls and stemware. And yes, these fragile objects are secured in oodles of protective wrapping.

Wilderness Gallery   Arts & Crafts
(✆03-755 7575; www.wildernessgallery.co.nz; 29 Tancred St; ⏲10.30am-1.30pm Tue-Sun, extended summer) Juergen Schacke's large-scale nature photography takes centre stage at this gallery/gift shop, which also sells an ex-

CHRISTOPHER BABCOCK/SHUTTERSTOCK ©

cellent range of NZ-made craft: woodwork, pottery and carved *pounamu*, in particular.

Expect hearty serves of pork, lamb, salmon, vegetarian pasta and a delicious Middle Eastern–style chicken on couscous.

🍴 EATING

Hokitika Sandwich Company
Sandwiches $

(📞03-429 2019; www.facebook.com/TheHoki tikaSandwichCompany; 83a Revell St; half/full sandwiches $9/18; ⏰10am-2pm Tue-Sat) To say this hip place is serious about sandwiches is an understatement. Everything's made to order and served on chunky slices of freshly baked bread, generously loaded with the best locally sourced goodies: free-range meat, organic vegetables, South Island cheeses and its own in-house condiments. Grab a seat on one of the communal tables and tuck in. Smoothies, too.

Stations Inn
Bistro $$

(📞03-755 5499; www.stationsinnhokitika. co.nz; 11 Blue Spur Rd; mains $29-39; ⏰6-10pm Tue-Sat) Attached to an out-of-the-way but upmarket motel-style complex 4km southeast of the town centre, this restaurant delivers the best bistro-style fare in Hokitika.

ℹ️ INFORMATION

Hokitika i-SITE (📞03-755 6166; www.hokitika info.co.nz; 36 Weld St; ⏰9am-5pm) One of NZ's best i-SITEs offers extensive bookings, including all bus services.

ℹ️ GETTING THERE & AWAY

Hokitika Airport (HKK; 📞03-756 8050; www. hokitikaairport.co.nz; Airport Dr) is on the town's eastern fringe and has the usual collection of rental-car counters. **Air New Zealand** (www. airnewzealand.com) has two flights most days to/from Christchurch.

InterCity (📞03-365 1113; www.intercity.co.nz) has a daily service between Greymouth ($28, 55 minutes) and Fox Glacier ($40, 3¼ hours) via Ross ($28, 25 minutes), Whataroa ($30, two hours) and Franz Josef ($38, 2½ hours). All buses stop outside both the National Kiwi Centre and the i-SITE.

QUEENSTOWN

In this Chapter

Queenstown at a Glance...

Queenstown is as much a verb as a noun, a place of doing that likes to spruik itself as the 'adventure capital of the world'. It's famously the birthplace of bungy jumping, and the list of adventures you can throw yourself into here is encyclopaedic – from alpine heliskiing to ziplining. It's rare that a visitor leaves without having tried something that ups their heart rate, but to pigeonhole Queenstown as just a playground is to overlook its cosmopolitan dining and arts scene, its fine vineyards, and the diverse range of bars that can make evenings as fun-filled as the days.

Two Days in Queenstown

Fuel up at **Bespoke Kitchen** (p225) before riding the **Skyline Gondola** (p222). Leap from **Kawarau Bridge** (p208) before drinks at **Atlas Beer Cafe** (p226) and dinner at **Rātā** (p226). Begin the next day with breakfast at **Yonder** (p225) before a tour of the nearby **Gibbston Valley wine region** (p216). Then grab a pie from **Fergbaker** (p225) before winding down with a quiet fireside glass of wine at **Bardeaux** (p227).

Four Days in Queenstown

Spend one day skiing the slopes (**the Remarkables** and **Coronet Peak** are on hand), and the next day maintaining the adrenaline with a ride on the **Shotover Jet** (p211). Or for something more low-key, a trip around **Lake Wakatipu** (p218) or to historic Arrowtown. Finish up at **Zephyr** (p228) for some live tunes.

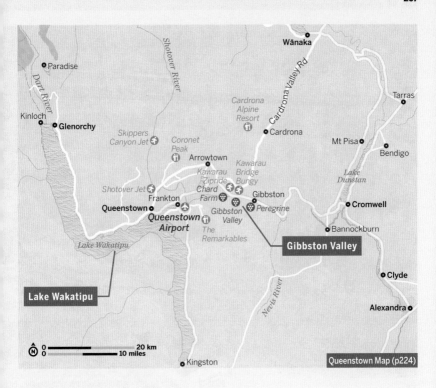

Lake Wakatipu

Gibbston Valley

Queenstown Map (p224)

Arriving in Queenstown

Queenstown airport (p305) lies 7km east of the town centre. Taxis charge around $50 for the journey between the airport and town. **Super Shuttle** (www.supershuttle.co.nz) runs a door-to-door shuttle ($20).

Long-haul buses (arriving from Christchurch, Te Anau, Dunedin, Franz Josef and beyond) stop outside the **Queenstown i-SITE** (p228).

Where to Stay

Lakefront accommodation isn't difficult to come by in Queenstown, but mid-range rooms are few and far between. Queenstown's hostels are competitive, however, and often come with an intriguing selection of extras – free GoPro hire, in-house saunas etc. Prices fluctuate widely with seasonal peaks (summer, from Christmas to February; winter, from June to September) so check hotel websites to see about discounts.

Kawarau Bridge

NICRAM SABOD/SHUTTERSTOCK ©

Extreme Queenstown

Many visitors who come to Queenstown try crazy things that they've never done before – often with a backdrop of stunning Central Otago scenery (...look forward to a good collection of 'I Did It!' souvenir T-shirts).

Great For...

☑ Don't Miss

Kawarau Bridge, the world's first commercial bungy-jump site.

Shotover St, particularly the two blocks between Stanley and Brecon Sts, is wall-to-wall with adventure-tour operators selling their products, interspersed with travel agencies and 'information centres' hawking the very same products. Adding to the confusion is the fact that some stores change their name from summer to winter, while some tour operators list street addresses that are primarily their pick-up points rather than distinct shopfronts for the business.

Bungy Jumping & Swings

AJ Hackett Bungy (☏ 03-450 1300; www. bungy.co.nz; The Station, cnr Camp & Shotover Sts), the bungy originator, now offers jumps from three sites in the Queenstown area, with giant swings available at two of them. It all started at the historic 1880 **Kawarau Bridge** (☏ 03-450 1300; www.bungy.co.nz;

AJ Hackett Bungy

NORMAN ALLCHIN/SHUTTERSTOCK ©

ℹ️ Need to Know

Head to Shotover St to get a handle on the baffling array of activities on offer in Queenstown.

✕ Take a Break

Recount tales of brave deeds over a craft beer or four at Smiths Craft Beer House (p228).

★ Top Tip

Planning on tackling several activities? Various combination tickets are available; try Queenstown Combos (p223).

Gibbston Hwy; adult/child $205/155), 23km from Queenstown, which became the world's first commercial bungy site in 1988. The 43m leap has you plunging towards the river, and is the only bungy site in the region to offer tandem jumps.

The Kawarau Bridge site also features the **Kawarau Zipride** (📞03-450 1300; www. bungy.co.nz; Gibbston Hwy; adult/child $50/40, 3-/5-ride pack $105/150), a zipline along the riverbank that reaches speeds of 60km/h. Multiride packs can be split between groups, making it a far cheaper alternative to the bungy.

The closest options to Queenstown are the **Ledge Bungy** (📞0800 286 4958; www.bungy.co.nz; Skyline Gondola; adult/child $205/155) and **Ledge Swing** (www.bungy. co.nz; Skyline Gondola; adult/child $165/115), set just beneath the top station of the Skyline

Gondola (p222). The drop is 47m, but it's 400m above town. From July to September you can even leap into the dark.

Last but most airy is the **Nevis Bungy** (📞03-450 1300; www.bungy.co.nz; bungy $275), the highest leap in New Zealand. From Queenstown, 4WD buses will transport you onto private farmland where you can jump from a specially constructed pod, 134m above the Nevis River. The **Nevis Swing** (📞03-450 1300; www.bungy.co.nz; adult/child $225/175, tandem $440) starts 160m above the river and cuts a 300m arc across the canyon on a rope longer than a rugby field – yes, it's the world's biggest swing. If you're keen to try more than one AJ Hackett experience, enquire about the range of combo tickets.

Adventure Sports

Shotover Canyon Swing & Fox (📞03-442 9186; www.canyonswing.co.nz; 34 Shotover St; swing $249, fox $169, swing & fox combo $299) 🚩 allows you to pick from any number of jump styles – backwards, in a chair, upside down – and then leap from a 109m cliff above the Shotover River, with 60m of free fall and a wild swing across the canyon at 150km/h. The Canyon Fox zipline, new in 2016, can have you whizzing across the Shotover Canyon more than 180m above the river. The price includes transfer from the Queenstown booking office, and if you liked the swing the first time, you can go again for $45.

Jump, slide, zipline and abseil your way through more canyons with **Canyoning Queenstown** (☏03-441 3003; www.canyonexplorers.nz; 39 Camp St; ⊙Oct-Apr),10 minutes' drive from town, or at the remote Routeburn and Dart Canyons. It also operates via ferrata trips, climbing cliffs that overlook Queenstown using metal rungs and safety cables.

Mountain Biking

Queenstown Bike Park (☏03-441 0101; www.skyline.co.nz; Skyline Gondola; day pass incl gondola adult/child $110/75; ⊙9am-7pm mid-Sep–mid-May) has more than 30 different trails – from easy (green) to extreme (double black) – radiating out from the top of the Skyline Gondola (p222). Once you've descended the 400m of vertical, simply jump on the gondola and do it all over again. The best trail for novice riders is the 6km-long **Hammy's Track**, which is studded with lake views and picnic spots.

If you're serious about getting into mountain biking Queenstown-style, **Vertigo** (☏03-442 8378; www.vertigobikes.co.nz; 4 Brecon St; rental half/full day from $39/59; ⊙8am-7pm Oct-May) is an essential first stop. Whether your fancy is trundling on the Queenstown Trail or bombing down the tracks of the Queenstown Bike Park, it hires out both hardtail and downhill bikes, and also runs skills-training clinics (from $159).

Water Sports

Go Orange Rafting (☏03-442 7340; www.goorange.co.nz; 35 Shotover St; rafting/helirafting from $189/299; ⊙7.30am-7pm) ⏰ Operates

White-water rafting on Shotover River

year-round on the churning Shotover River (Grades III to V) and calmer Kawarau River (Grades II to III). Half-day trips give you two to three hours on the water. Helirafting trips are an exciting alternative, and there are multiday trips on the Landsborough River. Rafters must be at least 13 years old and weigh more than 40kg.

Shotover Jet (☑03-442 8570; www.shotover jet.com; 3 Arthurs Point Rd, Arthurs Point; adult/child $159/89) ✈ Runs half-hour jetboat trips through the narrow Shotover Canyon, with lots of thrilling 360-degree spins and reaching speeds of 90km/h.

Skippers Canyon Jet (☑03-442 9434; www.skipperscanyonjet.co.nz; Skippers Rd; adult/child $159/85) ✈ Offers a 30-minute jetboat blast through the remote and hard-to-access Skippers Canyon, among the narrowest

gorges on the Shotover River. Trips pick up from The Station in Queenstown, taking around three hours in total.

Paraflights

Queenstown Paraflights (☑03-441 2242; www.paraflights.co.nz; Main Town Pier; solo/tandem/triple per person $199/129/99) offers a solo, tandem or triple paraflight, zipping along 180m above the lake, pulled behind a boat. Paraflights depart from the town pier.

GForce Paragliding (p223) runs tandem paragliding from the top of the gondola (early departures are $20 cheaper).

★ **Top Tip**
Like to watch? Kawarau Bridge bungy has a viewing platform, or you can sit in the cafe and watch them drop.

WIESOLE/GETTY IMAGES ©

Cardrona Alpine Resort (p214)

Winter Slopes

New Zealand is a premier southern-hemisphere destination for snow bunnies. Wintry pursuits here span all levels, from family-friendly ski areas to daredevil snowboarding terrain and pulse-quickening heliskiing. Queenstown is the epicentre of the action.

Great For...

❶ Need to Know

The Queenstown ski season lasts from June until the snow starts to thaw in September.

★ **Top Tip**

For webcams and updates on snow conditions, see www.snow.co.nz and www.nzski.com.

WADE MACHIN/SHUTTERSTOCK ©

Queenstown has two excellent ski fields: The Remarkables (p214) and Coronet Peak (p215). If you fancy a change of scenery, there's also **Cardrona Alpine Resort** (☏03-443 9284; www.cardrona.com; Cardrona Skifield Rd; daily lift passes adult/child $120/62; ◷8.30am-4pm) and **Treble Cone** (☏03-443 7443; www.treblecone.com; Treble Cone Access Rd; daily lift pass adult/child $149/75) ✎ nearby, accessed via Wānaka, an hour to the north of Queenstown. Coronet Peak is the only field to offer night skiing, which is an experience not to be missed if you strike a starry night. Roads around Queenstown become almost commuter busy on ski mornings and evenings, so taking the NZSki Snowline Express (p215) can mean one less vehicle holding up the show.

Outside the main ski season (June to September), heliskiing is an option for seri-ous, cashed-up skiers; try **Harris Mountains Heli-Ski** (☏03-442 6722; www.heliski.co.nz; 19 Shotover St; from $995; ◷Jul-Sep), **Alpine Heliski** (☏03-441 2300; www.alpineheliski.com; Info & Snow, 37 Shotover St; from $975; ◷Jul-Sep) or **Southern Lakes Heliski** (☏03-442 6222; www.southernlakesheliski.com; Torpedo 7, 20 Athol St; from $975).

The Remarkables

Remarkable by name, and remarkable by view, this **ski field** (☏03-441 1456; www.theremarkables.co.nz; Remarkables Ski Field Access Rd; daily lift pass adult/child $129/69) across the lake from Queenstown has a good smattering of intermediate, advanced and beginner runs. The access road is rough, but shuttles from Queenstown head here during the ski season,

Coronet Peak

so you don't have to worry about driving yourself.

Coronet Peak

New Zealand's oldest commercial ski field, opened in 1947, **Coronet Peak** (☏03-441 1516; www.coronetpeak.co.nz; Coronet Peak Rd; daily lift pass adult/child $129/69) offers excellent skiing and snowboarding for all levels thanks to its treeless slopes and multimillion-dollar snow-making system. It's also

the only resort to offer night skiing, staying open until 9pm on Fridays and Saturdays at the peak of the season (and on Wednesdays through July).

Equipment Hire

In winter, shops throughout Queenstown are full of ski gear for purchase and hire; **Small Planet Outdoors** (☏03-442 5397; www.smallplanetsports.com; 15-17 Shotover St; ⊙8am-8pm) is a reliable option.

Winter Festivals

Queenstown Winter Festival

Carnival

(www.winterfestival.co.nz; ⊙Jun) Four days of wacky ski and snowboard activities, live music, comedy, fireworks, a community carnival, parade, ball and plenty of frigid frivolity in late June.

Winter Pride

LGBT

(www.winterpride.co.nz; ⊙Aug/Sep) The South Island's biggest and best gay-and-lesbian event, held in late August/ early September.

> **Shuttles to the Snow**
>
> During the ski season, **NZSki Snowline Express** (☏0800 697 547; www.nzski.com; return $20) shuttles depart from outside the Snow Centre on Duke St every 20 minutes from 8am until 11.30am (noon for Coronet Peak), heading to both Coronet Peak and the Remarkables.

ASIATRAVEL/SHUTTERSTOCK ©

> ✕ **Take a Break**
>
> Warm up with a hot après-ski cocktail at Bond-lair-esque Bunker (p227).

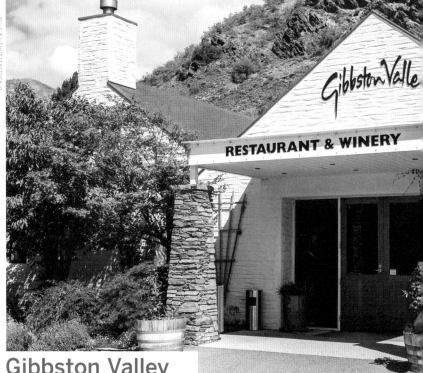

ROLF_52/SHUTTERSTOCK ©

Gibbston Valley

Queenstown's adrenaline junkies might be happiest dangling off a giant rubber band, but they might not realise they're in the heart of one of Central Otago's main wine subregions.

Great For...

☑ Don't Miss

The drive to picturesque Chard Farm along a precipitous 2km road.

Wineries

Strung along Gibbston Hwy (SH6) is an interesting and beautiful selection of vineyards. Almost opposite the Kawarau Bridge, a precipitous 2km gravel road leads to **Chard Farm** (☎03-442 8452; www.chard farm.co.nz; 205 Chard Rd; ☉10am-5pm) FREE, the most picturesque of the wineries. A further 1km along SH6 is **Gibbston Valley** (☎03-442 6910; www.gibbstonvalley.com; 1820 Gibbston Hwy; ☉10am-5pm), the area's oldest commercial winery. As well as tastings, it has a restaurant, a cheesery, tours of NZ's largest wine cave and bike hire. It also operates its own bus from Queenstown – consider taking the bus and then hiring a bike to get between cellar doors.

Another 3km along SH6, **Peregrine** (☎03-442 4000; www.peregrinewines.co.nz; 2127 Gibbston Hwy/SH6; ☉11am-5pm) FREE has

❶ Need to Know

Ask at the Queenstown i-SITE (p228) for maps and info about touring the valley.

✕ Take a Break

The earthy **Gibbston Tavern** (☏03-409 0508; www.gibbstontavern.co.nz; 8 Coalpit Rd; ⊙11am-8pm) stocks Gibbston wines and plates up good pizzas.

★ Top Tip

Stop at **Kinross Cottages** (☏03-746 7269; www.kinrosscottages.co.nz; 2300 Gibbston Hwy; r from $266; P ☏) for a boutique cellar-door experience; bookings recommended.

an impressive, award-winning cellar door – a bunker-like building with a roof reminiscent of a falcon's wing in flight. As well as tastings, you can take a stroll through the adjoining barrel room.

Gibbston River Trail

The **Gibbston River Trail**, part of the Queenstown Trail, is a walking and cycling track that follows the Kawarau River for 11km from the Kawarau Bridge, passing all of the wineries. From Peregrine, walkers (but not cyclists) can swing onto the **Peregrine Loop** (one hour, 2.7km), which crosses over old mining works on 11 timber and two steel bridges, one of which passes through the branches of a willow tree. A 30-minute loop trail from Waitiri Creek Wines heads to Big Beach on the Kawarau River, with views of Nevis Bluff.

Tours

Appellation Central Wine Tours (☏03-442 0246; www.appellationcentral.co.nz; from $169) Take a tipple at four or five wineries in Gibbston, Bannockburn and Cromwell, including platter lunches at a winery restaurant.

New Zealand Wine Tours (☏0800 666 778; www.nzwinetours.co.nz; from $235) Small-group (maximum seven people) or private winery tours, including lunch – platter, degustation or à la carte, depending on the tour – and an 'aroma room' experience.

Lake Wakatipu

Shaped like a perfect cartoon thunderbolt and framed on its southeastern edge by the spectacular Remarkables mountain range, beautiful Lake Wakatipu offers lake cruises, and easygoing adventures at sleepy Glenorchy.

Great For...

❶ Need to Know

Glenorchy Information Centre & Store (✎03-409 2049; www.glenorchyinfo centre.co.nz; 42-50 Mull St; ⊘8.30am-9pm)

★ **Top Tip**

DOC's *Head of Lake Wakatipu* and *Wakatipu Walks* brochures detail day walks in the area.

ROLF_52/SHUTTERSTOCK ©

This gorgeous lake has a 212km shoreline and reaches a depth of 379m (the average depth is more than 320m). Five rivers flow into it but only one (the Kawarau) flows out, making it prone to sometimes quite dramatic floods.

If the water looks clean, that's because it is. Scientists have rated Lake Wakatipu water as 99.9% pure – making it the second-purest lake water in the world. In fact, you're better off dipping your glass in the lake than buying bottled water. It's also very cold. That beach by Marine Pde may look tempting on a scorching day, but trust us, you won't want to splash about in water that hovers at around 10°C year-round.

Legend of the Lake

Māori tradition sees the lake's shape as the burnt outline of the evil giant Matau sleeping with his knees drawn up. Local lad Matakauri set fire to the bed of bracken on which the giant slept in order to rescue his beloved Manata, a chief's daughter who was kidnapped by the giant. The fat from Matau's body created a fire so intense that it burnt a hole deep into the ground.

Boat Trips

KJet   Boating
(☑03-409 0000; www.kjet.co.nz; Main Town Pier; adult/child/family $135/69/307; ☺9am-5pm) Skim, skid and spin around Lake Wakatipu and the Kawarau and Lower Shotover Rivers on these one-hour trips, leaving from the main town pier.

TSS Earnslaw   Cruise
(☑03-249 6000; www.realjourneys.co.nz; Steamer Wharf) The stately, steam-powered

Ben Lomond Summit

TSS *Earnslaw* was built in the same year as the *Titanic* (but with infinitely better results). Climb aboard for the standard 1½-hour Lake Wakatipu tour (adult/child $70/30), or take a 3½-hour excursion to the high-country Walter Peak Farm for a bike ride ($80/40), farm tour ($95/35) or horse trek ($159/95).

Hydro Attack · Boating

(✆0508 493 762; www.hydroattack.co.nz; Lapsley Butson Wharf; 25min ride $154; ✆9am-6pm Nov-Mar, 10am-4.30pm Apr-Oct) That shark you see buzzing about Lake Wakatipu is the

> ### ✗ Take a Break
>
> Glenorchy has a few cafes and a pub, and there's also a cafe-bistro at **Kinloch Lodge** (✆03-442 4900; www.kinlochlodge. co.nz; 862 Kinloch Rd; dm $45, r with/without bathroom from $195/120, cabin $435; 🛜) 🍴.

GIANTRABBIT/SHUTTERSTOCK ©

Hydro Attack – jump inside, strap yourself in and take a ride. This Seabreacher X watercraft can travel at 80km/h on the water, dive 2m underneath and then launch itself nearly 6m into the air. It's mesmerising to watch, let alone travel inside.

Viewpoints

Ben Lomond Track · Hiking

(www.doc.govt.nz) The popular track to Ben Lomond (1748m, six to eight hours return) culminates in probably the best accessible view in the area, stretching over Lake Wakatipu and as far as Tititea/Mt Aspiring.

Time Tripper · Viewpoint

(✆03-409 0000; www.timetripper.co.nz; Main Town Pier; adult/child $25/12; ✆9am-5pm) Six windows showcase life under the lake in this reverse aquarium (the people are behind glass) beneath the KJet office. Large brown trout abound, and look out for freshwater eels and scaup ducks, which dive past the windows. A KJet trip (p220) gets you free entry.

Glenorchy

The small town of Glenorchy sits on a rare shelf of flat land at the head of Lake Wakatipu. The hiking around here is sensational, and the town is also a base for horse treks, jetboat rides, helicopter flights and skydives. It's Queenstown on sedatives.

Two good short tracks here are the **Routeburn Flats** (four hours return), which follows the first section of the famous Routeburn Track, and **Lake Sylvan** (1½ hours return). If you like birds, the **Glenorchy Walkway** starts in the town centre and loops around Glenorchy Lagoon, switching to boardwalks for the swampy bits.

> ### ☑ Don't Miss
>
> The scenic 40-minute (46km) drive to Glenorchy, at the head of the lake northwest of Queenstown.

◉ SIGHTS

Queenstown Gardens   Park

(Park St) Set on its own tongue of land framing Queenstown Bay, this pretty park is the perfect city escape right within the city. Laid out in 1876, it features an 18-'hole' frisbee golf course (p223), a skate park, lawn-bowls club, tennis courts, **Queenstown Ice Arena** (☑03-441 8000; www.queenstownicearena.co.nz; 29 Park St; entry incl skate hire $19; ⊙hours vary), mature exotic trees (including large sequoias and some fab monkey puzzles by the rotunda) and a rose garden.

Skyline Gondola   Cable Car

(☑03-441 0101; www.skyline.co.nz; Brecon St; adult/child return $44/26; ⊙9am-9pm) Hop aboard for fantastic views as the gondola squeezes through pine forest to its grandstand location 400m above Queenstown. At the top there's the inevitable cafe,

> *fantastic views as the gondola squeezes through pine forest to its grandstand location*

restaurant, souvenir shop and observation deck, as well as the Queenstown Bike Park (p210), **Skyline Luge** (☑03-441 0101; www.skyline.co.nz; Skyline Gondola; 2/3/5 rides incl gondola adult $61/63/67, child $43/45/49; ⊙10am-8pm) ✐, Ledge Bungy (p209), Ledge Swing (p209), GForce Paragliding (p223) and Ziptrek Ecotours (p222). At night there are stargazing tours (including gondola, adult/child $99/54).

◑ ACTIVITIES

Queenstown Hill/Te Tapunui Time Walk   Hiking

Ascend 500m to the summit of Queenstown Hill/Te Tapunui for a 360-degree view over the lake and along the Remarkables. The walk takes around three hours return. Access is from Belfast Tce.

Ziptrek Ecotours   Adventure Sports

(☑03-441 2102; www.ziptrek.co.nz; Skyline Gondola; 🚻) ✐ Incorporating a series of flying foxes, this thrill-ride takes you whirring through the forest canopy, from treetop platform to treetop platform, high above

Skyline Luge

BOYLOSO/SHUTTERSTOCK ©

Queenstown. Choose from the two-hour, four-line Moa (adult/child $145/99); the gnarlier and faster three-hour, six-line Kea ($195/149); and the one-hour, two-line Keruru ($99), which evens with a 21m controlled drop.

Serious Fun Riverboarding
Adventure Sports

(☑03-442 5262; www.riverboarding.co.nz; Info & Track, 37 Shotover St; from $225) Steer buoyant sledges or bodyboards on the rapids and whirlpools of the Kawarau River. The gentlest option is bodyboard drifting ($255, January and February only), followed by sledging ($235, November to March) and full-on riversurfing ($235, September to May).

Frisbee Golf
Sports

(www.queenstowndiscgolf.co.nz; Queenstown Gardens) **FREE** A series of 18 chain baskets set among the trees of Queenstown Gardens. Local sports stores – and the Queenstown Ice Arena (p222) – sell or rent Frisbees and scorecards.

GForce Paragliding
Paragliding

(☑03-441 8581; www.nzgforce.com; Skyline Gondola; flight $239) Tandem paragliding from the top of the gondola (early departures are $20 cheaper).

Family Adventures
Rafting

(☑03-442 8836; www.familyadventures. co.nz; 39 Shotover St; adult/child $189/120; ☺Oct-Apr; 👪) These gentle (Grades I to II) and good-humoured rafting trips on the Shotover River are much loved by families as they're suitable for even three-year-olds. Trips depart from Browns Ski Shop and include a 45-minute scenic drive to the Skippers Canyon launch site, which *The Lord of the Rings* nuts will recognise as the Ford of Bruinen.

Queenstown Combos
Adventure Sports

(☑03-442 7318; www.combos.co.nz; The Station, cnr Shotover & Camp Sts) Sells combination tickets for many of the region's most fa-

History

The Queenstown region was deserted when the first British people arrived in the mid-1850s, although there is evidence of previous Māori settlement. Sheep farmers came first, but after two shearers discovered gold on the banks of the Shotover River in 1862, a deluge of prospectors followed.

Within a year the settlement was a mining town with streets, permanent buildings and a population of several thousand. It was declared 'fit for a queen' by the NZ government; hence Queenstown was born. Lake Wakatipu was the principal means of transport, and at the height of the boom there were four paddle steamers and 30 other craft plying the waters.

By 1900 the gold had petered out and the population was a mere 190. It wasn't until the 1950s that Queenstown became a popular holiday destination.

Shotover River
ı VIEWFINDER/SHUTTERSTOCK ©

mous activities – bungy, jetboating, skydiving, swings, rafting and helicopter flights.

🔒 SHOPPING

Vesta
Arts & Crafts

(☑03-442 5687; www.vestadesign.co.nz; 19 Marine Pde; ☺9am-5pm Mon-Sat) Arguably Queenstown's most interesting store, inside inarguably the town's oldest building; Vesta sells a collection of prints, jewellery and homeware as fascinating as

Queenstown

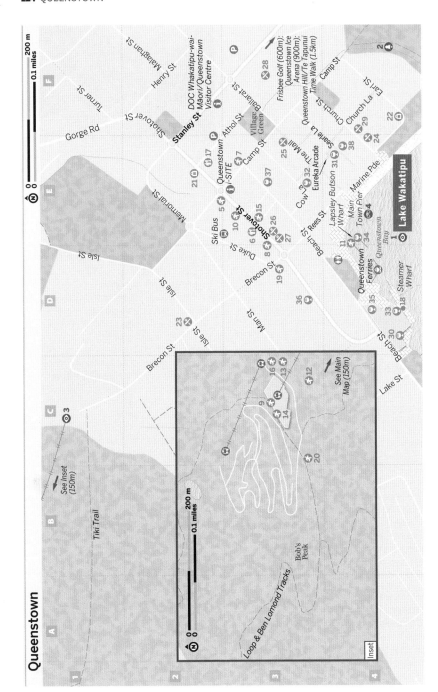

Lake Wakatipu

Queenstown

the original wallpaper and warped-by-time floorboards of the 1864 wooden cottage.

EATING

Fergbaker
Bakery $

(☑03-441 1206; 40 Shotover St; items $3-7.50; ☺6.30am-4.30am) The sweeter sister of Fergburger (p226) bakes all manner of tempting treats – and though most things look tasty with 3am beer goggles on, it withstands the daylight test admirably. Goodies include inventive pies (such as venison and portobello mushroom) and breads, filled rolls and a sugary wealth of sweet treats. If you're after gelato, call into **Mrs Ferg** next door.

Caribe Latin Kitchen
Latin American $

(☑03-442 6658; www.caribelatinkitchen.com; 36 The Mall; mains $8-16; ☺10.30am-11pm; ☑) One of the Mall's more characterful and colourful restaurants, Caribe is a small nook dishing out quality tacos, quesadillas

and burritos stuffed fuller than a piñata. The tiled decor plays to a Day of the Dead theme, and the few tables are brighter than a Mexican sun. Excellent value.

Bespoke Kitchen
Cafe $$

(☑03-409 0552; www.bespokekitchen.co.nz; 9 Isle St; mains $20-25; ☺8am-5pm; ☎☑) Occupying a light-filled corner site near the gondola, Bespoke delivers everything you'd expect of a smart Kiwi cafe. It has a mouthwatering selection of counter food, beautifully presented cooked options, outside seating in sight of the mountains and, of course, great coffee. Vegans will find plenty of choice, too.

Yonder
Cafe $$

(☑03-409 0994; www.yonderqt.co.nz; 14 Church St; mains $12-24; ☺8am-late; ☎) With a menu inspired by 'the things we've loved around our travels', this cafe brings to the table a cosmopolitan assortment of dishes: bacon butties, kimchi bowls, salmon poké bowls. There are power points and USB ports by

 **Arrowtown Detour**

Beloved by day-trippers from Queenstown, exceedingly quaint Arrowtown sprang up in the 1860s following the discovery of gold in the Arrow River. Today its pretty, treelined avenues retain more than 60 of their original gold-rush buildings, and history is so ingrained here that even the golf course wraps around the ruined cottages and relics of the town's gold-mining heyday. But don't be fooled by the rustic facades; Arrowtown has a thriving contemporary scene, with chic modern dining, a cool cinema and a couple of drinking dens to rival the finest in Queenstown.

The pace in Arrowtown is very different to that of Queenstown, just 20km away. Strolling Buckingham St, with its gold-era facades, is the major activity here; when you need something more, there are gentle bike rides along the valleys, or an expanding network of walks along the Arrow River and Bush Creek.

Arrowtown Visitor Information Centre (☏03-442 1824; www.arrowtown. com; 49 Buckingham St; ⊗8.30am-5pm) has local info and sells maps.

FILEDIMAGE/SHUTTERSTOCK ©

many of the indoor tables, but when the sun's out you'll want to be on the outdoor patio.

Blue Kanu Fusion $$
(☏03-442 6060; www.bluekanu.co.nz; 16 Church St; mains $29-36; ⊗4pm-late) Disproving the rule that all tiki houses are inherently tacky,

Blue Kanu serves up a food style it calls 'Polynasian' – Fijian *kokoda* (raw fish with coconut and lime) in one hand, XO pork dumplings in the other. It's relaxed and personable, and although the marriage of the Polynesian decor and chopsticks sounds impossible to pull off, it works.

Rātā International $$$
(☏03-442 9393; www.ratadining.co.nz; 43 Ballarat St; mains $42-48, 2-/3-course lunch $38/45; ⊗noon-late) After gaining Michelin stars for restaurants in London, New York and LA, chef-owner Josh Emett now wields his exceptional but surprisingly unflashy cooking back home in this upmarket yet informal back-lane eatery. Native bush, edging the windows and in a large-scale photographic mural, sets the scene for a short menu showcasing the best seasonal NZ produce.

Fergburger Burgers $$
(☏03-441 1232; www.fergburger.com; 42 Shotover St; burgers $13-20; ⊗8am-5am) Who knew a burger joint could ever be a destination restaurant? Such are the queues at Fergburger that it often looks like an All Blacks scrum out the front. The burgers are as tasty and satisfying as ever, but the wait can be horrendous and the menu has more choices than the place has seats.

🍸 DRINKING & NIGHTLIFE

Perky's Bar
(☏021 664 043; www.facebook.com/ perkysqueenstown; Lapsley Butson Wharf; ⊗noon-11pm) That hint of wobbliness you feel isn't the alcohol (yet), it's the fact that you're drinking on an old tour boat that's now permanently moored at the lakeshore. If you're feeling peckish, you're welcome to bring your own food aboard.

Atlas Beer Cafe Craft Beer
(☏03-442 5995; www.atlasbeercafe.com; Steamer Wharf; ⊗10am-late) There are usually 23 craft beers on tap at this pint-sized lakefront bar, headlined by brews from Dunedin's Emerson's Brewery and

Queenstown's Altitude; pick four to sample on a tasting paddle. It also serves excellent cooked breakfasts ($17 to $22), and simple substantial fare such as steaks and burgers.

Little Blackwood
Cocktail Bar

(☑03-441 8066; www.littleblackwood.com; Steamer Wharf; ⊘2pm-2am) Slink into the darkened interior of this slick bar for a sneaky afternoon cocktail, or perch yourself on the waterfront terrace for views over the lake.

Bardeaux
Wine Bar

(☑03-442 8284; www.goodgroup.co.nz; Eureka Arcade, off The Mall; ⊘4pm-4am) This small, cavelike wine bar is all class. Under a low ceiling are plush leather armchairs and a fireplace made from Central Otago schist. Whisky is king here, but the wine list is extraordinary, especially if you're keen to drop $4500 on a bottle once in your life. It's surprisingly relaxed for a place with such lofty tastes.

Bunker
Cocktail Bar

(☑03-441 8030; www.thebunker.co.nz; 14 Cow Lane; ⊘4pm-4am) Bunkered upstairs rather than down, this chi-chi little bar clearly fancies itself as the kind of place Sean Connery's James Bond might frequent, if the decor is anything to go by. Best of all is the outside terrace, with couches, a fire in winter and a projector screening classic movies onto the wall of a neighbouring building.

The Winery
Wine Bar

(☑03-409 2226; www.thewinery.co.nz; 14 Beach St; ⊘10.30am-late) Ignore the uninspiring location and settle in for a journey around NZ wine. Load up cash on a smart card and then help yourself to tasting pours or glasses of more than 80 NZ wines dispensed through an automated gas-closure system. There's also a whisky corner, and cheese and salami platters are available.

The burgers are as tasty and satisfying as ever

ROOTSTUDIO/SHUTTERSTOCK ©

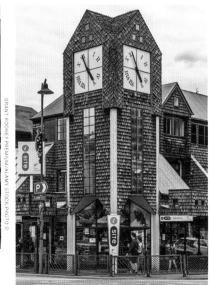

From left: Pub on Wharf; Queenstown i-Site; Perky's (p226)

Wines are arranged by varietals along the walls.

Smiths Craft Beer House
Craft Beer

(☏03-409 2337; www.smithscraftbeer.co.nz; 1st floor, 53 Shotover St; ⏰noon-late; 🛜) It's back to basics in everything but the taps, with bare concrete floors and industrial tables and chairs, but 36 creative NZ craft beers to sample. The folks behind the bar will chat brews as long as you'll listen, and there's a menu (mains $17 to $20) of burgers and po'boys (Louisiana-style sandwiches) to mop up the suds.

Pub on Wharf
Pub

(☏03-441 2155; www.pubonwharf.co.nz; 88 Beach St; ⏰10am-late) Schmick interior de-sign combines with handsome woodwork at this popular pub, with fake sheep heads to remind you that you're still in NZ. Mac's beers on tap, scrummy nibbles and a decent wine list make this a great place to settle in for the evening. There's live music every night and comedy occasionally.

Zephyr
Bar

(☏03-409 0852; www.facebook.com/zephyrqt; 1 Searle Lane; ⏰7pm-4am) Queenstown's hippest rock bar is located – as all such places should be – in a dark, grungy, concrete-floored space off a back lane. There's a popular pool table and live bands on Wednesday nights. Beer comes only in bottles, and there's a permanently raucous soundtrack.

ℹ INFORMATION

DOC Whakatipu-wai-Māori/Queenstown Visitor Centre
(☏03-442 7935; www.doc.govt. nz; 50 Stanley St; ⏰8.30am-4.30pm) Head here for advice about hiking tracks, as well as maps, backcountry hut passes, locator beacons, weath-er alerts and to check in for your Routeburn Track booking.

Queenstown i-SITE
(☏03-442 4100; www. queenstownsite.com; cnr Shotover & Camp Sts; ⏰8.30am-8pm) Friendly and informative despite being perpetually frantic, the saintly staff here can help with bookings and information on the Southern Lakes region and further afield.

CK TRAVELS/SHUTTERSTOCK ©

❶ GETTING THERE & AWAY

AIR

Air New Zealand (📞0800 737 000; www.airnewzealand.co.nz) flies directly to Queenstown from Auckland, Wellington and Christchurch, as well as Melbourne, Sydney and Brisbane.

Jetstar (📞0800 800 995; www.jetstar.com) also flies the Auckland and Wellington routes, along with Melbourne, Sydney and the Gold Coast.

Qantas (www.qantas.com) and **Virgin Australia** (www.virginaustralia.com) fly directly from Australia (Melbourne, Sydney and Brisbane).

BUS

Most buses and shuttles stop on Athol St or Camp St; check when you book.

InterCity (📞03-442 4922; www.intercity.co.nz) The main operator; daily destinations include Wānaka, Franz Josef, Dunedin and Christchurch.

Ritchies (📞03-441 4471; www.ritchies.co.nz; 📶) Operates the Expresslink shuttle to/from Wānaka four times daily ($30, 1¾ hours), with three stopping in Cromwell ($20, one hour).

❶ GETTING AROUND

Queenstown Ferries (📞03-441 1124; www.queenstownferries.co.nz; Steamer Wharf; single/return $9/15; ⏱departs Queenstown 7.45am-9.45pm Sun-Thu, to 10.45pm Fri & Sat) zip across the lake from the town centre to the Hilton Hotel on the Kelvin Peninsula (and four stops in between). Pay the driver on the boat either in cash or electronically.

Orbus (📞0800 672 8778; www.orc.govt.nz/orbusqt; cash/GoCard trip $5/2) has four main routes. Pick up a route map and timetable from the i-SITE (p228).

FIORDLAND

Fiordland at a Glance...

Brace yourself for sublime scenery on a breathtaking scale. In New Zealand's far southwest, Fiordland National Park's mountains, forests and mirror-smooth waters hold visitors in thrall. Framed by kilometre-high cliffs, Milford Sound was clawed away by glaciers over millennia. Leading here is the Milford Hwy, which reveals a magnificent alpine view at every bend, and the epic Milford Track, one of NZ's (and arguably, the planet's) best hiking trails. Shying away from attention is Doubtful Sound, the pristine 'place of silence', which leaves many admiring visitors speechless (doubtfulness doesn't often enter into it).

One Day in Fiordland

Kick-start your Fiordland adventures with a day trip to **Milford Sound** (p238), along the astonishingly pho-togenic **Te Anau–Milford Highway** (p242). Explore by boat, or to really experience the area's watery expanses, soaring cliffs and lush forest, consider a kayaking excursion. Kayaking is also popular on **Doubtful Sound** (p244), a much less-visited destination (if you feel like sidestepping the crowds).

Four Days in Fiordland

For an extended Fiordland experience, undertake one of New Zealand's Great Walks for three days and four nights. Once you've conquered the **Milford Track** (p234), take time to explore **Milford Sound** (p238) by boat, before returning to lakeside **Te Anau** (p246). You'll really have earned something delicious at the **Sandfly Cafe** (p248), or an ice-cold beer at the local pub.

Previous page: Milford Sound (p238)
MARCONI COUTO DE JESUS/SHUTTERSTOCK ©

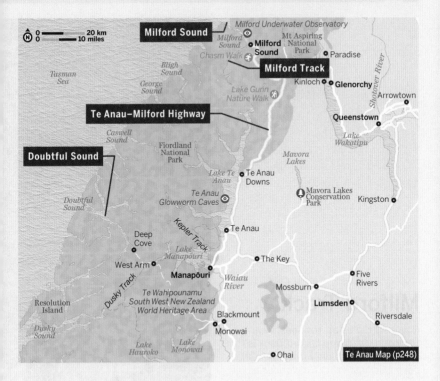

 0 ____ 20 km
0 ____ 10 miles

Milford Sound

Milford Underwater Observatory

Milford Sound

Milford Sound

Chasm Walk

Mt Aspiring National Park

Paradise

Milford Track

Bligh Sound

Kinloch ● **Glenorchy**

Tasman Sea

George Sound

Lake Gunn Nature Walk

Arrowtown

Te Anau–Milford Highway

Caswell Sound

Fiordland National Park

Queenstown

Doubtful Sound

Lake Wakatipu

Mavora Lakes

Lake Te Anau ● Te Anau Downs

Mavora Lakes Conservation Park

Kingston ●

Doubtful Sound

Te Anau Glowworm Caves

● Te Anau

Deep Cove

Lake Manapōuri

West Arm ●

Manapōuri

● The Key

Waiau River

Five Rivers

Resolution Island

Te Wahipounamu South West New Zealand World Heritage Area

Mossburn ●

Lumsden ●

Blackmount ●

Riversdale ●

Dusky Sound

Monowai

Lake Hauroko

Lake Monowai

● Ohai

Te Anau Map (p248)

Arriving in Fiordland

Fiordland is a long way from anywhere, but **Te Anau** has direct bus connections with Queenstown, Dunedin and Christchurch. Tour companies run return day trips to Milford Sound from Queenstown, but it's a long day in the saddle with just a couple of hours at Milford.

Where to Stay

Te Anau has a decent array of motels, B&Bs and hiker-friendly hostels. Accommodation can get booked out in the peak season when hiker numbers soar (December to February), so book early if possible. Closer to Doubtful Sound, Manapōuri also has some good places to stay.

Milford Track

Routinely touted as 'the finest walk in the world', the 54km Milford Track is a knockout, complete with rainforest, deep glaciated valleys, a glorious alpine pass and rampaging waterfalls.

Great For...

❶ Need to Know

See www.doc.govt.nz/milfordtrack for essential pre-trip planning and booking guidelines.

★ **Top Tip**

Between late October and mid-April, hut passes must be pre-booked, online or at a DOC visitor centre. Book early!

NUI RATTAPON/SHUTTERSTOCK ©

Milford track is hugely popular. Soon after bookings open (sometime between February and May, for the summer season starting in October), this Great Walk becomes fully booked – keep an eye on www.doc.govt.nz/milfordtrack to time it right.

During the Great Walks season (late October through April) the track can only be walked in one direction, starting from Glade Wharf. You must stay at Clinton Hut the first night, despite it being only one hour from the start of the track, and you must complete the trip in the prescribed three nights and four days. This is perfectly acceptable if the weather is kind, but when the weather turns sour you'll still have to push on across the alpine Mackinnon Pass and may miss some rather spectacular views. It's all down to the luck of the draw.

The Great Walk season also sees the track frequented by guided hiking parties, who stay at cosy, carpeted lodges with hot showers and proper food. If that sounds appealing, contact Ultimate Hikes (p237), the only operator permitted to run guided hikes on the Milford.

The track is covered by 1:70,000 *Parkmap 335-01 (Milford Track)*.

Bookings & Transport

The Milford Track is officially a Great Walk. Between late October and mid-April, you need to pre-book each of your three nights in the huts: Clinton Hut, Mintaro Hut and Dumpling Hut. Hut passes must be obtained in advance, either online via DOC or in person at a DOC visitor centre. Book early to avoid disappointment as the entire season books up very quickly.

Sandfly Point

DOC advises against tackling the Milford Track between early May and late October because of the significant risk of avalanches and floods, and the fact that bridges at risk of avalanche are removed. It's wet, very cold, and snow conceals trail markers. If you're a well-equipped hiking pro considering the Milford Track out of season, get DOC advice on weather conditions. During this low season, restrictions on walking the track in four days are removed.

The track starts at Glade Wharf, at the head of Lake Te Anau, accessible by a 1½-hour boat trip from Te Anau Downs, itself 29km from Te Anau on the road to Milford Sound. The track finishes at Sandfly Point, a 15-minute boat trip from Milford Sound village, from where you can return by road to Te Anau, around two hours away. You will be given options to book this connecting transport online, at the same time as you book your hut tickets.

Tracknet (p251) offers transport from Queenstown and Te Anau to meet the boats at Te Anau Downs and Milford Sound. Fiordland i-SITE (p249) and the Fiordland National Park Visitor Centre (p249) can advise on options to best suit you.

> ### ✕ Take a Break
>
> Back in Te Anau, celebrate completing the Milford Track with dinner at Kepler's (p249).

Tours

Real Journeys (📞 0800 656 501; www.real journeys.co.nz; 85 Lakefront Dr; ⏱ 7am-8.30pm Mar-Oct, 6.45am-9.30pm Nov-Apr) 🚶 You can count on sharp service and well-organised tours from this major player, which offers guided day-walks on the Milford Track.

Ultimate Hikes (📞 03-450 1940, 0800 659 255; www.ultimatehikes.co.nz; 5-day hikes incl food dm/s/d $2295/3330/5590; ⏱ Nov–mid-Apr) 🚶 Booking yourself onto a guided hike of the Milford Track with Queenstown-based Ultimate Hikes puts route planning and logistics in the capable hands of an experienced operator. The guides' expert knowledge of fauna and flora enhances the journey, and walkers will overnight in lodges with hot showers and proper food.

STOCKER1970/SHUTTERSTOCK ©

> ### ★ Did You Know?
>
> Almost 7500 hikers complete the 54km-long track each summer.

SOUTHERN LIGHTSCAPES AUSTRALIA/GETTY IMAGES ©

Milford Sound

The iconic image of Mitre Peak amid Milford Sound has long dominated New Zealand tourism marketing. Opportunities to explore the fabled body of water include boat cruises, kayaking and flight-seeing.

Great For...

☑ Don't Miss

At least one moment alone on the sound, just you and nature's beautiful oblivion.

The pot of gold at the end of Milford Hwy (SH94) is sublime Milford Sound (Piopiotahi). Rising above the fiord's indigo water is Mitre Peak (Rahotu), the deserved focal point of millions of photographs. Tapering to a cloud-piercing summit, the 1692m-high mountain appears sculpted by a divine hand.

In truth, it's the action of glaciers that carved these razor-edge cliffs. Scoured into the bare rock are pathways from tree avalanches, where entangled roots dragged whole forests down into darkly glittering water. When rain comes (and that's often), dozens of temporary waterfalls curtain the cliffs. Stirling and Lady Bowen Falls gush on in fine weather, with rainbows bouncing from their mists when sunlight strikes just right.

❶ Need to Know

Fill your tank in Te Anau before driving to Milford (no petrol stations en route). Bring snow chains in winter.

✕ Take a Break

At **Milford Sound Lodge** (☎03-249 8071; www.milfordlodge.com; SH94; powered camp-ervan sites per person $35, chalets $615-849; 🛜), travellers convene at Pio Pio Cafe for breakfast, dinner and good espresso.

★ Top Tip

Raining? Fear not: cruises on rainy Milford days have views of innumerable temporary waterfalls.

Milford Sound receives an estimated one million visitors annually, which makes it an almighty challenge to keep its beauty pristine. But out on the water, all human activity – cruise ships, divers, kayakers – seems dwarfed into insignificance.

Cruises

Fiordland's most accessible experience is a cruise on Milford Sound, usually lasting 90 minutes or more. A slew of companies have booking desks in the flash cruise terminal, a 10-minute walk from the main car park, but it's always wiser to book ahead.

Each cruise company claims to be quieter, smaller, bigger, cheaper or in some way preferable to the rest. What really makes a difference is timing. Most bus tours aim for 1pm sailings, so if you avoid that time of day there will be fewer people on the boat, fewer boats on the water and fewer buses on the road.

If you're particularly keen on wildlife, opt for a cruise with a nature guide on board. These are usually a few minutes longer than the standard 'scenic' cruises, and often on smaller boats. Most companies offer coach transfers from Te Anau for an additional cost. Day trips from Queens-town make for a very long 13-hour day.

Arrive 20 minutes before departure. All cruises visit the mouth of the sound, just 15km from the wharf, poking their prows into the choppy waves of the Tasman Sea. Shorter cruises visit fewer en route 'high-lights', which include Bowen Falls, Mitre Peak, Anita Bay and Stirling Falls.

Only possible to visit on trips run by Southern Discoveries and Mitre Peak Cruises, **Milford Underwater Observatory** (www.southerndiscoveries.co.nz; Harrison Cove; ⏱8am-5pm), New Zealand's only floating underwater observatory, showcases interactive displays on the natural environment of the fiord. The centre offers a chance to view corals, tube anemones and bottom-dwelling sea perch from 10m below the waterline.

Operators

Real Journeys (0800 656 501, 03-249 7416; www.realjourneys.co.nz; adult/child from $81/30) Milford's biggest and most venerable operator runs a popular 1¾-hour scenic cruise. More specialised is the 2¼-hour nature cruise (adult/child from $89/30), which homes in on wildlife with commentary from a nature guide. Overnight cruises (from $363) are also available, from which you can take nature tours in small boats en route. Gilded with a long list of awards since it was founded

in 1954, Real Journeys continues to be involved in local conservation efforts, from its minimal-impact cruises to fundraisers and charitable donations.

Cruise Milford (0800 645 367; www. cruisemilfordnz.com; adult/child from $99/18; 10.45am, 12.45pm & 2.45pm) Offering a more personal touch than some of the big-boat tours, Cruise Milford's smaller vessels head out three times a day on 1¾-hour cruises, divulging great info on everything from tectonics to wildlife.

Mitre Peak Cruises (0800 744 633, 03-249 8110; www.mitrepeak.com; adult/child from $95/30) Two-hour cruises in smallish boats (maximum capacity 75), allowing closer waterfall and wildlife viewing than larger vessels. The 4.30pm cruise is a good choice because many larger boats are heading back at this time.

Real Journeys cruise ship

Kayaking

Getting out on the water offers one of the best perspectives of Milford Sound. Rosco, from **Rosco's Milford Kayaks** (☏03-249 8500, 0800 476 726; www.roscosmilfordkayaks. com; 72 Town Centre, Te Anau; trips $115-225), is a colourful character, seasoned by decades of kayaking experience. He leads guided, tandem-kayak trips such as the Morning Glory ($225), a challenging paddle the full length of the fiord to Dale Point, and the Stirling Sunriser ($219), which ventures beneath the 151m-high Stirling Falls for a 'glacial facial'. Beginners can take it easy on a two-hour paddle on the sound ($115) assisted by water-taxi transfers.

Diving

For total immersion in Milford Sound's wildlife, a dive with **Descend Scubadiving** (☏027 337 2363; www.descend.co.nz; dives incl gear from $345) plunges you amid black coral and more than 150 species of fish. Descend's six-hour trips include a cruise in a 7m catamaran and two dives along the way. They offers excursions for experienced divers and novices. Transport, equipment, hot drinks and snacks included.

Sound Advice

'Milford Sound' is something of a misnomer. Sounds are sculpted by rivers, and fiords carved out by glaciers; Milford is the latter, but the name stuck.

ROBERT CHG/SHUTTERSTOCK ©

Chasm Walk, Cleddau River

ANGELA MEIER/SHUTTERSTOCK ©

Te Anau–Milford Highway

Milford Sound is deservedly famous, but the road linking Te Anau to the sound is also a world standout – wonderfully scenic and travelling deep into the heart of true wilderness.

Great For...

☑ Don't Miss

Hiking along one of the excellent tracks off the main road to hidden lakes and rivers.

Sometimes the journey is the destination, and that's certainly true of the 119km stretch of road between Te Anau and Milford Sound. The Milford Hwy (SH94) offers the most easily accessible experience of Fiordland in all its diversity, taking in expanses of beautiful beech forest, gentle river valleys, mirror-like lakes, exquisite alpine scenery and ending at arguably New Zealand's most breathtaking vista, Milford Sound.

The journey should take 2½ hours each way, but expect to spend time dawdling along walking trails and maxing out your photo storage. Most travellers embark on the Milford Hwy as a day trip from Te Anau, with a cruise on Milford Sound to break up the return journey, but the prospect of longer hikes or camping beneath jagged mountains might entice you to stay.

Kea bird

URMASS3/GETTY IMAGES ©

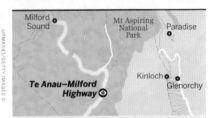

Milford Sound

Mt Aspiring National Park

Paradise

Te Anau–Milford Highway ⊚

Kinloch

Glenorchy

❶ Need to Know

Fill up with petrol in Te Anau. Allow at least 2½ hours to drive the full length of the highway.

✕ Take a Break

There are no eateries along the highway and only average ones in Milford Sound. Fill your hamper in Te Anau.

★ Top Tip

Kea (alpine parrots) hang around the Homer Tunnel. Don't feed them as it's bad for their health.

Hiking

Chasm Walk (SH94) About 9km before the end of the Te Anau–Milford Hwy, the 20-minute Chasm Walk affords staggering views over the churning Cleddau River. Pebbles caught in its frenetic currents have hollowed boulders into shapes reminiscent of a Salvador Dalí scene, while deep falls and thrashing waters give an unmistakable glimpse of nature's might. Wheelchair- and pram-friendly.

Lake Gunn Nature Walk (SH94) An easy 45-minute return walk loops through tall red-beech forest at this bewitching spot along the Milford Hwy, 77km north of Te Anau. Moss-clung logs and a chorus of birdsong create a fairy-tale atmosphere, and side trails lead to quiet lakeside beaches. The area was known to Māori as O Tapara, and served as a stopover for parties

heading to Anita Bay in search of *pounamu* (greenstone).

Milford Highway Checklist

Set your alarm clock Aim to leave Te Anau early (by 8am) or later in the morning (11am) to avoid the tour buses heading for midday sound cruises.

Read up Pick up DOC's *Fiordland National Park Day Walks* brochure ($2) from Fiordland i-SITE (p249) or Fiordland National Park Visitor Centre (p249), or download it at www.doc.govt.nz. Otherwise you risk zooming past the loveliest spots.

Allow loads of time The trip takes two to 2½ hours if you drive straight through, but take time to pull off the road and explore the many view points and nature walks along the way.

SARA MONICA/SHUTTERSTOCK ©

Doubtful Sound

Milford Sound gets all the attention, but the misty expanse of Doubtful Sound is even more spectacular. The area's remoteness is especially enhanced during an overnight stay on the water.

Remote Doubtful Sound is humbling in size and beauty. Carved by glaciers, it's one of New Zealand's largest fiords – almost three times the length of more popular Milford. Boats gliding through this maze of forested valleys have good chances of encountering fur seals and Fiordland penguins. Aside from haunting birdsong, Doubtful Sound deserves its Māori name, Pātea, the 'place of silence'.

Great For...

☑ Don't Miss

Dipping your kayak blades into mirror-flat water as you explore Doubtful Sound's mystic coves.

Getting There & Away

Until relatively recently, Doubtful Sound was isolated from all but intrepid explorers. Even Captain Cook only observed it from off the coast in 1770, because he was 'doubtful' that winds would be sufficient to blow the ship back to sea. Access improved when the road over Wilmot Pass opened in

❶ Need to Know

Doubtful Sound is a one-hour boat trip from Manapōuri to West Arm power station, followed by a 22km drive to Deep Cove.

✕ Take a Break

The Church (p251), in Manapōuri, is a merry pub (formerly a church) with exceptionally welcoming staff.

★ Top Tip

Manapōuri makes a logical base, although Te Anau (20km) and Queenstown (170km) pick-ups can be organised through cruise-boat operators.

1959 to facilitate construction of West Arm power station.

Boat and coach transfers from Manapōuri to Deep Cove are easily organised through tour operators, but time-consuming enough to deter some travellers...ideal for those who want to enjoy the silence.

Cruises

Day cruises allow about three hours on the water (once you've factored in transport time to the sound). Overnight cruises are pricey but preferable; they include meals plus the option of fishing and kayaking, depending on the weather.

Real Journeys (☏0800 656 501; www. realjourneys.co.nz) 🌿 A family-run tourism trailblazer, Real Journeys is ecofriendly, and just plain friendly. One-day Wilderness

Cruises (adult/child from $265/80) include a 2¾-hour journey aboard a modern catamaran with a specialist nature guide. The overnight cruise, which runs from September to May, is aboard the *Fiordland Navigator,* which sleeps 72 in en-suite cabins (quad-share $503, singles/doubles from $785/1570).

Deep Cove Charters (☏03-249 6828; https://doubtfulsoundcruise.nz; s $650, cabin tw/d $1450/1550; ⊗mid-Nov–mid-Mar) Overnight cruises on board the *Seafinn* (maximum 12 passengers) run by home-grown crew. There are options to kayak and fish, but it had us at 'crayfish lunch and venison supper included'.

Te Anau

Picturesque Te Anau is the main gateway to Milford Sound and three Great Walks: the Milford, Kepler and Routeburn Tracks. Firmly focused on servicing travellers and holidaymakers, there's a sizeable accommodation scene, an array of places to eat, and the chance to stock up on dehydrated food and hiking gear. And while Te Anau doesn't party nearly as hard as effervescent Queenstown, there are a few places to sink a beer – which will taste all the better after a long day of hiking, kayaking or driving the unforgettable Milford Hwy.

Te Anau stretches along Lake Te Anau, New Zealand's second-largest lake, whose glacier-gouged fiords spider into secluded forest on its western shore. To the east are the pastoral areas of central Southland, while west across Lake Te Anau lie the rugged mountains of Fiordland. A day or two in town is more than enough before you'll be itching to get out into the wilderness.

◎ SIGHTS

Te Anau Glowworm Caves   Cave

(☏0800 656 501; www.realjourneys.co.nz; adult/child $103/30) Stare up at constellations of glowworms on an underground boat ride. First described in Māori stories, this 200m-long cave system was lost in time until it was 'rediscovered' in 1948. Its sculpted rocks, waterfalls and whirlpools are impressive by themselves, but the bluish sparkle of glowworms, peculiar territorial larvae who lure prey with their come-hither lights, is the main draw. The caves can only be reached by a 2¼-hour guided tour with Real Journeys (p237), departing from its office on Lakefront Dr.

Mavora Lakes Conservation Park   Nature Reserve

(www.doc.govt.nz; Centre Hill Rd) Within the Snowdon State Forest, this conservation park's huge golden meadows sit alongside

> *Te Anau doesn't party nearly as hard as effervescent Queenstown*

Te Anau

WESTEND61/GETTY IMAGES ©

two lakes – North and South Mavora – fringed by forest and towered over by the impressive Thomson and Livingstone Mountains, whose peaks rise to more than 1600m. Hikers can overnight at **Mavora Lakes Campsite** (adult/child $8/4), a campground with two areas (north and south) in a sublime setting in the heart of the park. The north campsite is the starting point of the four-day, 50km Mavora–Greenstone Walkway.

The park, part of the Te Wāhipounamu (Southwest New Zealand) World Heritage Area, served as a *The Lord of the Rings* filming location to represent Silverlode and Nen Hithoel.

⊕ ACTIVITIES

Te Anau is primarily a way to access the great wilderness of Te Wāhipounamu (Southwest New Zealand) World Heritage Area, which boasts such crowd-pullers as Milford Sound. However, there's plenty to keep you occupied around the town itself, as well as out on the water and in the air.

Te Anau's **Lakeside Track** makes for a very pleasant stroll or cycle in either direction – north to the marina and around to the Upukerora River (about an hour return), or south past the Fiordland National Park Visitor Centre and Punanga Manu o Te Anau bird sanctuary to the Waiau River control gates and the start of the Kepler Track (50 minutes).

Lake2Lake   Cycling
(www.trailstrust.co.nz) A local-community initiative, this easy cycle trail along the Waiau River will eventually link Te Anau with Manapōuri, starting from the DOC visitor centre (p249). At the time of research the section between Balloon Loop, 19km from Te Anau, and Supply Bay Rd, 4.7km from Manapōuri, was not yet complete (though a detour along the highway is possible for this section).

Bike Fiordland (☑03-280 0116, 0800 960 096; www.wildridesfiordland.co.nz; 68 Town Centre; bike hire 2/4hr $30/39, full day $50, ebikes 2/4hr $55/75; ☺9am-6pm daily Nov-Apr,

 Classic Kiwiana

Rickety and eccentric, **Manapouri Motels & Holiday Park** (☑03-249 6624; www.manapourimotels.co.nz; 86 Cathedral Dr; unpowered/powered sites from $20/50, s/d from $100/120, without bathroom from $75; ☎) is a love-or-hate kind of place. Cabins are inexpensive, the campsite is quiet and the amenities block (with kitchen and laundry) functions nicely. But service is patchy and some of the accommodation needs a polish. If charm trumps comfort in your book, you'll appreciate the silvery lake views and the fleet of old Morris Minors.

Our pick is Motel H, the split-level, mock-Swiss Alpine unit.

Lake Manapōuri
PHUONG D. NGUYEN/SHUTTERSTOCK ©

10am-4pm Tue-Fri, to 3pm Sat May-Oct) offers regular shuttles to or from Balloon Loop ($78 including bike hire).

Southern Lakes Helicopters   Scenic Flights
(☑03-249 7167; www.southernlakeshelicopters. co.nz; Lakefront Dr) Offering flights over Te Anau for 30 minutes ($240), half-day heli-hike options to Luxmore Hut on the Kepler Track ($270), and longer trips with landings over Doubtful, Dusky and Milford Sounds (from $685), this operator's three decades of experience in Fiordland will reassure nervous flyers.

Fiordland Jet   Adventure Sports
(☑0800 253 826; www.fjet.nz; 84 Lakefront Dr; adult/child $159/79) Thrilling two-hour

Te Anau

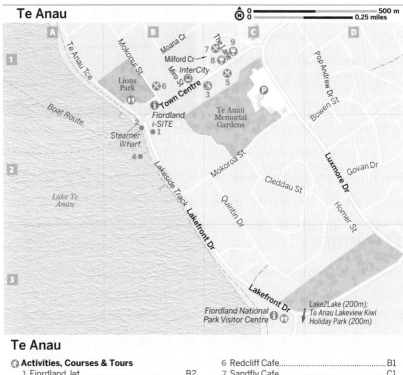

Te Anau

Activities, Courses & Tours
1	Fiordland Jet	B2
2	Real Journeys	B2
3	Rosco's Milford Kayaks	C1
4	Southern Lakes Helicopters	B2

Eating
5	Kepler's	C1
6	Redcliff Cafe	B1
7	Sandfly Cafe	C1

Drinking & Nightlife
8	Black Dog Bar	C1
9	Ranch Bar & Grill	C1

Entertainment
	Fiordland Cinema	(see 8)

jetboating trips on the Upper Waiau River (in *The Lord of the Rings*, the River Anduin), zipping between mountain-backed beech forest, with commentary on the area's natural (and fictional) highlights.

EATING

Te Anau's compact town centre has a good selection of cafes and restaurants, mostly modern NZ cuisine and fast food, plus a few surprises in the form of authentic Italian and South American.

The sizeable supermarket suits self-caterers (and is a god-send if you're stocking up for onward tramps and road trips).

Sandfly Cafe   Cafe $

(☎03-249 9529; 9 The Lane; mains $11.50-21; ☺7am-4.30pm; ☏) Popular both with locals and travellers, Sandfly serves up the town's best espresso alongside breakfasts, light meals of pasta or club sandwiches, and an impressive selection of sweet treats from caramel slices to berry friands. Sun yourself on the lawn, or try to get maximum mileage out of the free 15 minutes of wi-fi.

Kepler's   South American $$$

(☏03-249 7909; 90 Town Centre; mains $29-45; ☺5-9.30pm) Mountains of crayfish, mouthwatering ceviche and perfectly seared steaks are whisked to tables at this efficient but friendly family-run place. South American flair permeates the menu (quinoa salads, empanadas, Argentine *carménère*); but for Kiwi flare try the lamb – roasted whole over coals in the centre of the restaurant – with a generous pour of merlot.

Redcliff Cafe   Modern NZ $$$

(☏03-249 7431; www.theredcliff.co.nz; 12 Mokonui St; mains $32-40; ☺restaurant 11am-2pm & 5-9.30pm, bar 11am-late Sep-May) Housed in a replica settler's cottage, candlelit and cosy Redcliff Cafe offers well-executed, locally sourced food amid nostalgic decor (including old photos and antique sewing machines). Hearty meals include succulent slow-roasted pork belly with pear chutney or NZ prime beef with chimichurri. But Redcliff is just as good for a drink in the antique bar or on the sunny outdoor terrace.

Live music on Wednesday and Friday nights.

🍷 DRINKING & NIGHTLIFE

Black Dog Bar   Bar

(☏03-249 9089; www.blackdogbar.co.nz; 7 The Lane; ☺10am-late Oct-Apr, 2.30pm-late May-Sep; 🛜) Cocktails, Kiwi-style tapas, a smooth soundtrack and plump black sofas by an open fire...they all conspire to make Black Dog the most sophisticated watering hole in Te Anau. It's attached to the **Fiordland Cinema** (☏03 249 8844; www.fiordlandcinema.co.nz; 7 The Lane; adult/child $16/10; 🛜).

Ranch Bar & Grill   Pub

(☏03-249 8801; www.theranchbar.co.nz; 111 Town Centre; ☺8am-late) An open fire and chalet-style eaves heighten the appeal

of this popular local pub, most loved for its hefty Sunday roast dinners ($17.50), Thursday jam nights and sports matches on big screens. Show up for big pancake breakfasts (until 11.30am) or generous schnitzels and mostly meaty mains like surf 'n' turf and BBQ pork ribs ($28 to $45).

ℹ️ INFORMATION

Fiordland i-SITE (☏03-249 8900; www.fiordland.org.nz; 19 Town Centre; ☺9am-5pm May-Sep, 8.30am-7pm Oct-Apr) The official information centre, offering activity, accommodation and transport bookings.

Fiordland National Park Visitor Centre (DOC; ☏03-249 7924; www.doc.govt.nz; cnr Lakefront Dr & Te Anau–Manapōuri Rd; ☺8am-5pm daily Nov-Apr, 8.30am-4.30pm Mon-Fri, to 4pm Sat & Sun May-Oct) Can assist with Great Walks bookings, general hut tickets and information, with the bonus of a natural-history display and a shop stocking hiking supplies and essential topographical maps for backcountry trips.

ℹ️ GETTING THERE & AWAY

InterCity (☏03-442 4922; www.intercity.co.nz; Miro St) Services to Milford Sound (from $33, three hours, two to three daily) and Queenstown (from $33, 2¼ hours, four daily), and daily 8am buses to Gore (from $33, 1¾ hours), Dunedin (from $26, 4¾ hours) and Christchurch (from $42, 11¼ hours). Buses depart from a stop on Miro St outside Kiwi Country, at the Town Centre end.

Topline Tours (p251) Offers year-round shuttles between Te Anau and Manapōuri (from $25), and transfers from Te Anau to the Kepler Track trailheads at the control gates (from $5) and Rainbow Reach (from $10). Shuttles must be booked in advance.

Tracknet (p251) From November to April Te Anau–based Tracknet has at least three daily scheduled buses to/from Te Anau Downs ($29, 30 minutes), the Divide ($43, 1¼ hours) and Milford Sound ($55, 2¼ hours), two buses to/from Manapōuri ($25, 20 minutes), one to Invercargill ($51) and four daily to Queenstown

TRAVEL PIX/ALAMY ©

KWANG CHUN GAN/SHUTTERSTOCK ©

From left: Sandy Fly Cafe (p248); Frasers Beach; Pearl Harbour, Manapōuri

($49, 2¾ hours). In winter, services are by demand. Buses depart from near the **Te Anau Lakeview Kiwi Holiday Park** (☎03-249 7457, 0800 483 262; www.teanauholidaypark.co.nz; 77 Manapōuri–Te Anau Hwy; unpowered/powered sites $25/26, dm/s/d without bathroom from $36/59/80, d units from $379; P @ ☰).

Manapōuri

Manapōuri, 20km south of Te Anau, is the jumping-off point for cruises to Doubtful Sound. Most visitors head straight to Pearl Harbour for the ferry to West Arm across Lake Manapōuri, known to early Māori as Roto Ua or 'rainy lake', and later as Moturau, the 'many island lake'.

But little Manapōuri has a few tricks up its sleeve. The town can't compete with Te Anau's abundance of restaurants and motels but even the locals admit its mountain-backed lake views are more impressive. At 440m, Lake Manapōuri is the second-deepest lake in New Zealand. And with far fewer overnight visitors than Te Anau, you can enjoy the spectacular sunsets all to yourself.

ACTIVITIES

By crossing the Waiau River at **Pearl Harbour** (Waiau St) you can embark on day walks as detailed in DOC's *Fiordland Day Walks* brochure ($3 from the DOC office or download for free). A classic circuit with glimmering lake views (and occasional steep parts) is the **Circle Track** (3½ hours), or you can take the branch to **Hope Arm** (five to six hours return). Cross the Waiau River aboard a water taxi operated by **Adventure Manapouri** (☎021 925 577, 03-249 8070; www.adventuremanapouri.co.nz; water taxi per person return $20; ⏲Oct-May), departing Pearl Harbour at 11am daily and returning at 3pm (also available on demand by arrangement).

Running between the northern entrance to Manapōuri township and Pearl Harbour, the 30-minute **Frasers Beach** walk offers picnic and swimming spots as well as fantastic views across the lake.

EATING & DRINKING

The Church   Pub Food $$

(☑03-249 6001; www.facebook.com/pg/mana
pouri.co.nz; 23 Waiau St; mains $10-30; ⊙4-8pm
Tue, to 9pm Wed, noon-10pm Thu, to midnight
Fri & Sat, to 9pm Sun; 🛜) No need to head up
to Te Anau for a satisfying feed and a few
beers, hurrah! Plates heavy with steaks,
burgers and butter chicken are hauled to
tables in the mezzanine of this converted
church building, now a merry pub with
exceptionally welcoming staff.

GETTING THERE & AWAY

Topline Tours (☑03-249 8059; www.topline
tours.co.nz; 32 Caswell Rd) Offers year-round
shuttles between Te Anau and Manapōuri (from
$25). Note that shuttles must be booked in
advance.

Tracknet (☑0800 483 262; www.tracknet.net)
One to two daily buses to/from Te Anau ($25,
20 minutes) from November to April, and on
demand at other times of the year.

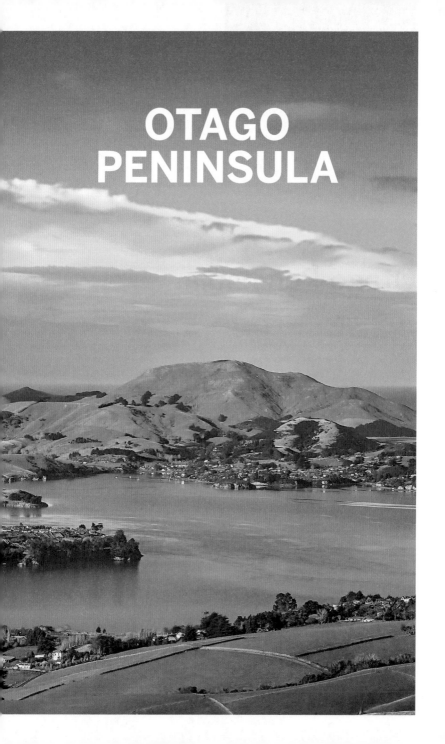

OTAGO
PENINSULA

Otago Peninsula

It's hard to believe that the Otago Peninsula – a picturesque haven of rolling hills, secluded bays, sandy beaches and cliff top vistas – is only half an hour's drive from downtown Dunedin. This small sliver of land is home to the South Island's most accessible diversity of wildlife, including albatrosses, penguins, fur seals and sea lions. The peninsula's only town is the petite Portobello, and despite a host of tours exploring the region, it maintains its quiet rural air. Back in Dunedin (aka the 'Edinburgh of the South'), New Zealand's oldest university provides plenty of student energy to sustain the local bars.

Two Days in the Otago Peninsula

Fuel-up for a day trip: grab breakfast at **No 7 Balmac** (p266) before exploring the peninsula. Must-sees include the **Penguin Place** (p260) and the big birds at the **Royal Albatross Centre** (p260). Back in Dunedin, dinner at **Bracken** (p266) awaits.

Four Days in the Otago Peninsula

On the next morning, grab your caffeine hit at Dunedin's **Insomnia by Strictly Coffee** (p266) or **Allpress** (p266) before trucking out to the peninsula again. **Nature's Wonders Naturally** (p259) wildlife reserve hosts yellow-eyed penguins, NZ fur seals and beautiful beaches. Back in the city, tour **Emerson's Brewery** (p263), rolling on to the bars around The Octagon.

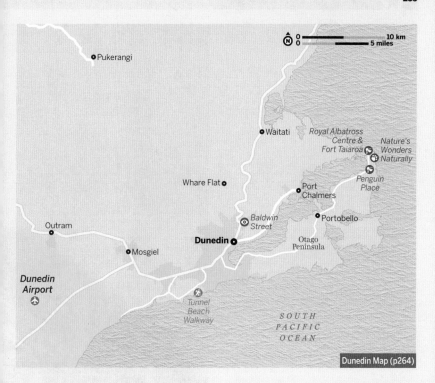

Dunedin Map (p264)

Arriving in the Otago Peninsula

Dunedin Airport (p305) There's no public transport to the airport, located 27km southwest of the city. A taxi to/from the city costs around $90. Pre-booked shuttle buses run door-to-door ($20).

Where to Stay

The Otago Peninsula is easily visited on a day trip from Dunedin, where there are myriad places to stay. There are some good accommodation options on the peninsula too – notably a motel, B&B and hostel) – worth considering if you don't fancy a drive back to the city after a wild evening with the penguins.

Blue penguin

Wildlife Watching

The Otago Peninsula is one of the best places on the South Island for wildlife spotting. Jagging into the ocean east of Dunedin, the peninsula provides safe, sheltered harbours for resident penguins and albatross, and nomadic sea lions. You might also spot a few passing whales or dolphins.

Great For...

☑ Don't Miss

Spying some slow-circling albatross at Taiaroa Head, the world's only mainland royal albatross colony.

ⓘ Need to Know

Visit Dunedin i-SITE (p267) for maps, directions, tour info and DOC walking guides.

BOB HILSCHER/SHUTTERSTOCK ©

Yellow-Eyed Penguins

One of the world's rarest penguins, the endangered hoiho (yellow-eyed penguin) is found along the Otago coast. It's estimated that less than 4000 of these penguins remain in the wild, with around 150 breeding pairs resident on deserted beaches in the southeast of the South Island during the 2016–17 breeding season.

The encroachment of humans on their habitat is one of the main causes of the penguins' decline. Penguins have been badly distressed by tourists using flash photography or traipsing through the nesting grounds; under no circumstances should you approach one. Even loud voices can disturb them. For this reason, the best way to see a hoiho in the wild is through an organised tour onto private land, such as through Nature's Wonders Naturally (p259) or Penguin Place (p260).

Blue Penguins

Nowhere near as rare as their yellow-eyed cousins, little penguins sometimes pop up in the oddest places (window-shopping in Ōamaru's Victorian Precinct, for instance). Also known as blue penguins, little blue penguins, kororā (in Māori) and fairy penguins (in Australia), these little cuties can spend days out at sea before returning to their colony just before dusk in batches known as rafts.

Although you might chance upon one at night, the best places to see them arrive en masse are at the Royal Albatross Centre (p260) on the Otago Peninsula.

Sea lions

Sea Lions

Sea lions are most easily seen on a tour, but are regularly present at Sandfly Bay, Allans Beach and Victory Beach on the Otago Peninsula. They are predominantly bachelor males vacationing from Campbell Island or the Auckland Islands. Give them plenty of space, as these powerful beasts can really motor over the first 20m.

Sanctuaries & Sights
Nature's
Wonders Naturally Wildlife Reserve
(☎03-478 1150; www.natureswonders.
co.nz; Taiaroa Head; adult/child Argo $99/45,
coach $45/22.50, boat $55/22.50; ☺tours
10.15am-sunset) What makes the improbably
beautiful beaches of this coastal sheep
farm different from other important wildlife

habitats is that (apart from pest eradication and the like) they're left completely alone. Many of the multiple private beaches haven't suffered a human footprint in years. The result is that yellow-eyed penguins can often be spotted (through binoculars) at any time of the day, and NZ fur seals laze around rocky swimming holes, blissfully unfazed by tour groups passing by.

Depending on the time of year, you might also see whales and little penguin chicks. The tour is conducted in 'go-anywhere' Argo vehicles by enthusiastic guides, at least some of whom double as true-blue Kiwi farmers. A less bumpy coach option

> ★ **Top Tip**
> Binoculars come in handy to spot wildlife during your excursions.

TIM WINTER/GETTY IMAGES ©

is also available, and there's also the *Albatross Express* boat tour, departing 3km south from Wellers Rock Wharf, devoted to spotting albatross and sea birds. Combo tours are available.

Penguin Place Bird Sanctuary

(☎03-478 0286; www.penguinplace.co.nz; 45 Pakihau Rd, Harington Point; adult/child $55/16; ⊙tours from 10.15am Oct-Mar, 3.45pm Apr-Sep) On private farmland, this reserve protects nesting sites of the rare yellow-eyed penguin (hoiho). The 90-minute tours cover 2km and focus on penguin conservation and close-up viewing from a system of hides. Bookings are recommended.

Royal Albatross Centre & Fort Taiaroa Bird Sanctuary

(☎03-478 0499; www.albatross.org.nz; Taiaroa Head; adult/child albatross $52/15, fort $26/10, combined $62/20; ⊙10.15am-sunset) Taiaroa Head (Pukekura), at the peninsula's northern tip, has the world's only mainland royal albatross colony, along with a late 19th-century military fort. The only public access to the area is by guided tour. There's an hour-long albatross tour and a 30-minute fort tour available, or the two can also be combined. Otherwise you can just call into the centre to have a look at the displays and grab a bite to eat in the cafe.

Albatross are present on Taiaroa Head throughout the year, but the best time to see them is from December to March, when one parent is constantly guarding the young while the other delivers food throughout the day. Sightings are most common in the afternoon when the winds pick up; calm days don't see as many birds in flight.

Little penguins swim ashore at Pilots Beach (just below the car park) around dusk to head to their nests in the dunes. For their protection, the beach is closed to the public every evening one hour before sunset, but viewing is possible from a specially constructed wooden platform (adult/child $35/10). Depending on the time of year, 50 to 200 penguins might waddle past. Photos are allowed, but no flashes.

Fort Taiaroa was built in 1885 in response to a perceived threat of Russian invasion. Its **Armstrong Disappearing Gun** was designed to be loaded and aimed underground, then popped up like the world's slowest jack-in-the-box to be fired.

Tours

Back to Nature Tours Bus

(☎0800 286 000; www.backtonaturetours.co.nz) ☞ The full-day Royal Peninsula tour (adult/ child $205/130) heads to points of interest around Dunedin before hitting the Otago Peninsula. Stops include Larnach Castle's gardens (castle entry is extra), Penguin

Royal Albatross Centre

Place and the Royal Albatross Centre. There's also a half-day option that visits various beaches ($85/55) and another tackling the Lovers Leap walking track ($99/55). It's possible to organise pick-ups from your accommodation.

Elm Wildlife Tours
Wildlife

(📞03-454 4121; www.elmwildlifetours.co.nz; tours from $103) 🌿 Well-regarded, small-group, wildlife-focused tours, with options to add the Royal Albatross Centre or a Monarch Cruise. Pick-up and drop-off from Dunedin is included.

Wild Earth Adventures
Kayaking

(📞03-489 1951; www.wildearth.co.nz; per person $115) Offers guided tours in double sea kayaks, with wildlife often sighted en route. Tours take between three and five hours, with pick-ups from The Octagon in Dunedin.

✕ Take a Break

Stay overnight at **Portobello Motel** (📞03-478 0155; www.portobellomotels.com; 10 Harington Point Rd, Portobello; d units $180; 🅿🛜), with studio units overlooking the bay.

★ Top Tip

The peninsula can be easily tackled as a day trip (or two) from Dunedin.

ERIK_V/GETTY IMAGES ©

Dunedin

Dunedin is full of hidden surprises. Firmly on the international street-art map since A-list Belgian aerosol artist ROA put up his beautiful tuatara at 7 Bath St in 2014, it now has artists from around the world vying for the best wall space in town. Many of them are drawn to the city's blossoming warehouse precinct, south of The Octagon, home to funky burger joints and vegan cafes. Dunedin also boasts a vibrant live-music scene, supported by the students of New Zealand's oldest university, and the wildlife-rich Otago Peninsula, which officially lies within the city limits.

And Dunedin has not forgotten its roots. The city is immensely proud of its Scottish heritage, never missing an opportunity to break out the haggis and bagpipes on civic occasions. In fact, the very name Dunedin is derived from the Scottish Gaelic name

it has now artists from around the world vying for the best wall space in town

University of Otago

for Edinburgh – Dùn Èideann – and the city even has its own tartan.

 SIGHTS

Olveston House
(☏ 03-477 3320; www.olveston.co.nz; 42 Royal Tce, Roslyn; adult/child $23/13; ⏱ tours 9.30am, 10.45am, noon, 1.30pm, 2.45pm & 4pm) Although it's a youngster by European standards, this spectacular 1906 mansion provides a wonderful window into Dunedin's past. Entry is via fascinating one-hour guided tours; it pays to book ahead. There's also a pretty little garden to explore (entry free) with a beautifully preserved 1921 Fiat 510 on display.

Until 1966 Olveston was the family home of the wealthy Theomin family, notable patrons of the arts who were heavily involved with endowing the Public Art Gallery. This artistic bent is evident in Olveston's grand interiors, which include works by Charles Goldie and Frances Hodgkins (a family friend). A particular passion was Japanese art, and the home is liberally peppered with

exquisite examples. The family was Jewish, and the grand dining table is set up as if for Shabbat dinner.

Toitū Otago Settlers Museum Museum

(📞03-477 5052; www.toituosm.com; 31 Queens Gardens; ⏰10am-5pm; 👪) **FREE** Storytelling is the focus of this excellent interactive museum, which traces the history of human settlement on the South Island. Pass through the new albatross *waharoa* (entranceway) by master carver James York to enter the engrossing Māori section, followed by a large gallery where floor-to-ceiling portraits of Victorian-era settlers stare out from behind their whiskers and lace. Walk through a re-created passenger-ship cabin (you can try out a bunk) and check out the fascinating array of obsolete technology.

Dunedin Public Art Gallery Gallery

(📞03-474 3240; www.dunedin.art.museum; 30 The Octagon; ⏰10am-5pm; 👪) **FREE** Gaze upon local and international art – including a small collection of Impressionists – at this expansive and airy gallery. Only a fraction of the collection is displayed at any given time, with most of the space given over to often-edgy temporary exhibitions with a focus on interactive art.

A new playspace (open 10am to 4.30pm) encourages kids to get crafty and hands-on.

University of Otago Historic Building

(www.otago.ac.nz; 362 Leith St) Founded in 1869, the University of Otago is NZ's oldest. Today the university is home to some 21,000 students, and is well worth a wander, with many magnificent bluestone buildings to admire. The historic heart – bounded by Leith, St David and Castle Sts – is the most photogenic part of the campus. Check the university website for a self-guided tour map. You can buy uni merch from the **visitor centre** (www.otago. ac.nz; cnr Cumberland & David Sts; ⏰9am-4.30pm Mon-Fri, 10.30am-3pm Sat).

 Baldwin Street

This **street** (North East Valley) proudly held the title of steepest street in the world until July 2019, when Ffordd Pen Llech in the Welsh town of Harlech was officially recognised as steeper by Guinness World Records. Dunedin went into shock and at the time of writing local surveyor Toby Stoff was mounting a challenge to the controversial decision. Stay tuned... However, not even the Welsh can deny that Baldwin St is pretty bloody steep, with a gradient of 1 in 2.86 (19 degrees).

GRACETHANG2/SHUTTERSTOCK ©

Emerson's Brewery Brewery

(📞03-477 1812; https://emersons.co.nz; 70 Anzac Ave; tours per person $28; ⏰tours 10am, noon, 2pm, 4pm & 6pm Oct-Mar, 11am, 2pm & 6pm Apr-Sep, restaurant 10am-late, cellar door 10am-8pm; 🅿) This impressive brick-and-glass structure is the flash home of Emerson's, the microbrewery founded by local-boy-made-good Richard Emerson in 1992. Forty-five-minute tours take you behind the scenes of the brewing process, ending with the all-important tasting. There's also a cellar door where you can fill a rigger with your favourite drop – or, if you'd like to linger longer, drop into the lively, cavernous restaurant for hearty meals (mains $17 to $35).

Otago Museum Museum

(📞03-474 7474; www.otagomuseum.nz; 419 Great King St, North Dunedin; ⏰10am-5pm) 🌿 **FREE** The centrepiece of this august institution is Southern Land, Southern

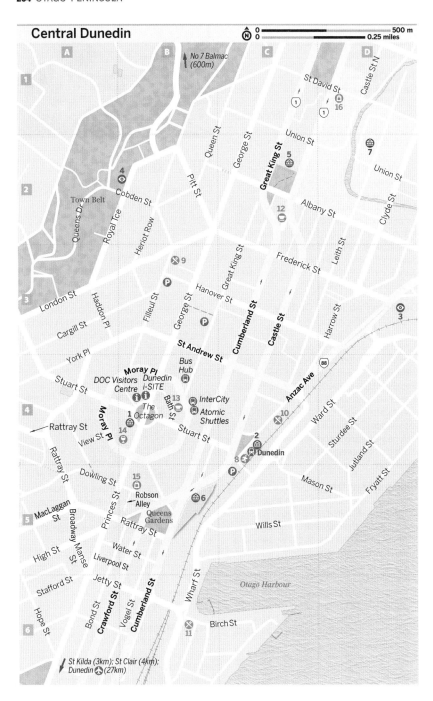

Central Dunedin

N

0 ——————— 500 m
0 ——————— 0.25 miles

A — B — C — D

1

No 7 Balmac
(600m)

St David St

1

16

Castle St N

Queen St

George St

Pitt St

Great King St

Union St

5

Union St

7

4

Cobden St

Town Belt

Royal Tce

Heriot Row

Queens Dr

Albany St

12

Clyde St

Leith St

London St

Haddon Pl

Cargill St

Fileul St

George St

Hanover St

Great King St

Frederick St

Cumberland St

Castle St

Harrow St

9

P

York Pl

Stuart St

Moray Pl

DOC Visitors
Centre

Dunedin
i-SITE

St Andrew St

Bus
Hub

The
Octagon

13

Bath St

InterCity

Atomic
Shuttles

Moray Pl

1

Rattray St

View St

14

Stuart St

2

Dunedin

Anzac Ave

88

10

Ward St

Sturdee St

Jutland St

3

Rattray St

Dowling St

15

Robson
Alley

8

P

Mason St

Fryatt St

MacLaggan
St

Broadway

Manse St

Princes St

Rattray St

Queens
Gardens

6

Wills St

High St

Water St

Liverpool St

Stafford St

Jetty St

Crawford St

Bond St

Vogel St

Cumberland St

Wharf St

Otago Harbour

Hope St

Birch St

11

St Kilda (3km); St Clair (4km);
Dunedin (27km)

Central Dunedin

People, showcasing Otago's cultural and physical past and present, from geology and dinosaurs to the modern day. The Tāngata Whenua Māori gallery houses an impressive *waka taua* (war canoe), wonderfully worn old carvings, and some lovely *pounamu* (greenstone) weapons, tools and jewellery. Other major galleries include Pacific Cultures, People of the World (including the requisite mummy), Nature, Maritime and the Animal Attic.

The **Tūhura Otago Community Trust Science Centre** (adult/child $15/10) boasts 45 hands-on interactive science displays, a Tropical Forest butterfly enclosure and a 7.5m-high double helix slide. There's also a **planetarium** ($12/7), which screens films on its 360-degree dome.

Guided tours depart from the information desk at 11am, 1pm, 2pm and 3pm daily ($15 per person).

ACTIVITIES

Dunedin Railways　　　　Rail
(☎03-477 4449; www.dunedinrailways.co.nz; Dunedin Railway Station, 22 Anzac Ave; ☺office 8am-5pm Mon-Fri, 8.30am-3pm Sat & Sun) Two scenic heritage train journeys set off from Dunedin's **railway station** (22 Anzac Ave; ☺8am-5pm Mon-Fri, 8.30am-3pm Sat & Sun). The best is the **Taieri Gorge Railway**, with narrow tunnels, deep gorges, winding tracks, rugged canyons and viaduct crossings. The four-hour return trip aboard 1920s heritage coaches travels to

Pukerangi (one way/return adult $72/115, child $19/29), 58km away, leaving at 9.30am and 3pm daily.

On Sundays Taieri Gorge trains carry on for another 20km from Pukerangi to Middlemarch (adult/child one way from Dunedin $81/21).

The **Seasider** heads north along the coast as far as Waitati (adult/child return $70/25, two hours) once or twice daily, depending on the season. Aim for a seat on the right-hand side of the train for better sea views.

Check the website for precise schedules.

Tunnel Beach Walkway　　Walking
(Tunnel Beach Rd, Blackhead) This short but extremely steep pathway (20 minutes down, 40 back up) brings you to a dramatic stretch of coast where the wild Pacific has carved sea stacks, arches and unusual formations out of the limestone. The tunnel is cut off at high tide so check tide times online or with the i-SITE (p267) before you set off. Strong currents make swimming here dangerous, but the views are spectacular.

The walkway takes its name from a hand-hewn stone tunnel at the bottom of the track, which civic father John Cargill had built to give his daughters access to secluded beachside picnics.

The track is 7km southwest of central Dunedin. You can take Bus 33 or 50 to Corstorphine, from there it's about a 2km walk.

SHOPPING

Hard to Find Books
Books

(☏03-471 8518; www.hardtofind.co.nz; 20 Dowling St; ☉10am-6pm) Bookworms will spend hours prowling the shelves of this sprawling store. With 140,000 catalogued books, and another 360,000 in storage, if you can't find it here, it probably doesn't exist.

EATING

Forage for cheap eats from around the world, from Khmer to Mexican, along George St, or hit the hip nosh spots in the converted warehouses along Vogel St. There's a cluster of relaxed bars and cafes in North East Valley, on the way to Baldwin St, while the beachy ambience of St Clair is great for a lazy brunch or sunset drinks.

Otago Farmers Market
Market $

(www.otagofarmersmarket.org.nz; Dunedin Railway Station; ☉8am-12.30pm Sat) This thriving market is all local, all edible (or drinkable) and mostly organic. Grab a freshly baked pastry and a flat white to sustain you while you browse, and stock up on fresh meat, seafood, veggies and cheese for your journey. Sorted.

Plato
Modern NZ $$$

(☏03-477 4235; www.platocafe.co.nz; 2 Birch St; mains lunch $20-25, dinner $36; ☉noon-2pm Wed-Sun, 6pm-late daily) The unpromising locale and kooky decor (including collections of toys and beer tankards) gives little indication of the seriously good food on offer at this relaxed eatery. Fresh fish and shellfish, including oysters in season, feature prominently. Try the house-brewed beer.

No 7 Balmac
Cafe $$$

(☏03-464 0064; www.no7balmac.co.nz; 7 Balmacewen Rd, Maori Hill; mains brunch $14-26, dinner $35-40; ☉7am-late Mon-Fri, from 8am Sat, 8am-5pm Sun; ☎) We wouldn't recommend walking to this sophisticated cafe at the top of Maori Hill, but luckily it's well worth the price of a cab. The fancy cafe fare stretches from smashing brunches to the likes of confit duck and applewood-grilled

pork and fennel. Take a stroll through the organic garden where many of the greens are sourced.

Bracken
Modern NZ $$$

(☏03-477 9779; www.brackenrestaurant.co.nz; 95 Filleul St; menus from $55; ☉11.30am-2pm & 5pm-late Tue-Sat) ✔ Bracken's seasonal tasting menus offer a succession of pretty little plates bursting with flavour. While the dishes are intricate, nothing's overly gimmicky, and the setting, in an old wooden house, is classy without being too formal. Meals can be paired with wine (from $45) or whisky (from $35).

✪ DRINKING & NIGHTLIFE

Pequeno
Cocktail Bar

(☏03-477 7830; www.pequeno.co.nz; behind 12 Moray Pl; ☉5pm-late Mon-Fri, from 7pm Sat) Head down the alley opposite the Rialto Cinema, with the black-and-white *kākāpō* street-art piece by Phelgm, to discover this intimate and sophisticated lounge bar. Music is generally laid-back, with regular live acts. The leather couches, fireplace, tapas menu and excellent wine and cocktail list make this backstreet bar perfect for a chilled night out.

Allpress
Coffee

(☏03-477 7162; www.allpressespresso.com; 12 Emily Siedeberg Pl; ☉8am-4pm Mon-Fri) The coffee at the Dunedin branch of this famous Kiwi roastery is just as smooth and rich as you'd expect. The simple cafe space fills with students from the nearby university, who come to sup espresso and nibble on cakes and salads from the small daily menu.

Insomnia by Strictly Coffee
Coffee

(☏03-479 0017; www.strictlycoffee.co.nz; 23 Bath St; ☉7.30am-4pm Mon-Fri) One of Dunedin's seriously serious coffee bars, Strictly Coffee is a stylish, retro option hidden down grungy Bath St. Different rooms provide varying views and artworks to enjoy while you sip and sup. The sunny courtyard is a great spot to partake in

Tunnel Beach Walkway (p265)

your morning caffeine hit – if you're over espresso, options include chemex and aeropress brews.

ℹ INFORMATION

The **Dunedin i-SITE** (☑03-474 3300; www. isitedunedin.co.nz; 50 The Octagon; ⊗8.30am-5.30pm Mon-Fri, from 8.45am Sat & Sun) incorporates the **DOC Visitor Centre** (Department of Conservation; ☑03-474 3300; www.doc.govt.nz; 50 The Octagon; ⊗8.30am-5.30pm Mon-Fri), providing a one-stop shop for all of your information needs, including Great Walks and hut bookings.

ℹ GETTING THERE & AWAY

AIR

Air New Zealand (☑0800 737 000; www. airnewzealand.co.nz) flies to/from Auckland, Wellington and Christchurch.

Jetstar (☑0800 800 995; www.jetstar.com) flies to/from Auckland.

Virgin Australia (☑0800 670 000; www. virginaustralia.com) flies to/from Brisbane, Australia.

BUS

Regional buses leave from Moray Pl, just around the corner from the **Bus Hub** (☑0800 672 8736; www.orc.govt.nz/public-transport/dunedin-buses; Great King St).

Atomic Shuttles (☑210 867 6001; www. atomictravel.co.nz; 331 Moray Pl) Buses to/from Christchurch, Timaru and Ōamaru daily.

Catch-a-Bus (☑03-449 2150; www.trailjourneys. co.nz) Bike-friendly shuttles to/from key Rail Trail towns.

InterCity (☑03-471 7143; www.intercity.co.nz; 331 Moray Pl) Coaches run to/from all South Island cities.

Queenstown (p205)

APEXPHOTOS/GETTY IMAGES ©

In Focus

Waitangi Treaty Grounds (p68)

History

Historians continue to unravel New Zealand's early history...with much of what they discover confirming traditional Māori narratives. In less than a thousand years NZ produced two new peoples: the Polynesian Māori and European New Zealanders (also known by their Māori name, Pākehā). NZ shares some of its history with the rest of Polynesia, and with other European settler societies, creating a unique cultural intermingling.

1280 CE

Based on evidence from archaeological digs, the most likely arrival date of east Polynesians in NZ, now known as Māori.

1500–1642

The 'classic period' of Māori culture, where weapon-making and artistic techniques were refined.

1642

First European contact: Abel Tasman arrives from the Dutch East Indies (Indonesia) but leaves after a sea skirmish with Māori.

Te Papa (p130)

Māori Settlement

The first settlers of NZ were the Polynesian forebears of today's Māori. Archaeologists and anthropologists continue to search for the details, but the most widely accepted evidence suggests they arrived in the 13th century. The DNA of Polynesian rat bones found in NZ, dated to centuries earlier, has been written off as unreliable (and certainly not conclusive evidence of earlier settlement). Most historians now agree on 1280 as the likeliest Māori arrival date. Scientists have sequenced the DNA of settlers buried at the Wairau Bar archaeological site on the South Island, and confirmed the settlers as originating from east Polynesia (though work is ongoing to pinpoint their origins more precisely). The genetic diversity of the buried settlers suggests a fairly large-scale settlement – a finding consistent with Māori narratives about numerous vessels reaching the islands.

Prime sites for first settlement were warm coastal gardens for the food plants brought from Polynesia (kumara or sweet potato, gourd, yam and taro), places with sources of workable stone for knives and adzes, and areas with abundant big game. New Zealand

1769
European contact recommences via James Cook and Jean de Surville. Despite violence, both communicate with Māori.

1772
Marion du Fresne's French expedition arrives. Relations with Māori start well, but a breach of Māori *tapu* (sacred law) leads to violence.

1790s
Whaling ships and sealing gangs arrive. Europeans depend on Māori contacts for essentials such as food, water and protection.

has no native land mammals apart from a few species of bat, but 'big game' is no exaggeration: the islands were home to a dozen species of moa (a large flightless bird) – the largest of which weighed up to 240kg, about twice the size of an ostrich – preyed upon by *Harpagornis moorei,* a whopping 15kg eagle that is now extinct. Other species of flightless birds and large sea mammals, such as fur seals, were easy game for hunters from small Pacific Islands. The first settlers spread far and fast, from the top of the North Island to the bottom of the South Island within the first 100 years. High-protein diets are likely to have boosted population growth.

By about 1400, however, with big-game supply dwindling, Māori economics turned from big game to small game – forest birds and rats – and from hunting to farming and fishing. A good living could still be made, but it required detailed local knowledge, steady effort and complex communal organisation, hence the rise of the Māori tribes. Competition for resources increased, conflict did likewise, and this led to the building of increasingly sophisticated *pā* (fortified villages), complete with wells and food-storage pits. Vestiges of *pā* earthworks can still be seen around the country (on the hilltops of Auckland, for example).

Around 1500 is considered the dawn of the 'classic period', when Māori developed a social structure and aesthetic that was truly distinct, rather than an offshoot of the parent Polynesian culture. Māori had no metals and no written language (and no alcoholic drinks or drugs). Traditional Māori culture from these times endures, including performance art like *kapa haka* (cultural dance) and unmistakable visual art, notably woodcarving, weaponry and *pounamu* (greenstone) carving.

Spiritual life was similarly distinctive. Below Ranginui (sky father) and Papatūānuku (earth mother) were various gods of land, forest and sea, joined by deified ancestors over time. The mischievous demigod Māui was particularly important. In legend, he vanquished the sun and fished up the North Island before meeting his death between the thighs of the goddess Hine-nui-te-pō in an attempt to bring immortality to humankind.

Enter Europe

The first authenticated contact between Māori and European explorers took place in 1642. Seafarer Abel Tasman had just claimed Van Diemen's Land (Tasmania) for the Dutch when rough winds steered his ships east, where he sighted New Zealand. Tasman's two ships were searching for southern land and anything valuable it might contain. Tasman was instructed to pretend to any natives he might meet 'that you are by no means eager for precious metals, so as to leave them ignorant of the value of the same'.

When Tasman's ships anchored in the bay, local Māori came out in their canoes to make the traditional challenge: friends or foes? The Dutch blew their trumpets, unwittingly challenging back. When a boat was lowered to take a party between the two ships, it was attacked and four crewmen were killed. Having not even set foot on the land, Tasman sailed away and didn't return; nor did any other European for 127 years. But the Dutch did leave a name: initially 'Statenland', later changed to 'Nova Zeelandia' by cartographers.

1818–36	**1840**	**1844**
Intertribal Māori 'Musket Wars' take place: tribes acquire muskets and win bloody victories against tribes without them.	On 6 February around 500 chiefs countrywide sign the Treaty of Waitangi. NZ becomes a nominal British colony.	Young Ngāpuhi chief Hōne Heke challenges British sovereignty. The ensuing Northland war continues until 1846.

English & French Arrivals

Contact between Māori and Europeans was renewed in 1769, when English and French explorers arrived, under James Cook and Jean de Surville – Cook narrowly pipped the latter to the post, naming Doubtless Bay before the French party dropped anchor there. The first French explorations ended sourly, with misunderstandings and violence; later expeditions were more fruitful. Meanwhile Cook made two more visits between 1773 and 1777. Exploration continued, motivated by science, profit and political rivalry.

Unofficial visits, by whaling ships in the north and sealing gangs in the south, began in the 1790s (though Māori living in New Zealand's interior remained largely unaffected). The first Christian missionaries established themselves in the Bay of Islands in 1814, followed by dozens of others: Anglican, Methodist and Catholic. Europe brought such things as pigs and potatoes, which benefited Māori and were even used as currency. Trade in flax and timber generated small European–Māori settlements by the 1820s. Surprisingly, the most numerous category of European visitor was probably American. New England whaling ships favoured the Bay of Islands for rest and recreation, which meant sex and drink. Their favourite haunt, the little town of Kororāreka (now Russell), was known as 'Gomorrah, the scourge of the Pacific'. New England visitors today might well have distant relatives among the local Māori.

The Musket Wars

The 'Musket Wars' of 1818–36 was a period of terrible intertribal Māori warfare. Because Northland had the majority of early contact with Europe, its Ngāpuhi tribe acquired muskets first. Under their great general Hongi Hika, Ngāpuhi then raided south, winning bloody victories against tribes without muskets. Once they acquired muskets, these tribes then saw off Ngāpuhi, but also raided further south in their turn. The domino effect continued to the far south of the South Island in 1836. The missionaries claimed that the Musket Wars then tapered off through their influence, but the restoration of the balance of power through the equal distribution of muskets was probably more important.

Māori–European Trade

One or two dozen bloody clashes dot the history of Māori–European contact before 1840 but, given the number of visits, inter-racial conflict was modest. Europeans needed Māori protection, food and labour, and Māori came to need European articles, especially muskets. Whaling stations and mission stations were linked to local Māori groups by intermarriage, which helped keep the peace.

The Māori population for 1769 has been estimated at between 85,000 and 110,000. The Musket Wars killed perhaps 20,000, and new diseases (including typhoid, tuberculosis and venereal disease) did considerable damage, too. Fortunately NZ had the natural quarantine

1860–69	1861	1863–64
The Taranaki wars, starting with the controversial swindling of Māori land by the government at Waitara.	Gold is discovered in Otago, resulting in the local population climbing from less than 13,000 to more than 30,000 in six months.	Waikato Land War: despite surprising successes, Māori are defeated and much land is confiscated.

of distance: infected Europeans often recovered or died during the long voyage, and small-pox, for example, which devastated indigenous North Americans, never arrived. By 1840 Māori had been reduced to about 70,000, a decline of at least 20%. Māori bent under the weight of European contact, but they certainly did not break.

Growing Pains

Māori tribes valued the profit and prestige brought by the Pākehā and wanted both, along with protection from foreign powers. Accepting nominal British authority was the way to get them. James Busby was appointed NZ's first British Resident in 1833, though his powers were largely symbolic. Busby selected the country's first official flag and established the Declaration of the Independence of New Zealand. But Busby was too ineffectual to curb rampant colonisation.

By 1840 the British government was overcoming its reluctance to undertake potentially expensive intervention in NZ. The British were eager to secure their commercial interests and they also believed, wrongly but sincerely, that Māori could not handle the increasing scale of unofficial European contact. In 1840 the two peoples struck a deal, symbolised by the treaty first signed at Waitangi on 6 February that year. The Treaty of Waitangi now has a standing not dissimilar to that of the Constitution in the US, but is even more contested. The original problem was a discrepancy between British and Māori understandings of it. The English version promised Māori full equality as British subjects in return for complete rights of government. The Māori version also promised that Māori would retain their chieftainship, which implied local rights of government. The problem was not great at first, because the Māori version applied outside the small European settlements. But as those settlements grew, conflict brewed.

Mass Migration

In 1840 there were only about 2000 Europeans in NZ, with the shanty town of Kororāreka the capital and biggest settlement. By 1850 six new settlements had been formed with 22,000 settlers between them. About half of these had arrived under the auspices of the New Zealand Company and its associates. The company was the brainchild of Edward Gibbon Wakefield, who also influenced the settlement of South Australia. Wakefield hoped to short-circuit the barbarous frontier phase of settlement with 'instant civilisation', but his success was limited. From the 1850s his settlers, who included a high proportion of upper-middle-class gentlefolk, were swamped by succeeding waves of immigrants that continued to wash in until the 1880s. These people were part of the great British and Irish diaspora that also populated Australia and much of North America, but the NZ mix was distinctive. Lowland Scots settlers were more prominent in NZ than elsewhere, for example, with the possible exception of parts of Canada. NZ's Irish, even the Catholics, tended to come from the north of Ireland. NZ's English tended to come from the counties close to London. Small groups of Germans, Scandinavians and Chinese made their way in, though the last faced

1867	**1893**	**1901**
All Māori men (rather than just individual land owners) are granted the right to vote.	NZ becomes the first country in the world to grant the vote to women, following a campaign led by Kate Sheppard.	New Zealand politely declines the invitation to join the new Commonwealth of Australia, but thanks for asking.

increasing racial prejudice from the 1880s, when the Pākehā population reached half a million.

Māori Resistance

The Māori tribes did not go down without a fight. Indeed, their resistance was one of the most formidable ever mounted against European expansion. The first clash took place in 1843 in the Wairau Valley, now a wine-growing district. A posse of settlers set out to enforce the myth of British control, but encountered the reality of Māori control. Twenty-two settlers were killed, including Wakefield's brother, Arthur, along with about six Māori. In 1845 more serious fighting broke out in the Bay of Islands, when Hōne Heke sacked a British settlement. Heke and his ally Kawiti baffled three British punitive expeditions, using a modern variant of the traditional *pā* fortification. Vestiges of these innovative earthworks can still be seen at Ruapekapeka (south of Kawakawa). Governor Grey claimed victory in the north, but few were convinced at the time. Grey had more success in the south, where he arrested the formidable Ngāti Toa chief Te Rauparaha, who until then wielded great influence on both sides of Cook Strait. Pākehā were able to swamp the few Māori living on the South Island, but the fighting of the 1840s confirmed that the North Island at that time comprised a European fringe around an independent Māori heartland.

In the 1850s settler population and aspirations grew, and fighting broke out again in 1860. The wars burned on sporadically until 1872 over much of the North Island. In the early years the King Movement, seeking to establish a monarchy that would allow Māori to assume a more equal footing with the European settlers, was the backbone of resistance. In later years some remarkable prophet-generals, notably Titokowaru and Te Kooti, took over. Most wars were small-scale, but the Waikato War of 1863–64 was not. This conflict, fought at the same time as the American Civil War, involved armoured steamships, ultra-modern heavy artillery, telegraph and 10 proud British regular regiments. Despite the odds, Māori forces won several battles, such as that at Gate Pā, near Tauranga, in 1864. But in the end they were ground down by European numbers and resources. Māori political, though not cultural, independence ebbed away in the last decades of the 19th century. It finally expired when police invaded its last sanctuary, the Urewera Mountains, in 1916.

From Gold Rush to Welfare State

From the 1850s to the 1880s, despite conflict with Māori, the Pākehā economy boomed. A gold rush on the South Island made Dunedin NZ's biggest town, and a young, mostly male population chased their fortunes along the West Coast. Fretting over the imbalance in this frontier society, the British government tried to entice women to settle in NZ. Huge amounts of wool were exported, and there were unwise levels of overseas borrowing for development of railways and roads. By 1886 the population reached a tipping point: the population of non-Māori people were mostly born in NZ. Many still considered Britain their distant home, but a new identity was taking shape.

1908	1914–18	1930s
NZ physicist Ernest Rutherford is awarded the Nobel Prize in chemistry for 'splitting the atom'.	In a country of just over one million people, about 100,000 NZ men serve overseas in WWI. Some 60,000 become casualties.	Maurice Schlesinger begins producing the Buzzy Bee, NZ's most famous children's toy.

Auckland Museum

KRUG_100/SHUTTERSTOCK ©

Depression hit in 1879, when wool prices slipped and gold production thinned out. Unemployment pushed some of the working population to Australia, and many of those who stayed suffered miserable working conditions. There was still cause for optimism: NZ successfully exported frozen meat in 1882, raising hopes of a new backbone for the economy. Forests were enthusiastically cleared to make way for farmland.

In 1890 the Liberals, NZ's first organised political party, came to power. They stayed there until 1912, helped by a recovering economy. For decades, social-reform movements such as the Woman's Christian Temperance Union (WCTU) had lobbied for women's freedom, and NZ became the first country in the world to give women the vote in 1893. (Another major WCTU push, for countrywide prohibition, didn't take off.) Old-age pensions were introduced in 1898, but these social leaps forward didn't bring universal good news. Pensions only applied to those falling within a very particular definition of 'good character', and the pension reforms deliberately excluded the population of Chinese settlers who had arrived to labour in the goldfields. Meanwhile, the Liberals were obtaining more and more Māori land for settlement. By now, the non-Māori population outnumbered the Māori by 17 to one.

Nation-Building

New Zealand had backed Britain in the Boer War (1899–1902) and WWI (1914–18), with dramatic losses in WWI. However, the bravery of Anzac (Australian and New Zealand Army Corps) forces in the failed Gallipoli campaign endures as a nation-building moment for NZ. In the 1930s NZ's experience of the Great Depression was as grim as any. The derelict farmhouses still seen in rural areas often date from this era. In 1935 a second reforming government took office, campaigning on a platform of social justice: the first Labour government, led by Australian-born Michael Joseph Savage. In WWII NZ formally declared war on Germany; 140,000 or so New Zealanders fought in Europe and the Middle East, while at home women took on increasing roles in the labour force.

1931

A massive earthquake in Napier and Hastings kills at least 256 people.

1939–45

NZ troops back Britain and the Allies during WWII; from 1942 around 45,000 Americans arrive to protect NZ from the Japanese.

1953

New Zealander Edmund Hillary and Nepalese Tenzing Norgay become the first men to reach the summit of Mt Everest.

By the 1930s giant ships were regularly carrying frozen meat, cheese and butter, as well as wool, on regular voyages from NZ to Britain. As the NZ economy adapted to the feeding of London, cultural links were also enhanced. New Zealand children studied British history and literature, not their own. New Zealand's leading scientists and writers, such as Ernest Rutherford and Katherine Mansfield, gravitated to Britain. Average living standards in NZ were normally better than in Britain, as were the welfare and lower-level education systems. New Zealanders had access to British markets and culture, and they contributed their share to the latter as equals. The list of 'British' writers, academics, scientists, military leaders, publishers and the like who were actually New Zealanders is long.

New Zealand prided itself on its affluence, equality and social harmony. But it was also conformist, even puritanical. The 1953 Marlon Brando movie, *The Wild One,* was banned until 1977. Full Sunday trading was not allowed until 1989. Licensed restaurants hardly existed in 1960, nor did supermarkets or TV. Notoriously, from 1917 to 1967, pubs were obliged to shut at 6pm (which, ironically, paved the way for a culture of fast, heavy drinking before closing time). Yet puritanism was never the whole story. Opposition to Sunday trading stemmed not so much from belief in the sanctity of the sabbath, but from the belief that workers should have weekends, too. Six o'clock closing was a standing joke in rural areas. There was always something of a Kiwi counterculture, even before imported countercultures took root from the 1960s onward.

In 1973 'Mother England' ran off and joined the budding EU. New Zealand was beginning to develop alternative markets to Britain, and alternative exports to wool, meat and dairy products. Wide-bodied jet aircraft were allowing the world and NZ to visit each other on an increasing scale. Women were beginning to penetrate first the upper reaches of the workforce and then the political sphere. Gay people came out of the closet, despite vigorous efforts by moral conservatives to push them back in. University-educated youths were becoming more numerous and more assertive.

The Modern Age

From the 1930s, Māori experienced both a population explosion and massive urbanisation. Life expectancy was lengthening, the birth rate was high, and Māori people were moving to cities for occupations formerly filled by Pākehā servicemen. Almost 80% were urban dwellers by the mid-1980s, a staggering reversal of the status quo that brought cultural displacement but simultaneously triggered a movement to strengthen pride in Māori identity. Immigration was broadening, too, first encouraging Pacific Islanders in, for their labour, and then (East) Asians for their capital.

Then, in 1984, NZ's next great reforming government was elected – the fourth Labour government, ostensibly led by David Lange, though in fact by Roger Douglas, the Minister of Finance. This government adopted a more market-led economic policy (dubbed 'Rogernomics'), delighting the right, and an anti-nuclear foreign policy, delighting the left. New Zealand's numerous economic controls were dismantled with breakneck speed. Revelling

1981	2011	2013
Springbok rugby tour divides the nation. Many New Zealanders show a strong anti-apartheid stance by protesting the games.	A severe earthquake strikes Christchurch, killing 185 people and badly damaging the central business district.	New Zealand becomes one of just 15 countries in the world to legally recognise same-sex marriage.

in their new freedom, NZ investors engaged in a frenzy of speculation, and suffered even more than the rest of the world from the economic crash of 1987.

In 1985 French spies sank the Greenpeace anti-nuclear protest ship *Rainbow Warrior* in Auckland Harbour, killing one crewman. The lukewarm American condemnation of the French act brought middle NZ in behind the anti-nuclear policy, which became associated with national independence.

From the 1990s, a change to a points-based immigration policy has woven an increasingly multicultural tapestry in NZ. Numbers of migrating Brits fell, while new arrivals from Pacific Islands, Asia, North Africa, the Middle East and other European countries increased, particularly to NZ's cities.

In 2017 NZ voted in a new face to show the world. Helmed by Jacinda Ardern, a coalition government was formed by Labour and NZ First, with support from the Green Party. New Zealand's third female prime minister has faced challenges satisfying the various elements of her governing coalition while trying to tackle a national housing crisis and effect bigger investment in education and health. Ardern's response to the 2019 Christchurch mosque attacks was widely admired for her compassion and leadership. The same can be said of her adept management of the corona virus pandemic in New Zealand, which was praised across the world. It's no wonder that her ascendancy has been touted as the dawn of a new period of major reform.

2017
Whanganui River is granted the same legal rights as a human being, a global first.

2017
Jacinda Ardern becomes NZ's youngest PM for 150 years, heralding a new direction for NZ politics.

2019
The Christchurch mosque shootings shocked NZ but the country's response inspired the world.

Thermal pool at Whakarewarewa Village (p86)

Environment

New Zealand's landforms have a diversity that you would expect to find across an entire continent: snow-dusted mountains, drowned glacial valleys, rainforests, dunelands and an otherworldly volcanic plateau. Straddling the boundary of two great colliding slabs of the earth's crust – the Pacific plate and the Indo-Australian plate – NZ is a plaything for nature's powerful forces.

The Land

New Zealand is a young country – its present shape is less than 10,000 years old. Having broken away from the supercontinent of Gondwanaland (which included Africa, Australia, Antarctica and South America) some 85 million years ago, it endured continual uplift and erosion, buckling and tearing, and the slow fall and rise of the sea as ice ages came and went.

Evidence of NZ's tumultuous past is everywhere. The South Island's mountainous spine – the 650km-long ranges of the Southern Alps – grew from the clash between plates at a rate of 20km over three million years; in geological terms, that's a sprint. Despite NZ's highest peak, Aoraki/Mt Cook, losing 10m from its summit overnight in a 1991 landslide (and a couple of dozen more metres to erosion), the Alps are overall believed to be some of the fastest-growing mountains in the world.

Tui

FILEDIMAGE/SHUTTERSTOCK ©

★ Native Birds

Kea Big cheeky parrot.

Kererū The New Zealand pigeon.

Kiwi Famously flightless national icon.

Pukeko Elegant swamp hen.

Tui Beautiful songbird.

Volcanoes

The North Island's most impressive landscapes have been wrought by volcanoes. Auckland is built on an isthmus peppered by some 48 scoria cones (cinder cones, or volcanic vents). The city's largest and most recently formed volcano, 600-year-old Rangitoto Island, is a short ferry ride from downtown. Another 300km south, the classically shaped cone of snowcapped Mt Taranaki overlooks tranquil dairy pastures.

But NZ's real volcanic heartland runs through the centre of the North Island, from the restless bulk of Mt Ruapehu in Tongariro National Park, northeast through the Rotorua lake district and out to NZ's most active volcano, White Island, in the Bay of Plenty, which tragically erupted in December 2019, killing 21 people. This great 350km-long rift valley – part of a volcano chain known as the 'Pacific Ring of Fire' – has been the seat of massive eruptions that have left their mark on the country physically and culturally. The volcano that created Lake Taupō last erupted 1800 years ago in a display that was the most violent (a VEI-7 score) anywhere on the planet within the past 2000 years.

You can experience the aftermath of volcanic destruction on a smaller scale at **Te Wairoa, the Buried Village** (☏07-362 8287; www.buriedvillage.co.nz; 1180 Tarawera Rd; adult/child $35/5; ⊙9am-5pm Oct-Feb, to 4.30pm Mar-Sep), near Rotorua on the shores of Lake Tarawera. Here, partly excavated and open to the public, lie the remains of a 19th-century Māori village overwhelmed when nearby Mt Tarawera erupted without warning. The famous Pink and White Terraces, spectacular naturally formed pools (and one of several claimants to the title 'eighth wonder of the world'), were destroyed overnight by the same upheaval.

Born of geothermal violence, Waimangu Volcanic Valley (p93) is the place to go to experience hot earth up close and personal amid geysers, silica pans, bubbling mud pools and the world's biggest hot spring. Alternatively, wander around Rotorua's Whakarewarewa village (p86), where descendants of Māori displaced by the eruption live in the middle of steaming vents and prepare food for visitors in boiling pools.

The South Island also displays evidence of volcanism – if the remains of the old volcanoes of Banks Peninsula weren't there to repel the sea, the vast Canterbury Plains, built from alpine sediment washed down the rivers from the Alps, would have eroded long ago.

Earthquakes

Earthquakes are common in NZ. Most only rattle the glassware, but a few have wrecked major towns. In 1931 an earthquake measuring 7.9 on the Richter scale levelled the Hawke's Bay city of Napier, causing huge damage and loss of life. Napier was rebuilt almost entirely in then-fashionable art-deco architectural style.

On the South Island, in September 2010 Christchurch was rocked by a magnitude 7.1 earthquake. Less than six months later, in February 2011, a magnitude 6.3 quake destroyed much of the city's historic heart and claimed 185 lives, making it the country's second-deadliest natural disaster; Christchurch is still recovering. Then in November 2016 an earthquake measuring 7.8 on the Richter scale struck Kaikōura – further up the coast – resulting in two deaths and widespread damage to local infrastructure. Roads and rail have since been rebuilt but the landscape stills wears the evidence.

Flora & Fauna

New Zealand's long isolation has allowed it to become a veritable warehouse of unique
and varied plants. Separation of NZ's landmass occurred before mammals appeared on the scene, leaving birds and insects to evolve in spectacular ways. As one of the last places on earth to be colonised by humans, NZ was for millennia a safe laboratory for risky evolutionary strategies. But the arrival of Māori, and later Europeans, brought new threats and sometimes extinction.

The now-extinct flightless moa, the largest of which grew to 3.5m tall and weighed more than 200kg, browsed open grasslands much as cattle do today (skeletons can be seen at Auckland Museum), while the smaller kiwi still ekes out a nocturnal living rummaging among forest leaf litter for insects and worms. One of the country's most ferocious-looking insects, the mouse-sized giant weta, meanwhile, has taken on a scavenging role elsewhere filled by rodents.

Many endemic creatures, including moa and the huia, an exquisite songbird, were driven to extinction, and the vast forests were cleared for timber and to make way for agriculture. Destruction of habitat and the introduction of exotic animals and plants have taken a terrible environmental toll – and New Zealanders are now fighting a rearguard battle to save what remains.

Trees

Distinctive native trees you're likely to spy on your travels include the colourful kowhai, a small-leaved tree growing to 11m, which in spring has drooping clusters of bright-yellow flowers (informally considered NZ's national flower); the pohutukawa, a beautiful coastal tree of the northern North Island that bursts into vivid red flower in December, earning the nickname 'Christmas tree'; and a similar crimson-flowered tree, the rata. Rata species are found on both islands; the northern rata starts life as a climber on a host tree (that it eventually chokes).

The few remaining pockets of mature centuries-old kauri are stately emblems of former days. Their vast trunks and towering, epiphyte-festooned limbs reach well over 50m high, reminders of why they were sought after in colonial days for spars and building timber.

Other native timber trees include the distinctive rimu (red pine) and the long-lived totara (favoured for Māori war canoes). NZ's perfect pine-growing conditions encouraged one of the country's most successful imports, *Pinus radiata,* which grow to maturity in 35 years (and sometimes less). Plantation forests are now widespread through the central North Island – the southern hemisphere's biggest, Kaingaroa Forest, lies southeast of Rotorua.

New Zealand also has an impressive 200 species of ferns, and almost half grow nowhere else on the planet. Most easily recognised are the mamaku (black tree fern) – which grows to 20m and can be seen in damp gullies throughout the country – and the 10m-high ponga

An Ancient Lizard

The largest native reptile in NZ is the tuatara, a crested lizard that can grow up to 50cm long. Thought to be unchanged for more than 220 million years, these endearing creatures can live for up to a century. Meet them at Auckland Zoo (p50), Hokitika's National Kiwi Centre (p201), and other zoos and sanctuaries around NZ.

(silver tree fern) with its distinctive white underside. The silver fern is a national symbol and adorns sporting and corporate logos, as well as shop signs, clothing and jewellery.

Environmental Issues

New Zealand's reputation as an Eden, replete with pristine wilderness and eco-friendly practices, has been repeatedly placed under the microscope. The industry most visible to visitors, tourism, appears studded in green accolades, with environmental best practices employed in areas as broad as heating insulation in hotels to minimum-impact wildlife-watching. But mining, offshore oil and gas exploration, pollution, biodiversity loss, funding cuts and questionable urban planning have provided endless hooks for bad-news stories.

Water quality is arguably the most serious environmental issue faced by New Zealanders and one the government started to tackle seriously in 2019. Research from diverse sources suggests that the health of New Zealand's waterways has been in decline, the primary culprit: 'dirty dairying' – cow effluent leaching into freshwater ecosystems, carrying with it high levels of nitrates, as well as bacteria and parasites such as *E. coli* and giardia. A 2017 government push to make 90% of rivers and lakes swimmable by 2040 was met with initial scepticism about the metrics involved, but there's a strong impetus to make NZ's waterways worthy of the country's clean and green reputation.

Another ambitious initiative kicked off in 2016: Predator Free 2050. The aim is to rid NZ of introduced animals that prey on native flora and fauna. The worst offenders are possums, stoats and rats, which eat swathes of forest and kill wildlife, particularly birds. However, controversy rages at the Department of Conservation's (DOC) use of 1080 poison (sodium fluoroacetate) to control these pests, despite it being sanctioned by prominent environmental groups as well as the Parliamentary Commissioner for the Environment. Vehement opposition to 1080 is expressed by such diverse camps as hunters and animal-rights activists, who cite detriments such as by-kill and the potential for poison passing into waterways. Proponents of its use argue that it's biodegradable and that aerial distribution of 1080 is the only cost-effective way to target predators across vast, inaccessible parts of NZ. Still, 'Ban 1080' signs remain common in rural communities and the controversy is unlikely to end until the poison is banned.

As well as its damaging impact on waterways, the $12 billion dairy industry – the country's biggest export earner – generates 48% of NZ's greenhouse gas emissions. Some farmers are cleaning up their act, lowering emissions through improved management of fertilisers and higher-quality feed, and major players DairyNZ and Fonterra have pledged support. But when it comes to contributing to climate change, the dairy industry isn't NZ's only dirty habit. New Zealand might be a nation of avid recyclers and solar-panel enthusiasts, but it also has the world's fourth-highest ratio of motor vehicles to people.

There have been fears about safeguarding the principal legislation governing the NZ environment, the 1991 *Resource Management Act,* in the face of proposed amendments. NGOs and community groups – ever-vigilant and already making major contributions to the welfare of NZ's environment – will find plenty to keep them occupied in coming years. But with an eco-conscious prime minister, Jacinda Ardern, leading a coalition government, New Zealanders are hopeful of a greener future – Ardern has pledged an ambitious goal of reducing net greenhouse gas emissions to zero by 2050.

With more trains, 100% renewable energy sources and planting 100 million trees per year, NZ could take a lead in the global response to our current climate emergency.

Māori carving with pearlescent eyes

Māori Culture

Māori culture is as diverse as its people. Some are engaged with traditional cultural networks and pursuits; others are adapting traditions and placing these in dialogue with a globalised New Zealand culture. As a visitor you'll immediately notice that indigenous language and cultural understandings are imbued in everyday life, though areas where there's a larger proportion of Māori families living today are mainly on the North Island.

People of the Land

The indigenous Māori are New Zealand's *tangata whenua* (people of the land), and the Māori spiritual relationship with the land has grown over hundreds of years. Once a predominantly rural population, many Māori people now live in urban centres, away from their traditional homelands, but it's still the practice in formal settings to introduce oneself by reference to 'home': an ancestral mountain, river, sea or lake, or an ancestor.

The Māori concept of *whanaungatanga* – family relationships – is central to the culture: families spread out from the *whānau* (extended family) to the *hapū* (subtribe) and *iwi* (tribe) and even, in a sense, beyond the human world and into the natural and spiritual worlds.

If you're looking for a Māori experience in NZ you'll find it – in conversations, galleries, gigs, cultural performances, on an organised tour...

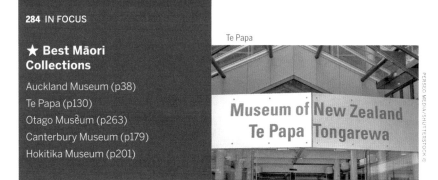

Te Papa

PERSED MEDIA/SHUTTERSTOCK ©

Māori Then

Some three millennia ago people began moving eastward into the Pacific, sailing against the prevailing winds and currents (hard to go out, easier to return safely). Some stopped at Tonga and Samoa, and others settled the small central East Polynesian tropical islands.

The Māori colonisation of Aotearoa began from an original homeland known to Māori as Hawaiki. Skilled navigators and sailors travelled across the Pacific, using many navigational tools – currents, winds, stars, birds and wave patterns – to guide their large, double-hulled ocean-going craft to a new land. The first of many was the great navigator Kupe, who arrived, the story goes, chasing a giant octopus named Muturangi. But the distinction of giving NZ its well-known Māori name – Aotearoa – goes to his wife, Kuramārōtini, who cried out, '*He ao, he ao tea, he ao tea roa!*' (A cloud, a white cloud, a long white cloud!).

Kupe and his crew journeyed around the land, and many places around Cook Strait (between the North and South Islands) and the Hokianga in Northland still bear the names that the crew gave them and the marks of their passage. Kupe returned to Hawaiki, leaving from (and naming) Northland's Hokianga. He gave other seafarers valuable navigational information. And then the great *waka* (ocean-going craft) began to arrive.

The *waka* that the first settlers arrived on, and their landing places, are immortalised in tribal histories. Well-known *waka* include *Tākitimu, Kurahaupō, Te Arawa, Mātaatua, Tainui, Aotea* and *Tokomaru*. There are many others. Māori trace their genealogies back to those who arrived on the *waka* (and further back as well).

What would it have been like, making the transition from small tropical islands to a much larger, cooler landmass? Goodbye breadfruit, coconuts, paper mulberry; hello moa, fernroot, flax – and immense space (relatively speaking). New Zealand has more than 15,000km of coastline. Rarotonga, by way of contrast, has a little over 30km. There was land, lots of it, and flora and fauna that had developed more or less separately from the rest of the world for 80 million years. There was an untouched, massive fishery. There were great seaside mammalian convenience stores – seals and sea lions – as well as a fabulous array of birds.

The early settlers went on the move, pulled by love, trade opportunities and greater resources; pushed by disputes and threats to security. When they settled, Māori established *mana whenua* (regional authority), whether by military campaigns or by the peaceful methods of intermarriage and diplomacy. Looking over tribal history it's possible to see the many alliances, absorptions and extinctions that went on.

Histories were carried by the voice, in stories, songs and chants. Great stress was placed on accurate learning – after all, in an oral culture where people are the libraries, the past is always a generation or two away from oblivion.

Māori lived in *kāinga* (small villages), which often had associated gardens. Housing was cosy by modern standards – often it was hard to stand upright while inside. From time to time people would leave their home base and go to harvest seasonal foods. When peaceful life was interrupted by conflict, people would withdraw to *pā* (fortified villages).

And then Europeans began to arrive.

Māori Today

Today's culture is marked by developments in the arts, business, sport and politics. Many historical grievances still stand, but some *iwi* (Ngāi Tahu and Tainui, for example) have settled major historical grievances and are significant forces in the NZ economy. Māori have also addressed the decline in Māori language use by establishing *kōhanga reo*, *kura kaupapa* and *wānanga* (Māori-language preschools, schools and universities). There is now a generation of people who speak Māori as a first language. There is a network of Māori radio stations, and Māori TV attracts a committed viewership. A recently revived Māori event is becoming more and more prominent – Matariki (Māori New Year). The constellation Matariki (also known as the Pleiades) begins to rise above the horizon in late May or early June and its appearance traditionally signals a time for learning, planning and preparing as well as singing, dancing and celebrating.

Visiting Marae

As you travel around NZ, you will see many *marae* complexes. Often *marae* are owned by a descent group. They are also owned by urban Māori groups, schools, universities and church groups, and they should only be visited by arrangement with the owners.

Marae complexes include a *wharenui* (meeting house), which often embodies an ancestor. Its ridge is the backbone, the rafters are ribs, and it shelters the descendants. There is a clear space in front of the *wharenui*, the *marae ātea*. Sometimes there are other buildings: a *wharekai* (dining hall); a toilet and shower block; perhaps even classrooms, play equipment and the like.

Hui (gatherings) are held at *marae*. Issues are discussed, classes conducted, milestones celebrated and the dead farewelled. Te reo Māori (the Māori language) is prominent, and sometimes the only language used.

Religion

Christian churches and denominations are prominent in the Māori world, including televangelists, mainstream churches for regular and occasional worship, and two major Māori churches (Ringatū and Rātana). But in the (non-Judeo-Christian) beginning there were the *atua Māori*, the Māori gods, and for many Māori the gods are a vital and relevant force still. It is common to greet the earth mother and sky father when speaking formally at a *marae* (meeting house). The gods are represented in art and carving, sung of in *waiata* (songs) and invoked through *karakia* (prayer and incantation) when a meeting house is opened, when a *waka* is launched, even (more simply) when a meal is served. They are spoken of in the *marae* and in wider Māori contexts. The traditional Māori creation story is well known and widely celebrated.

Arts & Media

You can stay up to date with what's happening in the Māori arts scene by listening to *iwi* stations (www.irirangi.net) or tuning into Māori TV (www.maoritelevision.com) for regular features on Māori arts. Māori TV went to air in 2004, an emotional time for many Māori who could at last see their culture, their concerns and their language in a mass medium. More than 90% of content is NZ made, and programs are in both Māori and English: they're subtitled and accessible to everyone. If you want to really get a feel for the rhythm and meter of spoken Māori from the comfort of your own chair, switch to Te Reo (www.maoritelevision.com/tv/te-reo-channel), a Māori-language-only channel.

E-Tangata (e-tangata.co.nz) is an online magazine run by the Mana Trust specialising in stories that reflect the experiences of Māori and Pasifika in Aotearoa.

Steamed green-lip mussels

Food & Drink

Travellers, bring your appetites! Eating is a highlight of any visit to New Zealand, from fresh seafood and gourmet burgers to farmers market fruit-and-veg and crisp-linen fine dining. Drinking here, too, presents boundless opportunities to have a good time, with coffee, craft beer and wine of world renown.

Modern NZ

Once upon a time (yet not that long ago) NZ subsisted on a modest diet of 'meat and three veg'. Though small-town country pubs still serve menus of roasted meats and battered fish, overall NZ's culinary sophistication has evolved. In larger towns, kitchens thrive on bending conventions and absorbing influences from around the planet, all the while keeping local produce central to the menu.

Immigration has been key to this culinary rise – particularly migrants from Europe, Asia and the Middle East – as has an adventurous breed of local restaurant-goers and the elevation of Māori and Pacific Islander flavours and ingredients to the mainstream.

Restaurants today are fusing contrasting ingredients and traditions into ever more innovative fare. The phrase 'Modern NZ' has been coined to classify this unclassifiable technique: a melange of East and West, a swirl of Atlantic and Pacific Rim, and a dash of authentic French and Italian.

Traditional staples still hold sway (lamb, beef, venison, green-lipped mussels), but dishes are characterised by interesting flavours and fresh ingredients rather than fuss, clutter or snobbery. Spicing ranges from gentle to extreme, seafood is plentiful and meats are tender and full flavoured. Enjoy!

When touring the menus of NZ, keep an eye out for these local delights: kina (sea urchin), paua (abalone; a type of sea snail), kumara (sweet potato, often served as chips), whitebait (tiny fish, often cooked into fritters or omelettes) and the humble kiwifruit.

To Market, To Market

There are more than 50 farmers markets held around NZ. Most happen on weekends and are upbeat local affairs, where visitors can meet local producers and find fresh regional produce. A mobile coffee cart is usually present, and tastings are offered by enterprising and innovative stall holders. Bring a carrier bag, and get there early for the best stuff! Check out www.farmersmarkets.org.nz for major market locations, and ask locally about smaller, and seasonal, markets.

Cafes & Coffee

Since the early 2000s, New Zealanders have cottoned on to coffee culture in a big way. Caffeine has become a nationwide addiction: there are Italian-style espresso machines in virtually every cafe, boutique roasters are de rigueur and, in urban areas, a qualified barista (coffee maker) is the norm. Auckland, Christchurch and student-filled Dunedin have borne generations of coffee aficionados, but Wellington takes top billing as NZ's caffeine capital. The cafe and bean-roasting scene here rivals the most vibrant in the world, and is very inclusive and family friendly. Join the arty local crew and dunk yourself into it over a late-night conversation or an early-morning recovery.

Vegetarians & Vegans

More than 10% of New Zealanders are vegetarian (more in the North than the South Island), and numbers are rising. Most large urban centres have at least one dedicated vegetarian cafe or restaurant; see the Vegetarians New Zealand website (www.vegetarians.co.nz) for listings. Almost all restaurants and cafes offer some vegetarian menu choices (although sometimes only one or two). Many diners also provide gluten-free and vegan options.

Pubs, Bars & Beer

Kiwi pubs were once male bastions with dim lighting, smoky air and beer-soaked carpets – these days they're more of a family affair. Sticky floors and pie-focused menus still abound in rural parts of NZ, but pubs are generally where parents take their kids for lunch, friends mingle for sav blanc and tapas, and locals of all ages congregate to roar at live sports screenings. Food has become integral to the NZ pub experience, along with the inexorable rise of craft beer in the national drinking consciousness.

Myriad small, independent breweries have popped up around the country in the last decade. Wellington, in particular, offers dozens of dedicated craft-beer bars, with revolving beers on tap and passionate bar staff who know all there is to know about where the beers

★ **Best Restaurants**

Mister D (p122), Napier

Noble Rot (p143), Wellington

Cassia (p56), Auckland

Twenty Seven Steps (p184), Christchurch

Rātā (p226), Queenstown

Wine tasting, Marlborough wine region

have come from, who made them and what's in them. A night on the tiles here has become less about volume and capacity, more about selectivity and virtue.

Aside from the food and the fancy beer, the NZ pub remains a place where all Kiwis can unite with a common purpose: to watch their beloved All Blacks play rugby on the big screen – a raucous experience to say the least!

Wine Regions

Like the wine industry in neighbouring Australia, the NZ version has European migrants to thank for its status and success – visionaries who knew good soils and good climate when they saw them, and planted the first vines. New Zealand's oldest vineyard – Mission Estate Winery (p121) in Hawke's Bay – was established by French Catholic missionaries in 1851 and is still producing top-flight wines today.

Since then, NZ cool-climate wines have conquered the world, a clutch of key regions producing the lion's share of bottles. Organised day tours via minivan or bicycle are a great way to visit a few select wineries.

Auckland Region Vineyards established in the early 1900s unfurl across the countryside around Auckland, producing swell syrah and pinot gris to the north and chardonnay to the west. A short ferry ride from Auckland, Waiheke has a hot, dry microclimate that just happens to be brilliant for growing reds and rosés.

Marlborough New Zealand's biggest and most widely known wine region sits at the top of the South Island, where a microclimate of warm days and cool nights is perfect for growing sauvigon blanc.

Hawke's Bay The North Island's sunny East Coast is NZ's second-largest producer – chardonnay and syrah are the mainstays. The Gisborne region a bit further north also produces terrific chardonnays, along with great pinot gris.

Wairarapa Just over the hills from Wellington, the Wairarapa region – centred on boutiquey Martinborough – produces winning pinot noir.

Central Otago Reaching from Cromwell in the north to Alexandra in the south and Gibbston near Queenstown in the west, the South Island's Central Otago region produces sublime riesling and pinot noir.

Māori dance on Waitangi Day (p22)

CHAMELEONSEYE/SHUTTERSTOCK ©

Arts & Music

Māori music and arts extends back to New Zealand's early, unrecorded history but its motifs endure today in diverse forms. European settlers imported artistic styles, but it took a century for post-colonial NZ to hone its distinctive identity. In the first half of the 20th century it was writers and visual artists who led the charge, but in the decades that followed music and movies catapulted the nation's creativity into the world's consciousness.

Literature

In 2013, 28-year-old Eleanor Catton became only the second NZ writer to ever win the Man Booker Prize, for her epic historical novel *The Luminaries,* set on the West Coast. Lloyd Jones came close in 2007 when his novel *Mister Pip* was shortlisted, but it had been a long wait between drinks since Keri Hulme took the prize in 1985 for her haunting novel *The Bone People*.

Katherine Mansfield's work had begun a Kiwi tradition in short fiction, and for years the standard was carried by novelist Janet Frame, who won the Commonwealth Writers' Prize in 1989 for *The Carpathians.*

Less recognised internationally, Maurice Gee has gained the nation's annual top fiction gong six times, most recently with *Blindsight* in 2006. A new author on New Zealanders' must-read lists is Catherine Chidgey: look for her heart-rending novel *The Wish Child* (2016).

Hobbiton (p62)

FADHLI ADNAN/SHUTTERSTOCK ©

★ New Zealand Oscar Winners

Anna Paquin (Best Supporting Actress, 1993; *The Piano*)

Russell Crowe (Best Actor, 2000; *Gladiator*)

Peter Jackson (Best Director, 2003; *The Lord of the Rings: The Return of the King*)

Bret McKenzie (Best Original Song, 2011; 'Man or Muppet,' *The Muppets*)

Cinema & TV

Sir Peter Jackson's NZ-made *The Lord of the Rings* and *The Hobbit* trilogies were the best thing to happen to NZ tourism since Captain Cook. The uniting factor in NZ film and TV is the landscape, which provides a haunting gothic backdrop. Jane Campion's *The Piano* (1993) and *Top of the Lake* (2013), Brad McGann's *In My Father's Den* (2004) and Jackson's *Heavenly Creatures* (1994) all use magically lush scenery to couch disturbing violence.

When Kiwis do humour, it is as resolutely black as their rugby jerseys, yet the HBO-produced TV musical parody *Flight of the Conchords* – featuring a mumbling, bumbling Kiwi folk-singing duo trying to get a break in New York – found surprising international success. Also packaging offbeat NZ humour for an international audience, Taika Waititi is a household name after directing *What We Do in the Shadows* (2014), *Hunt for the Wilderpeople* (2016) and Marvel's *Thor: Ragnarok* (2017).

Visual Arts

Traditional Māori art has a distinctive visual style with well-developed motifs that have been embraced by NZ artists of every race. In the painting medium, these include the cool modernism of Gordon Walters and the more controversial pop-art approach of Dick Frizzell's *Tiki* series. Also look for the intricate, collage-like paintings of Niuean-born, Auckland-raised John Pule.

Charles Frederick Goldie painted a series of controversial, realist portraits of Māori, who were feared to be a dying race. Recalibrating the ways in which Pacific Islander and Māori people are depicted in art, Lisa Reihana wowed the Venice Biennale in 2017 with her multimedia work *In Pursuit of Venus*.

Music

NZ music began with the *waiata* (singing) developed by Māori following their arrival in the country. These days, the liveliest place to see Māori music being performed is at traditional *kapa haka* song-and-dance competitions.

Rock & Metal

New Zealand's most acclaimed rock exports are the revered indie label Flying Nun and the music of the Finn Brothers. Started in 1981 by Christchurch record-store owner Roger Shepherd, many of Flying Nun's early groups came from Dunedin, where local musicians produce lo-fi indie-pop.

Something heavier? Hamilton heavy-metal act Devilskin's 2014 debut album hit the top spot on NZ's charts, as did their punchy 2016 follow-up *Be Like the River*.

Reggae, Hip-Hop & Dance

The genres of music that have been adopted most enthusiastically by Māori and Polynesian New Zealanders have been reggae (in the 1970s) and hip-hop (in the 1980s), which has led to distinct local forms. In Wellington, a thriving jazz scene took on a reggae influence to create a host of groups that blended dub, roots and funky jazz – most famously Fat Freddy's Drop.

The local hip-hop scene has its heart in the suburbs of South Auckland, which have a high concentration of Māori and Pacific Island residents. This area is home to one of New Zealand's foremost hip-hop labels, Dawn Raid. It's most successful artist is Savage, who sold a million copies of his single 'Swing' after it was featured in the movie *Knocked Up*. Within New Zealand, the most well-known hip-hop acts are Scribe, Che Fu and Smashproof. Popular dance music artists include Salmonella Dub, Concord Dawn and Shapeshifter.

The Brothers Finn

There are certain tunes that all Kiwis can sing along to, given a beer and the opportunity. A surprising proportion of these were written by Tim and Neil Finn, many of which have been international hits. Tim Finn first came to prominence in the 1970s group Split Enz, who amassed a solid following in Australia, NZ and Canada before disbanding in 1985. Neil then formed Crowded House with two Australian musicians (Paul Hester and Nick Seymour) and one of their early singles, 'Don't Dream It's Over', hit number two on the US charts. Tim and Neil have both released a number of solo albums, as well as releasing material together as the Finn Brothers.

Classical & Opera

In the 1950s Douglas Lilburn became one of the first internationally recognised NZ classical composers. More recently the country has produced a number of world-renowned musicians in this field, including legendary opera singer Dame Kiri Te Kanawa, million-selling classic-to-pop singer Hayley Westenra, composer John Psathas and composer/percussionist Gareth Farr (who also performs in drag under the name Lilith LaCroix).

Movers & Shakers

Since 2000, the NZ music scene has hit its stride after the government convinced commercial radio stations to adopt a voluntary quota of 20% local music. Since then Kiwi bands have had enough commercial airplay to gain large folllowings, though social media, streaming and YouTube have all played their part in the rising popularity of many NZ artists.

The soul/dance/reggae fusion outfit Six60 are now playing at a level previously only international bands enjoyed in NZ, selling out 50,000-seat venues like Auckland's Western Springs, and hip-hop artist Kings had the longest running NZ with his single 'Don't Worry 'Bout it' at number one for 33 weeks in 2017.

On the female solo artist front check out Benee, Bailey Wiley, Tammi Neilson and Hollie Smith. New Zealand also produced internationally acclaimed pop electronica bands like the Drax Project and Broods.

The biggest name in Kiwi music today is Lorde, a singer-songwriter from Devonport on Auckland's North Shore. Known less regally to her friends as Ella Yelich-O'Connor, Lorde was 16 years old when she cracked the number-one spot on the US Billboard charts in 2013 with her magical, schoolyard-chant-evoking, Grammy-winning hit 'Royals'. Her debut album *Pure Heroine* spawned a string of hits and sold millions of copies worldwide, while moody follow-up *Melodrama* instantly topped charts in NZ and the US upon its release in 2017.

Skyline Gondola (p222), Queenstown

CHAMELEONSEYE/SHUTTERSTOCK ©

Survival Guide

Directory A–Z

Accessible Travel

Kiwi accommodation generally caters fairly well for travellers with mobility issues, with most hostels, hotels and motels equipped with one or two wheelchair-accessible rooms. (B&Bs aren't required to have accessible rooms.) Many tourist attractions similarly provide wheelchair access, with wheelchairs often available. For advice on local attractions with maximum accessibility, ask at i-SITE visitor centres.

Tour operators with accessible vehicles operate from most major centres. Key cities are also serviced by 'kneeling' buses (buses that hydraulically stoop down to kerb level to allow easy access), and many taxi companies offer wheelchair-accessible vans. Large car-hire firms (Avis, Hertz etc) provide cars with hand controls at no extra charge (but advance booking is required, of course). Air New Zealand accommodates travellers in wheelchairs.

Download Lonely Planet's free Accessible Travel guides from https://shop.lonely planet.com/categories/accessible-travel.

Activities

Out and about, the DOC has been hard at work improving access to short walking trails (and some of the longer ones). Tracks that are wheelchair accessible are categorised as 'easy access short walks': the Cape Reinga Lighthouse Walk and Milford Foreshore Walk are two prime examples.

If cold-weather activity is more your thing, see Snow Sports NZ's page on adaptive winter sports: www.snowsports.co.nz/get-involved/adaptive-snow-sports.

Resources

Access4All (www.facebook.com/Access4all.Ltd) Now only a Facebook page, but a travel company with good links to accommodation and other accessible essentials.

Firstport (www.firstport.co.nz) Includes a high-level overview of transport in NZ, including mobility taxis and accessible public transport.

Mobility Parking (www.mobilityparking.org.nz) Apply for an overseas visitor mobility parking permit ($35 for 12 months) and have it posted to you before you even reach NZ (for a further $10).

Accommodation

Book beds well in advance in peak tourist seasons: November through March (particularly local summer holidays from Christmas to late January), at Easter, and during winter (June to September) in snowy resort towns like Queenstown and Wānaka.

Motels and pubs Most towns have low-rise, midrange motels. Even small towns usually have a pub with rooms.

Holiday parks Ideal if you're camping or touring in a campervan. Choose from unpowered tent sites, simple cabins and en suite units.

Hostels Backpacker hostels include beery, party-prone joints and family-friendly 'flashpackers'.

Pods Small private spaces from airport hotels to glass pods in the forest.

Hotels From small-town pubs to slick global-chain operations – with commensurate prices.

Lodges Luxurious in every sense, from the architecture to the locations, NZ has a stunning array of splash-out-worthy retreats.

B&Bs

Bed and breakfast (B&B) accommodation in NZ pops up in the middle of cities, in rural hamlets and on stretches of isolated coastline, with rooms offered in everything from suburban bungalows to stately manors.

Breakfast may be 'continental' (a standard offering of cereal, toast and tea or coffee); a heartier version with yoghurt, fruit, home-baked bread or muffins; or

Book Your Stay Online

For more accommodation reviews by Lonely Planet authors, check out http://hotels.lonely planet.com/newzealand. You'll find independent reviews, as well as recommendations on the best places to stay. Best of all, you can book online.

a stomach-loading cooked breakfast (eggs, bacon, sausages; though, with notice, vegetarians are increasingly well catered for). Some B&B hosts may also cook dinner for guests and advertise dinner, bed and breakfast (DB&B) packages.

Midrange B&B tariffs are typically in the $160 to $250 bracket (per double), though upwards of $350 per double is not unusual. Some hosts charge cheeky prices for what is, in essence, a bedroom in their home, though room-sharing websites like Airbnb have impacted this market in NZ too.

Booking Services

Local visitor information centres are generally excellent for accommodation in the area; many can also make bookings on your behalf.

Lonely Planet (www.lonely planet.com/hotels) Find independent reviews, as well as recommendations on the best

places to stay – and then book them online.

Automobile Association (www.aa.co.nz/travel) Online accommodation bookings (especially good for motels, B&Bs and holiday parks).

Bach Care (www.bachcare. co.nz) Rental listings for apartments of all sizes, including many beachfront options.

Book a Bach (www.booka bach.co.nz) Apartment and holiday-house bookings.

Holiday Houses (www.holiday houses.co.nz) Holiday-house rentals across NZ.

Jasons (www.jasons.co.nz) Long-running travel service with myriad online booking options.

New Zealand Bed & Breakfast (www.bnb.co.nz) Great for all sorts of B&Bs.

Rural Holidays NZ (www. ruralholidays.co.nz) Farm and homestay listings across NZ.

Stay Native (https://explore. staynative.co.nz) Lists indigenous-run sustainable activities and hosts.

Camping & Holiday Parks

Campers and campervan drivers converge on NZ's hugely popular 'holiday parks', pitching up in powered and unpowered sites, cheap bunk rooms (dorm rooms), cabins (using the shared bathroom facilities) or fully self-contained units (often called motels or tourist flats). Features often include well-equipped communal kitchens, dining areas, games and TV rooms,

and playgrounds for kids to run riot. In cities, holiday parks are usually a fair way from the action, but in smaller towns they can be impressively central or near lakes, beaches, rivers and forests.

The nightly cost of holiday-park tent sites is usually $20 to $30 per adult, with children charged half price; powered campervan sites can be anything from $35 to around the $50 mark. Cabin/unit accommodation normally ranges from $90 to $150 per double.

The 'glamping' scene has not really taken hold in NZ as it has in other places, but expect to see more bell tents popping up over the next year or two as rural property owners look to diversify their incomes.

Farmstays

Farmstays open the door to the agricultural side of NZ life, with visitors encouraged to get some dirt beneath their fingernails at orchards and on dairy, sheep and cattle farms. Costs can vary widely, with bed and breakfast generally costing $90 to $150. Some farms have separate cottages where you can fix your own food; others offer low-cost, shared, backpacker-style accommodation.

Farm Helpers in NZ (www.farmhelpers.co.nz) hosts an online database of hundreds of farms across the country providing lodging in exchange for four to six hours' work per day. Registration costs $40.

WWOOFing

If you don't mind some hard work, an economical way of travelling around NZ involves doing some voluntary work as a member of the international **Willing Workers On Organic Farms** (WWOOF; 02-2052 6624; www.wwoof.co.nz; 9am-3pm Mon-Fri) scheme. Down on the farm, in exchange for a short, hard day's work, owners provide food, accommodation and some hands-on organic farming experience. Contact farm owners a week or two beforehand to arrange your stay, as you would for a hotel or hostel – don't turn up unannounced!

A one-year online membership costs $40 for an individual or a couple. A farm-listing book, which is mailed to you, costs an extra $10 to $30, depending on where in the world your mailbox is. You should have a Working Holiday visa when you visit NZ, as the immigration department considers WWOOFers to be working.

Hostels

New Zealand is packed to the rafters with backpacker hostels, both independent and part of large chains, ranging from small, homestay-style affairs with a handful of beds to refurbished hotels and towering modern structures in the big cities. Hostel bed prices

listed by Lonely Planet are nonmember rates, usually $30 to $50 per night.

Hostel Organisations

Budget Backpacker Hostels (www.bbh.co.nz) A network of more than 160 hostels. Membership costs $35 for 12 months and entitles you to stay at member hostels at rates listed in the annual (free) *BBH Backpacker Accommodation* booklet. Nonmembers pay 10% more per night. Pick up a membership card from any member hostel or order one online.

YHA New Zealand (www.yha. co.nz) Over 35 hostels in prime NZ locations. The YHA is part of the Hostelling International network (www.hihostels. com), so if you're already an HI member in your own country, membership entitles you to use NZ hostels. If you don't already have a home membership, you can join at major NZ YHA hostels or online for $25, valid for 12 months (it's free for under 18s). Nonmembers pay 10% more per night. Membership has other perks, such as discounts on some car-hire providers, restaurants and cafes, travel insurers, DOC hut passes and more.

Base Backpackers (www. stayatbase.com) Chain with seven hostels around NZ: Auckland, Rotorua, Taupō, Wellington, Wānaka, Queenstown and Paihia. Expect clean dorms, women-only areas and party opportunities aplenty. Offers flexible seven-night 'Bed Hopper'' accommodation passes for A$225 (bookable online). Passes are valid in five affiliate

hostels too, and can be bought for longer periods.

Haka Lodges (www.hakalodges. com) A local chain with five snazzy hostels in Auckland, Queenstown, Christchurch, Taupō and Paihia. Rates are comparable to other hostels around NZ, dorms are no bigger than six beds and quality is high. Private en suites, female-only dorms, and tours are also available.

Pubs, Hotels & Motels

The least expensive form of NZ hotel accommodation is the humble pub. Some are full of character (and characters); others are grotty, ramshackle places that are best avoided (especially if travelling solo). Check whether there's a band playing the night you're staying, or you could be in for a sleepless night. In the cheapest pubs, singles/ doubles might cost as little as $50/80 (with a shared bathroom down the hall); $70/90 is more common.

At the top end of the hotel scale are five-star international chains, resort complexes and architecturally splendid boutique hotels, all of which charge a hefty premium for their mod cons, snappy service and/or historic opulence. We quote 'rack rates' (official advertised rates) for such places, but discounts and special deals often apply.

New Zealand's towns have a glut of often nondescript low-rise motels and 'motor lodges', charging

$90 to $200 for double rooms. These tend to be squat structures skulking by highways on the edges of towns. The best ones have been thoroughly modernised, but some have been neglected with decor mired in the 1990s (or earlier). Expect basic facilities, namely tea- and coffee-making equipment, fridge and TV. Prices vary with standards.

Rental Accommodation

The basic Kiwi holiday home is called a 'bach' (short for 'bachelor', as they were historically used by single men as hunting and fishing hideouts); in Otago and Southland they're known as 'cribs'. These are simple self-contained cottages that can be rented in rural and coastal areas, often in isolated locations, and sometimes include surf, fishing or other outdoor gear hire in the cost. Prices are typically $150 to $250 per night, which isn't bad for a whole house or self-contained bungalow. For more upmarket holiday houses, expect to pay anything from $250 to $500 per double.

Customs Regulations

For the low-down on what you can and can't bring into NZ, see the New Zealand

Climate

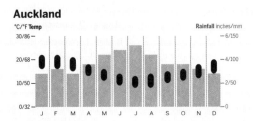

Auckland

Christchurch

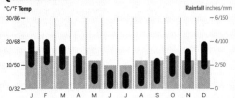

Queenstown

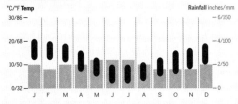

Customs Service website (www.customs.govt.nz). Per-person duty-free allowances:

- Three 1125mL (max) bottles of spirits or liqueur
- 4.5L of wine or beer
- 50 cigarettes, or 50g of tobacco or cigars
- Dutiable goods up to the value of $700

It's a good idea to declare any unusual medicines. Hiking gear (boots, tents etc) will be checked and may need to be cleaned before being allowed in. You must declare any plant or animal products (including anything made of wood), and food of any kind. Weapons and firearms are either prohibited or require a permit and safety testing. Don't take these rules lightly – noncompliance penalties will really hurt your wallet.

Discount Cards

The internationally recognised **International Student Identity Card** is produced by the ISIC

Association (www.isic.org), and issued to full-time students aged 12 and over. It provides over 150,000 discounts across more than 130 countries – on accommodation, transport, entertainment and attractions. The same folks also produce the **International Youth Travel Card**, available to travellers aged under 31 who are not full-time students, with equivalent benefits to the ISIC. Similar is the **International Teacher Identity Card**, available to teaching professionals. All three cards are $30 and can be bought online.

The **New Zealand Card** (www.newzealandcard.com) is a $35 discount pass that'll score you between 5% and 50% off a range of accommodation, tours, sights and activities. Browse participating businesses before you buy. A one-year **Budget Backpacker Hostels** (www.bbh.co.nz) membership card costs $35 and entitles you to discounts at BBH member hostels, usually snipping 10% off the price per night.

Travellers aged over 60 with some form of identification (eg an official seniors card from your home country) are often eligible for concession prices.

Electricity

To plug yourself into the electricity supply (230V AC, 50Hz), use a three-pin adaptor (the same as in Australia; different to British three-pin adaptors).

**Type I
230V/50Hz**

Food

Most eating options are casual walk-ups (pubs, cafes and takeaways) but book top-end restaurants well in advance.

Restaurants Open for dinner and lunch. 'Modern NZ' = locally sourced, top-quality fare with international influences.

Cafes Locally roasted beans, expert baristas, savvy breakfast-to-lunch food and family-friendly.

Takeaways Fish and chips, kebabs, burgers...the big internationals are here, but quality local outfits give them a run for their money.

Pubs & bars You can get a bite to eat at most Kiwi bars and pubs – from standard stodge to delicately wrought tapas and farmer-sized steaks.

Supermarkets In all sizeable towns – often open until 9pm.

Health

New Zealand poses minimal health risks to travellers. Diseases such as malaria and typhoid are unheard of, poisonous snakes and other dangerous animals are absent, and there are currently no dangerous insect-borne diseases. The biggest risks to travellers involve exploring the great outdoors: hikers must be clued-up on rapidly changing weather and diligent about sharing any plans to visit remote areas. Drivers must be very careful on NZ's notoriously winding, often-narrow roads.

Before You Go
Health Insurance

Health insurance is essential for all travellers, even to safe, wealthy countries such as New Zealand. While healthcare in NZ is of a high quality and not overly expensive by international standards, considerable costs can be built up and repatriation is pricey.

If you don't have a health insurance plan that covers you for medical expenses incurred overseas, buy a travel insurance policy – see www.lonelyplanet.com/travel-insurance. Find out in advance if your insurance plan will make payments directly to providers or reimburse you later for overseas health expenditures. Check whether your policy covers the activities you're planning to do in NZ (eg rock climbing or winter sports) and whether there's a limit on the number of days of cover for the activity.

Medications

Bring any prescribed medications for your trip in their original, clearly labelled containers. It is also wise to bring a signed and dated letter from your physician describing your medical conditions and medications (including generic names), and any requisite syringes or needles.

Vaccinations

New Zealand has no vaccination requirements for any traveller, but the World Health Organization recommends that all travellers should be covered for chickenpox, diphtheria, hepatitis B, measles, mumps, pertussis (whooping cough), polio, rubella, seasonal flu, tetanus and tuberculosis, regardless of their destination. Ask your doctor for an international certificate of vaccination (or 'the yellow booklet') in which they will list all the vaccinations you've received.

In New Zealand

Availability & Cost of Healthcare

New Zealand's public hospitals offer a high standard of care (free for residents). All travellers are covered for medical care resulting from accidents that occur while in NZ (eg motor-vehicle accidents or adventure-activity accidents) by the Accident Compensation Corporation (www.acc.co.nz). Costs incurred due to treatment of a medical illness that occurs while in NZ will only be covered by travel insurance. For more details, see www.health.govt.nz.

The 24-hour **Healthline** (☑0800 611 116; www.health line.govt.nz) offers health advice throughout NZ (free from local mobile phones or landlines). Interpreters are available.

Environmental Hazards

New Zealand's numerous biting insects are an irritation rather than a serious health risk, but hypothermia and drowning are genuine threats.

Biting Insects

Wear long, loose clothing and use an insect repellent containing 20% or more DEET to ward off sandflies and mosquitoes, which are particularly common in lake areas and tree-lined clearings. Bites are intensely itchy, but fortunately don't spread disease.

Hypothermia

Hypothermia, a dangerous drop in body temperature, is a significant risk to travellers in NZ, especially during winter and year-round at altitude. Mountain ranges and/or strong winds produce a high chill factor, which can cause hypothermia even in moderate temperatures. Early signs include the inability to perform fine movements (such as doing up buttons), shivering and a bad case of the 'umbles' (fumbles, mumbles, grumbles, stumbles).

To treat, minimise heat loss: remove wet clothing, add dry clothes with wind- and waterproof layers, and consume carbohydrates and water or warm liquids (not caffeine) to allow shivering to build the internal temperature. In severe hypothermia cases, shivering actually stops – this is a medical emergency requiring rapid evacuation in addition to the above measures.

Drowning

New Zealand has exceptional surf beaches across its 15,000km coastline. The power of the surf can fluctuate as a result of the varying slope of the seabed: rips and undertows are common, and drownings do happen. Check with local surf lifesaving organisations before jumping in the sea, always heed warning signs at beaches, and be realistic about your own limitations and expertise.

Infectious Diseases

Aside from the same sexually transmitted infections that are found worldwide (take normal precautions), giardiasis and (following an outbreak in 2019) measles are the main infectious diseases to be aware of when travelling in NZ.

Giardiasis

The giardia parasite is widespread in NZ waterways: drinking untreated water from streams and lakes is not recommended. Using water filters and boiling or treating water with iodine are effective ways of preventing the disease. The parasite can also latch on to swimmers in rivers and lakes (try not to swallow water), or through contact with infected animals. Symptoms consist of diarrhoea, vomiting, stomach cramps, abdominal bloating and wind. Effective treatment is available (tinidazole or metronidazole).

Pharmaceuticals

Over-the-counter medications are widely available in NZ through private chemists (pharmacies). These include painkillers, antihistamines, skincare products and sunscreen. Some medications, such as antibiotics, are only available via a prescription obtained from a general practitioner. If you take regular medications, bring an adequate supply and details of the generic name, as brand names differ from country to country.

Tap Water

Tap water throughout New Zealand is generally safe to drink, and public taps with nondrinkable water tend to be labelled as such. However, water quality has faced pollution challenges in some places. Very occasionally, a warning may be issued that tap water must be boiled – your accommodation should inform you if this happens.

Insurance

○ A watertight travel-insurance policy covering theft, loss and medical problems is essential when travelling. Some policies specifically exclude designated 'dangerous activities', such as scuba diving, bungy jumping, white-water rafting, skiing and even hiking. If you plan on doing any of these things (a distinct possibility in NZ!), make sure your policy covers you fully.

○ It's worth mentioning that, under NZ law, you cannot sue for personal injury (other than exemplary damages). Instead, the country's Accident Compensation Corporation (www.acc.co.nz) administers an accident compensation scheme that provides accident insurance for NZ residents and visitors to the country, regardless of fault. This scheme, however, does not negate the necessity for your own comprehensive travel-insurance policy, as it doesn't cover you for such things as income loss, treatment at home or ongoing illness.

○ Consider a policy that pays doctors or hospitals directly, rather than you paying on the spot and claiming later. If you have to claim later, keep all documentation. Some policies ask you to call a centre in your home country where an immediate assessment of your problem is made. Check that the policy covers ambulances and emergency medical evacuations by air.

○ Worldwide travel insurance is available at www.lonelyplanet.com/travel-insurance. You can buy, extend and claim online anytime – even if you're already on the road.

Internet Access

Getting online in NZ is easy in all but remote locales. Expect abundant wi-fi in cafes and accommodation in big towns and cities, but thrifty download limits elsewhere.

Wireless Access

Wi-fi You'll be able to find wi-fi access around the country, from hotel rooms and pub beer gardens to hostel dorms. Usually you have to be a guest or customer to log in, and you should be issued with an access code. Sometimes it's free, sometimes there's a charge, and often there's a limit on time or data.

Hotspots The country's main telecommunications company is Spark New Zealand (www.spark.co.nz), which has more than 1000 wireless hotspots around the country, recognisable by the company's pink-and-white phone boxes and wi-fi signs. You can purchase prepaid access cards or a prepaid number from the login page at any wireless hotspot using your credit card, while all Spark mobile and broadband plans come with up to 1GB of free daily data. See the website for hotspot listings.

Equipment and ISPs If you've brought your tablet or laptop, consider buying a prepay USB modem (aka a 'dongle') with a local SIM card: both Spark and Vodafone (www.vodafone.co.nz) sell these from $65.

Legal Matters

If you are questioned or arrested by police, it's your right to ask why, to refrain from making a statement, and to consult a lawyer in private.

A binding referendum on the decriminalisation of marijuana will be held in New Zealand in 2020, but for the time being it remains illegal, with the threshold for presumption of supply standing at 28g, or 100 joints. Anyone caught carrying this or other illicit drugs will have the book thrown at them.

Drink-driving is a serious offence and remains a significant problem in NZ. The legal blood alcohol limit is 0.05% for drivers aged 20 years and over, and zero for those under 20.

LGBT+ Travellers

The gay tourism industry in NZ isn't as high profile as it is in some other developed nations, but LGBTQI+ communities are prominent in Auckland and Wellington, with myriad support organisations across both islands.

New Zealand has progressive laws protecting human rights: same-sex marriage and adoption by same-sex couples were legalised in 2013 (ahead of anywhere else in the Asia-Pacific region). Generally speaking, Kiwis are fairly relaxed and accepting about same-sex relations and gender fluidity, but that's not to say that homophobia and/or transphobia don't exist. Rural communities tend to be more conservative, and public displays of affection may attract unwelcome attention.

Resources

There are loads of websites dedicated to gay and lesbian travel in NZ. Gay Tourism New Zealand (www.gaytourismnewzealand.com) is a starting point, with links to various sites. Other worthwhile websites include the following:

- www.gaynz.net.nz
- www.lesbian.net.nz
- www.gaystay.co.nz

Check out the nationwide monthly magazine *express* (www.gayexpress.co.nz) for the latest happenings, reviews and listings on the NZ gay scene. RainbowYOUTH (www.ry.org.nz) supports queer and gender-diverse people between 13 and 28, and New Zealand Awaits (www.newzealandawaits.com) is a local operator specialising in tours serving LGBT+ travellers.

Practicalities

Newspapers Check out Auckland's *New Zealand Herald* (www.nzherald.co.nz), Wellington's *Dominion Post* (www.stuff.co.nz/dominion-post) or Christchurch's *The Press* (www.stuff.co.nz/the-press).

TV Watch one of the national government-owned TV stations – including TVNZ 1, TVNZ 2, Māori TV or the 100% Māori-language Te Reo.

Radio Tune in to Radio New Zealand (www.radionz.co.nz) for news, current affairs, classical and jazz. Radio Hauraki (www.hauraki.co.nz) cranks out rock.

Weights & measures New Zealand uses the metric system.

Festivals & Events

Auckland Pride Festival (www.aucklandpridefestival.org.nz) Two-and-a-bit weeks of rainbow-hued celebrations in February.

Big Gay Out (www.biggayout.co.nz) Part of February's Auckland Pride Festival, this flagship day features live music, DJs, stalls, art and more.

Winter Pride (www.winterpride.co.nz) Ten days and two weekends of inclusive partying in and around Queenstown every August/September.

Maps

New Zealand's **Automobile Association** (AA; ☎0800 500 222; www.aa.co.nz/travel) sells maps. Scan the larger bookshops, or try the nearest Department of Conservation (DOC) office or visitor information centre for topo maps.

Map geeks will also love www.topomap.co.nz.

Online, log onto AA Maps (www.aamaps.co.nz) to pinpoint exact NZ addresses.

Money

ATMs & Eftpos

Branches of the country's major banks provide ATMs (cashpoints) across the country, but you may not find them in the very smallest towns. It's gener-

ally better to decline the on-the-spot conversion rate ATMs will offer, although this depends on your home bank's rates and market movements.

Many NZ businesses use Eftpos (electronic funds transfer at point of sale), allowing you to use your bank card (credit or debit) to make direct purchases and often withdraw cash as well. With over 52,500 devices connected to its New Zealand network, the system is close to universal. Just like at an ATM, you'll need your PIN unless it's a small purchase where contactless payment is available.

Credit Cards

Credit cards are widely accepted for everything from a hostel bed to a bungy jump, and are pretty much essential for car hire. Credit cards can also be used for over-the-counter cash advances at banks and from ATMs, but be aware that such transactions incur charges. Diners Club and American Express cards are not as widely accepted as Visa and MasterCard.

Debit Cards

Debit cards enable you to draw money directly from your home bank account using ATMs, banks or Eftpos facilities. Any card connected to the international banking network (Cirrus, Maestro, Visa Plus and Eurocard) should work with your PIN. Fees will vary depending on your home

bank; check before you leave. Alternatively, companies such as Travelex offer prepaid currency cards with set withdrawal fees and a balance you can top up from your personal bank account while on the road.

Exchange Rates

Australia	A$1	NZ$1.05
Canada	C$1	NZ$1.17
China	¥10	NZ$2.21
Eurozone	€1	NZ$1.71
Japan	¥100	NZ$1.43
Singapore	S$1	NZ$1.14
UK	UK£1	NZ$1.99
US	US$1	NZ$1.55

For current exchange rates, see www.xe.com.

Money Changers

Changing foreign currency (and to a lesser extent travellers cheques) is usually no problem at NZ banks or at licensed money changers (eg Travelex) in major tourist areas, cities and airports. However, withdrawing directly from ATMs usually secures the most favourable rates.

Taxes & Refunds

The Goods and Services Tax (GST) is a flat 15% tax on all domestic goods and services. New Zealand prices listed by Lonely Planet include GST. There's no GST refund available when you leave the country.

Tipping

Tipping is completely optional in NZ.

Guides Your kayaking guide or tour-group leader would happily accept tips; $10 is kind.

Restaurants The total on your bill is all you need to pay. If you like, reward good service with 5% to 10%.

Taxis If you round up your fare, don't be surprised if the driver hands back your change.

Opening Hours

Opening hours vary seasonally depending on where you are. Most places close on Christmas Day and Good Friday.

Banks 9am to 4.30pm Monday to Friday; some also 9am to noon Saturday

Cafes 7am or 8am to 3pm or 4pm

Post offices 8.30am to 5pm Monday to Friday; larger branches also 9.30am to 1pm Saturday

Pubs and bars noon to late ('late' varies by region, and by day)

Restaurants noon to 2.30pm and 6pm to 9pm

Shops and businesses 9am to 5.30pm Monday to Friday and 9am to noon or 5pm Saturday

Supermarkets 7am to 9pm

Public Holidays

New Zealand's main public holidays are as follows:

New Year 1 and 2 January
Waitangi Day 6 February

Easter Good Friday and Easter Monday; March/April

Anzac Day 25 April

Queen's Birthday First Monday in June

Labour Day Fourth Monday in October

Christmas Day 25 December

Boxing Day 26 December

For an up-to-date list of provincial anniversaries, see www.govt.nz/browse/work/public-holidays-and-work/public-holidays-and-anniversary-dates.

School Holidays

The Christmas holiday season, from mid-December to late January, is part of the summer school vacation: expect some transport and accommodation to be booked out in advance and queues at tourist attractions. There are three shorter school-holiday periods during the year: from mid to late April, early to mid-July, and late September to mid-October. For exact dates, see the Ministry of Education website (www.education.govt.nz).

Safe Travel

New Zealand is no more dangerous than other developed countries, but take normal safety precautions, especially after dark on city streets and in remote areas.

o Kiwi roads are often made hazardous by map-distracted tourists, wide-cornering campervans and traffic-ignorant sheep.

o Avoid leaving valuables in vehicles: theft is a problem, even in remote areas.

o New Zealand's climate is unpredictable: hypothermia is a risk in high-altitude areas.

o At the beach, beware of rips and undertows that can drag swimmers out to sea.

Telephone

New Zealand uses regional two-digit area codes for long-distance calls, which can be made from any landline or mobile. If you're making a local call (ie to someone else in the same town), you don't need to dial the area code. But if you're dialling within a region (even if it's to a nearby town with the same area code), you do.

To make international calls from NZ, the international access code is ☎00. If dialling NZ from overseas, the country code is ☎64, followed by the appropriate area code minus the initial '0'.

Mobile Phones

It's simple to buy a local SIM card and prepaid account at outlets in airports and large towns (provided your mobile is unlocked).

Mobile coverage is good in built-up areas and most of the North Island, but can be patchy in places on the South Island.

Local carriers can set you up with a NZ Travel SIM and phone number from around $20.

Pay Phones

Local calls from payphones cost $1 for the first 15 minutes, and 20c per minute thereafter, though coin-operated machines are scarce (and if you do find one, chances are the coin slot will be gummed up). You're better off relying on a phonecard. Calls to mobile phones or numbers outside the locality attract higher rates.

Premium-Rate & Toll-Free Calls

o Numbers starting with ☎0900 sometimes charge nearly $2 per minute (more from mobiles). These numbers cannot be dialled from payphones, and sometimes not from prepaid mobile phones.

o Toll-free numbers in NZ have the prefix ☎0800 or ☎0508, and can be called from anywhere in the country, though they may not be accessible from certain areas or from mobile phones.

o Numbers beginning with ☎0508, ☎0800 or ☎0900 cannot be dialled from outside NZ.

Emergency & Important Numbers

Regular numbers have a two-digit area code followed by a seven-digit number. When dialling within a region, the area code is required.

NZ's country code	☎64
International access code	☎00
Emergency (Ambulance, Fire, Police)	☎111
Directory Assistance (charges apply)	☎018

Phonecards

New Zealand has a wide range of phonecards available, which can be bought at hostels, newsagents and post offices for a fixed-dollar value (usually $5, $10, $20 and $50). These can be used with any public or private phone by dialling a toll-free access number and then the PIN number on the card. Shop around – rates vary from company to company.

Time

o New Zealand is 12 hours ahead of GMT/UTC and two hours ahead of Australian Eastern Standard Time (AEST).

o The Chathams are 45 minutes ahead of NZ's main islands.

o In summer, NZ observes daylight saving time: clocks are wound forward by one hour on the last Sunday in September; clocks are wound back on the first Sunday of April.

Toilets

Toilets in NZ are sit-down Western style. Public toilets are plentiful, and are usually reasonably clean with working locks and plenty of toilet paper.

Tourist Information

The website for the official national tourism body, Tourism New Zealand (www. newzealand.com), is an excellent place for pre-trip research. The site has information in several languages, including German, Spanish, French, Chinese and Japanese.

Local Tourist Offices

Almost every Kiwi city or town seems to have a visitor information centre. The bigger centres stand united within the outstanding i-SITE network (www. newzealand.com/travel/

i-sites) – more than 80 info centres affiliated with Tourism New Zealand. The i-SITE centres have trained staff, information on local activities, itineraries and attractions, and they provide free brochures and maps. Staff can also book activities, transport and accommodation.

Bear in mind that some information centres only promote accommodation and tour operators who are paying members of the local tourist association, and that staff shouldn't recommend any providers over others.

There's also a network of 19 Department of Conservation (DOC; www.doc.govt. nz) visitor centres to help you plan outdoor activities and make bookings (particularly for hiking tracks and huts). The visitor centres – in national parks, regional centres and major cities – usually also have displays on local flora and fauna.

Visas

Visitors need an NZeTA (New Zealand Electronic Travel Authority). In addition, tourists are expected to pay an International Visitor Conservation and Tourism Levy (IVL; NZ$35). See www.immigration. govt.nz.

Visa application forms are available from NZ

diplomatic missions overseas, travel agents and **Immigration New Zealand** (☑0508 558 855, 09-914 4100; www.immigration.govt.nz). Immigration New Zealand has more than 25 offices overseas, including the US, UK and Australia – consult the website for exact requirements and the list of nationals entitled to a visa waiver. Such entrants to NZ must still obtain a NZeTA, unless they're NZ nationals or Australians travelling on Australian passports. NZeTAs take from 10 minutes to three days to come through, and cost $9 through the Immigration Department's app, or $12 through its website.

Women Travellers

New Zealand is generally a very safe place for female travellers, although the usual sensible precautions apply (for all genders): avoid walking alone at night; never hitchhike alone; and if you're out on the town, have a plan for how to get back to your accommodation safely. Sexual harassment is not a widely reported problem in NZ, but of course that doesn't mean it doesn't happen. See www.women travel.co.nz for tours aimed at solo women.

Transport

Getting There & Away

New Zealand is a long way from almost everywhere – most travellers jet in from afar. Flights, cars and tours can be booked online at lonelyplanet.com/bookings.

Entering the Country

Entering NZ is a fairly straightforward affair and customs officials are relatively friendly, provided you have all your paperwork in order and follow the rules around what you need to declare to maintain NZ's biosecurity. Most airlines will not let you check in to your flight to NZ without your 90-day NZeTA (New Zealand Electronic Travel Authority) pre-approved.

Air

New Zealand's abundance of seasonal activities and attractions means that airports here are busy most of the year. If you want to fly at a particularly popular time (eg over the Christmas period), book well in advance.

The high season for flights into NZ is during summer (December to

February), with slightly less of a premium on fares over the shoulder months (October/November and March/April). The low season generally tallies with the winter months (June to August), though this is still a busy time for airlines servicing the ski fields.

Airlines Flying To/From New Zealand

● New Zealand's international carrier is Air New Zealand (www.airnewzealand.co.nz), which flies to runways across Europe, North America, eastern Asia, Australia and the Pacific, and has an extensive network across NZ.

● Winging in with direct flights from Australia, Virgin Australia (www.virginaustralia.com), Qantas (www.qantas.com.au), Jetstar (www.jetstar.com) and Air New Zealand are the key players.

● Joining Air New Zealand from North America, other operators include Air Canada (www.aircanada.com) and American Airlines (www.aa.com) – the latter has direct flights from Los Angeles to Auckland.

● From Europe, the options are a little broader, with Lufthansa (www.lufthansa.com) and Virgin Atlantic (www.virginatlantic.com) entering the fray. Flights go via major Middle Eastern or Asian airports. Several other airlines stop in NZ on broader round-the-world routes.

● From Asia and the Pacific there are myriad options, with direct flights from China, Japan, Singapore, Malaysia, Thailand and Pacific Island nations.

International Airports

A number of NZ airports handle international flights, with Auckland receiving the most traffic:

Auckland Airport (AKL; ☏09-275 0789; www.aucklandairport.co.nz; Ray Emery Dr, Māngere)

Christchurch Airport (CHC; ☏03-358 5029; www.christchurchairport.co.nz; 30 Durey Rd)

Dunedin Airport (DUD; ☏03-486 2879; www.dunedinairport.co.nz; 25 Miller Rd, Momona; ☎)

Queenstown Airport (ZQN; ☏03-450 9031; www.queenstownairport.co.nz; Sir Henry Wrigley Dr, Frankton)

Wellington Airport (WLG; ☏04-385 5100; www.wellingtonairport.co.nz; Stewart Duff Dr, Rongotai)

Note that Hamilton, Rotorua and Palmerston North airports are capable of handling direct international arrivals and departures, but are not currently doing so.

Sea

Cruise Ship If you're travelling from Australia and content with a slow pace, try P&O (www.pocruises.com.au) and Princess (www.princess.com) for cruises to New Zealand.

Yacht It is possible (though by no means straightforward) to make your way between NZ, Australia and the Pacific Islands by crewing on a yacht. Try asking around at harbours, marinas, and yacht and sailing clubs. Popular yachting harbours in NZ include the Bay of Islands and Whangārei (both in Northland), Auckland and Wellington. March and April are the best months to look for boats heading to Australia. From Fiji, October to November is a peak departure season to beat the cyclones that soon follow in that region.

Climate Change & Travel

Every form of transport that relies on carbon-based fuel generates CO_2, the main cause of human-induced climate change. Modern travel is dependent on aeroplanes, which might use less fuel per kilometre per person than most cars but travel much greater distances. The altitude at which aircraft emit gases (including CO_2) and particles also contributes to their climate change impact. Many websites offer 'carbon calculators' that allow people to estimate the carbon emissions generated by their journey and, for those who wish to do so, to offset the impact of the greenhouse gases emitted with contributions to portfolios of climate-friendly initiatives throughout the world. Lonely Planet offsets the carbon footprint of all staff and author travel.

Getting Around

Air

Those who have limited time to get between NZ's attractions can make the most of a widespread (and very reliable and safe) network of intra- and inter-island flights.

Airlines in New Zealand

The country's major domestic carrier, Air New Zealand, has an aerial network covering most of the country, often operating under the Air New Zealand Link moniker on less-popular routes. Australia-based Jetstar also flies between main urban areas. Between them, these two airlines carry the vast majority of domestic passengers in NZ.

Beyond this, several small-scale regional operators provide essential transport services to outlying islands, such as Great Barrier Island (in the Hauraki Gulf), Stewart Island and the Chathams. There are also plenty of scenic- and charter-flight operators around NZ, not listed here. Operators include the following:

Air Chathams (☎0800 580 127; www.airchathams. co.nz) Services to the remote Chatham Islands from Wellington, Christchurch and Auckland. Auckland–Whakatāne flights also available.

Air New Zealand (☎0800 737 000; www.airnewzealand.co.nz) Offers flights between 20-plus domestic destinations, plus myriad overseas hubs.

Barrier Air (☎0800 900 600; www.barrierair.kiwi) Connects Auckland with Great Barrier Island and Kaitāia.

FlyMySky (☎0800 222 123; www.flymysky.co.nz) At least three flights daily from Auckland to Great Barrier Island.

Golden Bay Air (☎0800 588 885; www.goldenbayair.co.nz) Flies regularly to Takaka in Golden Bay from Wellington and Nelson. Also connects to Karamea for Heaphy Track hikers.

Jetstar (☎0800 800 995; www.jetstar.com) Joins the dots between key tourism centres: Auckland, Wellington, Christchurch, Dunedin, Queenstown, Nelson, Napier, New Plymouth and Palmerston North.

Sounds Air (☎0800 505 005; www.soundsair.co.nz) Numerous flights daily between Picton and Wellington, plus flights from Wellington to Blenheim, Nelson, Westport and Taupō. Also flies Blenheim to Christchurch, Paraparaumu and Napier, and Nelson to Paraparaumu.

Stewart Island Flights (☎03-218 9129; www.stewartisland flights.co.nz) Flies between Invercargill and Stewart Island three times daily.

Sunair (☎0800 786 247; www. sunair.co.nz) Numerous North Island connections between Hamilton, Tuaranga, Great Barrier Island, Gisborne, Whangārei and Whitianga.

Bicycle

Touring cyclists proliferate in NZ, particularly over summer. The country is clean, green and relatively uncrowded, and has lots of cheap accommodation (including camping) and abundant fresh water. The roads are generally in good nick, and the climate is typically mild. Road traffic is the biggest danger: trucks overtaking too close to cyclists are a particular threat. Bikes and cycling gear are readily available to hire or buy in the main centres, and bicycle-repair shops are common.

By law all cyclists must wear an approved safety helmet (or risk a $55 fine); it's also vital to have good reflective safety clothing. Cyclists who use public transport will find two- and three-tier exterior racks on all Christchurch buses (and many elsewhere) where bikes can be secured for free. Some of the smaller shuttle-bus companies also have storage space for bikes, but may impose a surcharge.

If importing your own bike or transporting it by plane within NZ, check with the relevant airline for costs and the degree of dismantling and packing required.

See www.nzta.govt.nz/walking-cycling-and-public-transport for more bike safety and legal tips, and check out the New Zealand Cycle Trail – a network of 22 'Great Rides' across NZ.

Hire

Rates offered by most outfits for hiring road or mountain bikes are usually around $25 for a short hire to $60 per day. Longer-term hire is usually available, at reduced rates. Hire basic bikes from your accommodation (hostels, holiday parks etc), or better machines from bike shops in the larger towns.

Boat

New Zealand may be an island nation, but there's virtually no long-distance water transport around the country. Obvious exceptions include the boat services between Auckland and various islands in the Hauraki Gulf, the inter-island ferries plying the Cook Strait between Wellington and Picton, and the passenger ferry that negotiates Foveaux Strait between Bluff and the town of Oban on Stewart Island.

If you're cashed-up, consider the cruise liners that chug around the NZ coastline as part of broader South Pacific itineraries: P&O Cruises (www.pocruises.com.au) is a major player.

Bus

Bus travel in NZ is easy-going and well organised, with services transporting you to the far reaches of both islands (including the start/end of various walking tracks)...but it can be expensive, tedious and time-consuming.

New Zealand's main bus company is **InterCity** (www.intercity.co.nz), which can drive you to just about anywhere on the North and South Islands and offers fares as low as $1(!). InterCity also has a sightseeing arm called **GreatSights New Zealand** (www.great sights.co.nz) handling scenic routes such as Queenstown to Mt Cook and Milford Sound.

The low-fare bus company **Skip** (www.skip.travel) only operates on the North Island at present.

Privately run shuttle buses can transport travellers to some trailheads or collect them from the end point of a hike; advance booking essential.

Seat Classes & Smoking

There are no allocated economy or luxury classes on NZ buses (very democratic), and smoking on the bus is a definite no-no.

InterCity has a sleeper class on overnight services between Auckland and Wellington, stopping at Hamilton, Palmerston North and three other intervening towns. You'll get a 1.8m-long bed and small pillow; bring a sleeping bag, pillowcase and maybe earplugs. See www.intercity.co.nz for details.

Reservations

Over summer (December to February), school holidays and public holidays, book a week or two ahead for seats on popular routes. At other times, a day or two ahead is usually fine. The best prices are generally available online, and in advance.

Bus Passes

If you're covering a lot of ground, InterCity offers a range of passes, priced according to your proposed itinerary and length of journey. If the itineraries and fare schemes offered suit you, this can be cheaper than paying as you go, but do the maths before buying and note that you'll be locked into using one network. Passes are usually valid for 12 months.

InterCity offers a discount of around 10% on standard fares for students and YHA, ISIC, HI, Nomads, BBH or VIP backpacker card holders, on selected services. Senior discounts only apply to NZ citizens.

Nationwide Passes

FlexiPass A hop-on/hop-off InterCity pass, allowing travel to pretty much anywhere in NZ, in any direction, including the Interislander ferry across Cook Strait. The pass is purchased in blocks of travel time: the minimum is 15 hours ($132) and the maximum 60 ($459). The average cost of each block becomes cheaper the more hours you buy. You can top up the pass if you need more time.

TravelPass Hop-on/hop-off, fixed-itinerary nationwide passes offered by InterCity. With names like Aotearoa Explorer and Island Loop, these passes link tourist hotspots across either or both islands, and range from simple regional itineraries costing as little as $125 to grand, country-wide circuits worth

$1045. See www.intercity.
co.nz/bus-pass/travel
pass-overview for details.

North Island Passes

InterCity offers six hop-on/
hop-off, fixed-itinerary
North Island TravelPasses,
from short $125 runs be-
tween Auckland and Paihia,
to $405 trips from Auckland
to Wellington via the big
sights in between. See www.
intercity.co.nz/bus-pass/
travelpass-overview for
details.

South Island Passes

On the South Island,
InterCity offers six hop-on/
hop-off, fixed-itinerary
TravelPasses, from the
Picton-to-Queenstown
Westcoast Passport ($125)
to the Scenic South loop
($549). See www.intercity.
co.nz/bus-pass/travel
pass-overview for details.

Shuttle Buses

As well as InterCity's network, regional shuttle buses
fill in the gaps between the
smaller towns. Operators
include the following (see
www.tourism.net.nz/
transport/bus-and-coach-
services for a complete list),
offering regular scheduled
services and/or bus tours
and charters:

Abel Tasman Travel (www.
scenicnzabeltasman.co.nz)
Traverses the road between
Nelson and Marahau, on the
fringe of Abel Tasman National
Park.

Atomic Shuttles (www.atomic
travel.co.nz) Has services from
Christchurch to Dunedin and

Greymouth, stopping at points
of interest along the way.

Catch-a-Bus South (www.
catchabussouth.co.nz) Invercargill and Bluff to Dunedin and
Queenstown.

Cook Connection (www.cook
connect.co.nz) Triangulates
between Mt Cook, Twizel and
Lake Tekapo.

East West Coaches (www.
eastwestcoaches.co.nz) Offers
a service between Christchurch
and Westport via Lewis Pass,
and Greymouth via Arthur's
Pass.

Go Kiwi Shuttles (www.go-
kiwi.co.nz) Links Auckland with
Whitianga on the Coromandel
Peninsula daily.

Hanmer Connection (www.
hanmerconnection.co.nz)
Daily services between Hanmer
Springs and Christchurch.

Headfirst Travel (www.travel
headfirst.com) Does a loop
from Rotorua to Waitomo (with
an option to finish in Auckland).

Tracknet (www.tracknet.
net) Track transport (Milford,
Hollyford, Routeburn, Kepler)
with Queenstown, Te Anau
and Invercargill connections.
Services are sparser in winter.

Trek Express (www.trek
express.co.nz) Shuttle services
to all hiking tracks in the top
half of the South Island (eg
Heaphy, Abel Tasman, the Ghost
Trail).

Car & Motorcycle

The best way to explore NZ
in depth is to have your own
wheels. It's easy to hire cars
and campervans, though
it's worth noting that fuel
costs can be eye-watering.
Alternatively, if you're in NZ

for a few months, you might
consider buying your own
vehicle.

Automobile Association (AA)

New Zealand's **Automobile
Association** (AA; ☐0800
500 222; www.aa.co.nz/travel)
provides emergency break-
down services, distance
calculators and accommo-
dation guides (from holiday
parks to motels and B&Bs).

Members of overseas
automobile associations
should bring their mem-
bership cards – many of
these bodies have reciprocal
agreements with the AA.

Driving Licences

International visitors to NZ
can use their home-country
driving licence – if your
licence isn't in English,
it's a good idea to carry a
certified translation with
you. Alternatively, use an
International Driving Permit
(IDP), which will usually be
issued on the spot (valid
for 12 months) by your
home country's automobile
association.

Fuel

Fuel (petrol, aka gasoline)
is available from service
stations across NZ: unless
you're cruising around in
something from the 1970s,
you'll be filling up with
'unleaded', or LPG (gas).
LPG is not always stocked
by rural suppliers – if you're
on gas, it's safer to have
dual-fuel capability. Aside
from remote locations like
Milford Sound and Mt Cook,
petrol prices don't vary

much from place to place: per-litre costs at the time of research were hovering around $2.40.

Hire

Campervan

Check your rear-view mirror on any far-flung NZ road and you'll probably see a shiny white campervan (aka mobile home, motor home, RV), packed with liberated travellers, mountain bikes and portable barbecues, cruising along behind you.

Most towns of any size have a campsite or holiday park with powered pitches (where you can plug your vehicle in) for around $50 per night. There are also 250-plus vehicle-accessible Department of Conservation (DOC; www.doc.govt.nz) campsites around NZ, priced from $20 per adult. Weekly Campsite Passes for hired campervans slice up to 50% off the price of stays in some of these campsites; check the DOC website for info, and make sure your intended site(s) offer the discount.

You can hire campervans from dozens of companies. Prices vary with season, vehicle size and length of hire, and it pays to book months in advance.

A small van for two people typically has a mini kitchen and fold-out dining table, the latter transforming into a double bed when dinner is done and dusted. Larger, 'superior' two-berth vans include shower and toilet. Four- to six-berth

campervans are the size of trucks (and similarly sluggish) and, besides the extra space, usually contain a toilet and shower.

Over summer, rates offered by the main firms for two-/four-/six-berth vans booked three months in advance start at around $120/150/230 per day (though they rise much higher, depending on model) for hire for two weeks or more. Rates drop to $60/75/100 per day during winter.

Major operators include the following:

Apollo (☏0800 113 131, 09-889 2976; www.apollocamper.co.nz)
Britz (☏09-255 3910, 0800 081 032; www.britz.co.nz) Also does 'Britz Bikes' (add a mountain or city bike from $16 per day) and electric campervans.
Maui (☏09-255 3910, 0800 688 558; www.maui-rentals.com)
Wilderness Motorhomes (☏09-282 3606; www.wilderness.co.nz)

Car

Competition between car-hire companies in NZ is fierce, particularly in the big cities and Picton. Remember that if you want to travel far, you need to specify unlimited kilometres. Some (but not all) companies require drivers to be at least 21 years old – ask around.

International car-hire firms don't generally allow you to take their vehicles between islands on the Cook Strait ferries. Instead,

you leave your car at either Wellington or Picton terminal and pick up another car once you've crossed the strait. This saves you paying to transport a vehicle on the ferries, and is a pain-free exercise. However, some local car-hire firms (such as Apex) are fine with you taking your rental vehicle on the ferry and will even book your ferry ticket for you.

International Rental Companies

The big multinational companies have offices in most major cities, towns and airports. Firms sometimes offer one-way rentals (eg collect a car in Auckland, leave it in Wellington), but there are usually restrictions and fees.

The major companies offer a choice of either unlimited kilometres, or 100km (or so) per day free, plus so many cents per subsequent kilometre. Daily rates in main cities typically start at around $40 per day for a compact, late-model, Japanese car, and from $70 for medium-sized cars (including GST, unlimited kilometres and insurance).

Avis (☏09-526 2847, 0800 655 111; www.avis.co.nz)
Budget (☏09-529 7788, 0800 283 438; www.budget.co.nz)
Europcar (☏0800 800 115; www.europcar.co.nz)
Hertz (☏0800 654 321; www.hertz.co.nz)

Thrifty (☑️0800 737 070, 03-359 2721; www.thrifty.co.nz)

Local Rental Companies

Local hire firms proliferate. These are almost always cheaper than the big boys – sometimes half the price – but the cheap rates obviously have strings attached: vehicles are often older, depots might be further away from airports/city centres, and with less formality sometimes comes a less-protective legal structure for renters.

Rentals from local firms start at around $30 or $40 per day for the smallest option. It's cheaper if you hire for a week or more, and there are often low-season and weekend discounts.

Affordable, independent operators with national networks include the following:

Ace Rental Cars (☑️0800 502 277, 09-303 3112; www.acerentalcars.co.nz)

Apex Rentals (☑️03-595 2315, 0800 500 660; www.apexrentals.co.nz)

Ezi Car Rental (☑️0800 545 000, 09-254 4397; www.ezicarrental.co.nz)

Go Rentals (☑️0800 467 368, 09-974 1598; www.gorentals.co.nz)

Omega Rental Cars (☑️09-377 5573, 0800 525 210; www.omegarentalcars.com)

Pegasus Rental Cars (☑️0800 803 580; www.rentalcars.co.nz)

Transfercar (☑️09-630 7533; www.transfercar.co.nz) Relocation specialists with massive money-saving deals on one-way car hire.

Motorcycle

Born to be wild? New Zealand has great terrain for motorcycle touring, despite the fickle weather in some regions. Most of the country's motorcycle-hire shops are in Auckland and Christchurch, where you can hire anything from a little 50cc moped (aka nifty-fifty) to a throbbing 750cc touring motorcycle and beyond. Recommended operators (who also run guided tours) offer rates beginning around $100 per day:

New Zealand Motorcycle Rentals & Tours (☑️09-486 2472; www.nzbike.com)

Te Waipounamu Motorcycle Tours (☑️03-372 3537; www.motorcycle-hire.co.nz)

Insurance

Rather than risk paying out wads of cash if you have an accident, you can take out your own comprehensive insurance policy, or (the usual option) pay an additional fee per day to the hire company to reduce your excess. This brings the amount you must pay in the event of an accident down from around $1500 or $2000 to around $200 or $300. Smaller operators offering cheap rates often have a compulsory insurance excess, taken as a credit-card bond, of around $900.

Many insurance agreements won't cover the cost of damage to glass (including the windscreen) or tyres, and insurance coverage is often invalidated on beaches and certain rough (4WD)

unsealed roads – read the fine print.

See www.acc.co.nz for info on NZ's Accident Compensation Corporation (ACC) insurance scheme (fault-free personal injury insurance).

Road Hazards

A higher percentage of international drivers are involved in road accidents in NZ – suggesting something about the challenges its roads pose. Kiwi traffic is usually pretty light, but it's easy to get stuck behind a slow-moving truck or campervan – pack plenty of patience, and know your road rules before you get behind the wheel. There are also lots of slow wiggly roads, one-way bridges and plenty of gravel roads, all of which require a more cautious driving approach. And watch out for sheep!

To check road conditions, call ☑️0800 444 449 or see www.nzta.govt.nz/traffic.

Road Rules

○ Kiwis drive on the left-hand side of the road; cars are right-hand drive. Give way to the right at intersections.

○ All vehicle occupants must wear a seatbelt or risk a $150 fine. Small children must be belted into approved safety seats.

○ Always carry your licence when driving.

○ Drink-driving is a serious offence and remains a significant problem in NZ, despite widespread campaigns and severe penalties. The legal blood-alcohol limit is 0.05% for drivers aged over 20, and zero for those under 20.

● At single-lane bridges (of which there are a surprisingly large number), a smaller red arrow pointing in your direction of travel means that you give way.

● Speed limits on the open road are generally 100km/h; in built-up areas the limit is usually 50km/h. Speed cameras and radars are used extensively.

● Be aware that not all rail crossings have barriers or alarms. Approach slowly and look both ways.

● Don't pass other cars when the centre line is yellow.

● It's illegal to drive while using a mobile phone.

Local Transport

Bus, Train & Tram

New Zealand's larger cities have extensive bus services but, with a few honourable exceptions, they are mainly daytime, weekday operations; weekend services can be infrequent or nonexistent. Negotiating inner-city Auckland is made easier by Link buses; Hamilton has a free city-centre loop bus; Christchurch has city buses and the historic tramway. Most main cities have late-night buses for boozy Friday and Saturday nights. Don't expect local bus services in more remote areas.

The only cities with decent local train services are Auckland and Wellington, with four and five suburban routes respectively.

Taxi

The main cities have plenty of taxis and even small towns may have a local service. Taxis are licensed, metered, and generally reliable and trustworthy.

Ridesharing

With the global explosion of ride-sharing apps, there are plenty of hungrily circling alternatives to traditional taxis in Kiwi cities. They're still principally a city-based convenience, you can expect surge pricing at busy times, and fares are usually similar across the different providers. Here are a few of the most common:

Uber (www.uber.com) The original, and still easily the biggest. Covers Auckland, Wellington, Christchurch, Hamilton, Tauranga, Dunedin and Queenstown.

Ola (www.ola.co.nz) Trades on more equitable profit-sharing; currently servicing Auckland, Wellington and Christchurch.

Zoomy (www.zoomy.co.nz) Kiwi-owned, serving Auckland, Wellington and Christchurch.

Train

Train Passes

Great Journeys of New Zealand's **Flexi** and **Flexi Plus** passes allow you to break your journey and change bookings up to 24 hours before departure. Both types of pass require you to book your seats a minimum of 24 hours before you want to travel, and have discounts for early birds and kids.

Language

New Zealand has three official languages: English, Māori and NZ sign language. Although English is what you'll usually hear, Māori has been making a comeback. You can use English to speak to anyone in New Zealand, but there are some occasions when knowing a small amount of Māori is useful, such as when visiting a *marae,* where often only Māori is spoken. Some knowledge of Māori will also help you interpret the many Māori place names you'll come across.

Kiwi English

Like the people of other English-speaking countries in the world, New Zealanders have their own, unique way of speaking the language. The flattening of vowels is the most distinctive feature of Kiwi pronunciation. For example, in Kiwi English, 'fish and chips' sounds more like 'fush and chups'. On the North Island sentences often have 'eh!' attached to the end. In the far south a rolled 'r' is common, which is a holdover from that region's Scottish heritage .

Māori

The Māori have a vividly chronicled history, recorded in songs and chants that dramatically recall the migration to New Zealand from Polynesia as well as other important events. Early missionaries were the first to record the language in a written form using only 15 letters of the English alphabet.

Māori is closely related to other Polynesian languages such as Hawaiian, Tahitian and Cook Islands Māori. In fact, New Zealand Māori and Hawaiian are quite similar, even though more than 7000km separates Honolulu and Auckland.

The Māori language was never dead – it was always used in Māori ceremonies – but over time familiarity with it was definitely on the decline. Fortunately, recent years have seen a revival of interest in it, and this forms an integral part of the renaissance of *Māoritanga* (Māori culture). Many Māori people who had heard the language spoken on the *marae* for years but had not used it in their day-to-day lives, are now studying it and speaking it fluently. Māori is taught in schools throughout New Zealand, some TV programs and news reports are broadcast in it, and many English place names are being renamed in Māori. Even government departments have been given Māori names.

In many places, Māori have come together to provide instruction in their language and culture to young children; the idea is for them to grow up speaking both Māori and English, and to develop a familiarity with Māori tradition. It's a matter of some pride to have fluency in the language. On some *marae* only Māori can be spoken.

Pronunciation

Māori is a fluid, poetic language and surprisingly easy to pronounce once you remember to split each word (some can be amazingly long) into separate syllables. Each syllable ends in a vowel. There are no 'silent' letters.

Most consonants in Māori – *h, k, m, n, p, t* and *w* – are pronounced much the same as in English. The Māori *r* is a flapped sound (not rolled) with the tongue near the front of the mouth. It's closer to the English 'l' in pronunciation.

The *ng* is pronounced as in the English words 'singing' or 'running', and can be used at the beginning of words as well as at the end. To practise, just say 'ing' over and over, then isolate the 'ng' part of it.

The letters *wh,* when occuring together, are generally pronounced as a soft English 'f'. This pronunciation is used in many place names in New Zealand, such as Whakataneand Whakapapa (all pronounced as if they begin with a soft 'f'). There is some local variation: in the region around the Whanganui River, for example, *wh* is pronounced as in the English word 'when'.

The correct pronunciation of the vowels is very important. The examples below are a rough guideline – it helps to listen carefully to someone who speaks the language well. Each vowel has both a long and a short sound, with long vowels often denoted by a line over the letter or a double vowel. We have not indicated long and short vowel forms in this book.

Vowels

a	as in 'large', with no 'r' sound
e	as in 'get'
i	as in 'marine'
o	as in 'pork'
u	as the 'oo' in 'moon'

Vowel Combinations

ae, ai	as the 'y' in 'sky'
ao, au	as the 'ow' in 'how'
ea	as in 'bear'
ei	as in 'vein'
eo	as 'eh-oh'
eu	as 'eh-oo'
ia	as in the name 'Ian'
ie	as the 'ye' in 'yet'
io	as the 'ye o' in 'ye old'
iu	as the 'ue' in 'cue'
oa	as in 'roar'
oe	as in 'toe'
oi	as in 'toil'
ou	as the 'ow' in 'how'
ua	as the 'ewe' in 'fewer'

Greetings & Small Talk

Māori greetings are becoming increasingly popular – don't be surprised if you're greeted with *Kia ora*.

Welcome!	*Haere mai!*
Hello./Good luck./ Good health.	*Kia ora.*
Hello. *(to one person)*	*Tena koe.*
Goodbye. *(to person staying)*	*E noho ra.*
Goodbye. *(to person leaving)*	*Haere ra.*
How are you? *(to one person)*	*Kei te pehea koe?*
Very well, thanks./ That's fine.	*Kei te pai.*

Māori Geographical Terms

The following words form part of many Māori place names in New Zealand, and indicate the meaning of these place names. For example: Waikaremoana is the Sea *(moana)* of Rippling *(kare)* Waters *(wai)*, and Rotorua means the Second *(rua)* Lake *(roto)*.

ana – cave
ara – way, path or road
awa – river or valley
heke – descend
iti – small
kahurangi – treasured possession; special greenstone
kainga – village
manga – stream or tributary
maunga – mountain
moana – sea or lake
motu – island
nui – big or great
nuku – distance
o – of, place of...
one – beach, sand or mud
pa – fortified village, usually on a hilltop
poto – short
puke – hill
puna – spring; hole; fountain
rangi – sky; heavens
raro – north
roa – long
roto – lake
rua – hole in the ground; two
tahuna – beach; sandbank
tata – close to; dash against; twin islands
tawaha – entrance or opening
tonga – south
uru – west
wai – water
waingaro – lost; waters that disappear in certain seasons
waka – canoe
wera – burnt or warm; floating
whanga – harbour, bay or inlet
whare – house
whenua – land or country
whiti – east

GLOSSARY

Anzac – Australia and New Zealand Army Corps

Aoraki – Māori name for Mt Cook, meaning 'Cloud Piercer'

Aotearoa – Māori name for NZ, most often translated as 'Land of the Long White Cloud'

aroha – love

bach – holiday home (pronounced 'batch'); see also crib

choice/chur – fantastic; great

crib – the name for a bach in Otago and Southland

football – rugby, either union or league; occasionally soccer

Great Walks – set of nine popular tramping tracks within NZ

greenstone – jade; *pounamu*

haka – any dance, but usually a war dance

hangi – oven whereby food is steamed in baskets over embers in a hole; a Māori feast

hapu – subtribe or smaller tribal grouping

Hawaiki – original homeland of the Māori

hei tiki – carved, stylised human figure worn around the neck; also called a *tiki*

hongi – Māori greeting; the pressing of foreheads and noses, and sharing of life breath

hui – gathering; meeting

iwi – large tribal grouping with common lineage back to the original migration from *Hawaiki*; people; tribe

jandals – contraction of 'Japanese sandals'; flip-flops; thongs; usually rubber footwear

kauri – native pine

Kiwiana – things uniquely connected to NZ life and culture, especially from bygone years

kumara – Polynesian sweet potato, a Māori staple food

Kupe – early Polynesian navigator from *Hawaiki*, credited with the discovery of the islands that are now NZ

mana – spiritual quality of a person or object; authority or prestige

Māori – indigenous people of NZ

Māoritanga – things Māori, ie Māori culture

marae – sacred ground in front of the Māori meeting house; more commonly used to refer to the entire complex of buildings

Maui – figure in Māori (Polynesian) mythology

mauri – life force/principle

moa – large, extinct flightless bird

moko – tattoo; usually refers to facial tattoos

nga – the (plural); see also *te*

ngai/ngati – literally, 'the people of' or 'the descendants of'; tribe (pronounced 'kai' on the South Island)

Pakeha – Māori for a white or European person

Pasifika – Pacific Island culture

paua – abalone; iridescent paua shell is often used in jewellery

pavlova – meringue cake topped with cream and kiwifruit

PI – Pacific Islander

pounamu – Māori name for greenstone

powhiri – traditional Māori welcome onto a *marae*

rip – dangerously strong current running away from the shore at a beach

tapu – strong force in Māori life, with numerous meanings; in its simplest form it means sacred, forbidden, taboo

te – the (singular); see also *nga*

te reo – literally 'the language'; the Māori language

tiki – short for *hei tiki*

tiki tour – scenic tour

tramp – bushwalk; trek; hike

tuatara – prehistoric reptile dating back to the age of dinosaurs

Waitangi – short way of referring to the Treaty of Waitangi

Behind the Scenes

Acknowledgements

Climate map data adapted from Peel MC, Finlayson BL & McMahon TA (2007) 'Updated World Map of the Köppen-Geiger Climate Classification', *Hydrology and Earth System Sciences*, 11, 1633–44.

Cover photograph: Waiau River and Lake Manapōuri, Fiordland National Park, South Island; Danita Delimont Stock/AWL Images©

This Book

This 3rd edition of Lonely Planet's *Best of New Zealand* guidebook was researched and written by Tasmin Waby, Brett Atkinson, Andrew Bain, Peter Dragicevich, Monique Perrin and Charles Rawlings-Way. The previous two editions were written by Charles, Brett, Andrew and Peter, along with Sarah Bennett, Samantha Forge, Anita Isalska, Sofia Levin and Lee Slater. This guidebook was produced by the following:

Senior Product Editors Kate Chapman, Kathryn Rowan

Regional Senior Cartographer Diana Von Holdt

Product Editors Sandie Kestell, Fergus O'Shea

Book Designer Fergal Condon

Assisting Editor Victoria Harrison

Assisting Cartographers Mark Griffiths, Corey Hutchison

Cover Researcher Brendan Dempsey-Spencer

Thanks to Amy Lynch, Angela Tinson

Send Us Your Feedback

We love to hear from travellers – your comments keep us on our toes and help make our books better. Our well-travelled team reads every word on what you loved or loathed about this book. Although we cannot reply individually to postal submissions, we always guarantee that your feedback goes straight to the appropriate authors, in time for the next edition. Each person who sends us information is thanked in the next edition, the most useful submissions are rewarded with a selection of digital PDF chapters.

Visit lonelyplanet.com/contact to submit your updates and suggestions or to ask for help. Our award-winning website also features inspirational travel stories, news and discussions.

Note: We may edit, reproduce and incorporate your comments in Lonely Planet products such as guidebooks, websites and digital products, so let us know if you don't want your comments reproduced or your name acknowledged. For a copy of our privacy policy visit lonelyplanet.com/privacy.

Index

A

Symbols & Map Key

Look for these symbols to quickly identify listings:

◉ Sights
✪ Activities
◉ Courses
◉ Tours
✪ Festivals & Events

✪ Eating
◉ Drinking
✪ Entertainment
◉ Shopping
ℹ Information & Transport

These symbols and abbreviations give vital information for each listing:

🌿 Sustainable or green recommendation

FREE No payment required

☎ Telephone number
🕓 Opening hours
ℙ Parking
🚭 Nonsmoking
❄ Air-conditioning
@ Internet access
📶 Wi-fi access
🏊 Swimming pool

🚌 Bus
⛴ Ferry
🚊 Tram
🚆 Train
📋 English-language menu
🥗 Vegetarian selection
👪 Family-friendly

Find your best experiences with these Great For... icons.

 Art & Culture
 Beaches
 Budget
 Cafe/Coffee
🚲 Cycling
📐 Detour
🍷 Drinking
📺 Entertainment
🎆 Events
🏙 Family Travel
🍽 Food & Drink

 History
 Local Life
 Nature & Wildlife
 Photo Op
 Scenery
 Shopping
 Short Trip
 Sport
 Walking
❄ Winter Travel

Sights

🏖 Beach
🐦 Bird Sanctuary
☸ Buddhist
🏰 Castle/Palace
✝ Christian
☯ Confucian
🕉 Hindu
☪ Islamic
卍 Jain
✡ Jewish
❶ Monument
🏛 Museum/Gallery/ Historic Building
🏚 Ruin
⛩ Shinto
☬ Sikh
☯ Taoist
🍇 Winery/Vineyard
🐾 Zoo/Wildlife Sanctuary
◉ Other Sight

Points of Interest

🏄 Bodysurfing
⛺ Camping
☕ Cafe
🛶 Canoeing/Kayaking
● Course/Tour
🤿 Diving
🍸 Drinking & Nightlife
🍴 Eating
🎭 Entertainment
♨ Sento Hot Baths/ Onsen
🛍 Shopping
⛷ Skiing
🛌 Sleeping
🤿 Snorkelling
🏄 Surfing
🏊 Swimming/Pool
🚶 Walking
🏄 Windsurfing
◉ Other Activity

Information

💲 Bank
🏛 Embassy/Consulate
➕ Hospital/Medical
@ Internet
👮 Police
✉ Post Office
📞 Telephone
🚻 Toilet
ℹ Tourist Information
● Other Information

Geographic

🏖 Beach
⊷ Gate
🏠 Hut/Shelter
🗼 Lighthouse
🔭 Lookout
▲ Mountain/Volcano
🌴 Oasis
🌳 Park
)(Pass
🧺 Picnic Area
💧 Waterfall

Transport

✈ Airport
Ⓑ BART station
⊗ Border crossing
🅣 Boston T station
🚌 Bus
🚡 Cable car/Funicular
🚲 Cycling
⛴ Ferry
Ⓜ Metro/MRT station
🚝 Monorail
ℙ Parking
⛽ Petrol station
Ⓢ Subway/S-Bahn/ Skytrain station
🚕 Taxi
🚉 Train station/Railway
🚊 Tram
Ⓤ Underground/ U-Bahn station
● Other Transport

Kiwi wanderlust, giving up staff jobs to chase his diverse roots around much of Europe. Over the last 15 years he's written over 100 books for Lonely Planet on an oddly disparate collection of countries, all of which he's come to love. He once again calls Auckland, New Zealand, his home – although his current nomadic existence means he's often elsewhere.

Monique Perrin

Monique is a freelance writer, organic gardener, keen bushwalker and wannabe singer-songwriter. She has covered Tibet, Philippines, Australia and India for Lonely Planet. Monique has worked all over the world, including for the UN in Sri Lanka and as a journalist in Hong Kong. Her secret love is unearthing the hidden highlights of her awesome home town: Sydney.

Charles Rawlings-Way

Charles is an indefatigable travel, walking, food and music writer (all the good things). After dabbling in the dark arts of architecture, cartography, project management and busking for some years, Charles hit the road for Lonely Planet in 2005 and hasn't stopped travelling since. He has penned more than 40 titles for Lonely Planet, including guides to Singapore, Toronto, Canada, Tonga, New Zealand, the South Pacific, every state in Australia (including his native terrain of Tasmania and current homeland of South Australia), as well as countless articles. He's also the author of a best-selling rock biography on Glasgow band Del Amitri, *These Are Such Perfect Days*, which was published in 2018. Follow Charles at @crawlingsway.

Our Story

A beat-up old car, a few dollars in the pocket and a sense of adventure. In 1972 that's all Tony and Maureen Wheeler needed for the trip of a lifetime – across Europe and Asia overland to Australia. It took several months, and at the end – broke but inspired – they sat at their kitchen table writing and stapling together their first travel guide, *Across Asia on the Cheap*. Within a week they'd sold 1500 copies. Lonely Planet was born.

Today, Lonely Planet has offices in Franklin, Dublin, Beijing, and Delhi, with more than 600 staff and writers. We share Tony's belief that 'a great guidebook should do three things: inform, educate and amuse'.

Our Writers

Tasmin Waby

London-born to Kiwi parents, Tasmin was raised in Australia, for which she is incredibly grateful. As well as travelling, learning and writing, Tasmin is madly in love with cartography, wild swimming and starry skies. When not on assignment she lives on a narrowboat in England, raising two hilarious school-aged children and a fat Russian Blue cat called Millie.

Brett Atkinson

Brett is based in Auckland, New Zealand, but is frequently on the road for Lonely Planet. He's a full-time travel and food writer specialising in adventure travel, unusual destinations and surprising angles on more well known destinations. Craft beer and street food are Brett's favourite reasons to explore places, and he is featured regularly on the Lonely Planet website, as well as in newspapers, magazines and websites across New Zealand and Australia. Since becoming a Lonely Planet author in 2005, Brett has covered areas as diverse as Vietnam, Sri Lanka, the Czech Republic, New Zealand, Morocco, California and the South Pacific.

Andrew Bain

Andrew is an Australia-based writer specialising in outdoors and adventure. He's cycled and trekked across every continent bar the icy one, and is the author of *Headwinds,* the story of his 20,000km bike ride around Australia. He's written Lonely Planet titles such as *A Year of Adventures, Walking in Australia* and *Cycling Australia*. Find Andrew on Instagram at @bainonbike.

Peter Dragicevich

After a successful career in niche newspaper and magazine publishing, both in his native New Zealand and in Australia, Peter finally gave into

More Writers

STAY IN TOUCH LONELYPLANET.COM/CONTACT

IRELAND Digital Depot, Roe Lane (off Thomas St), Digital Hub, Dublin 8, D08 TCV4, Ireland

USA 230 Franklin Road, Building 2B, Franklin, TN 37064; 615 988 9713;

Although the authors and Lonely Planet have taken all reasonable care in preparing this book, we make no warranty about the accuracy or completeness of its content and, to the maximum extent permitted, disclaim all liability arising from its use.

All rights reserved. No part of this publication may be copied, stored in a retrieval system, or transmitted in any form by any means, electronic, mechanical, recording or otherwise, except brief extracts for the purpose of review, and no part of this publication may be sold or hired, without the written permission of the publisher. Lonely Planet and the Lonely Planet logo are trademarks of Lonely Planet and are registered in the US Patent and Trademark Office and in other countries. Lonely Planet does not allow its name or logo to be appropriated by commercial establishments, such as retailers, restaurants or hotels. Please let us know of any misuses: lonelyplanet.com/ip.

 twitter.com/ lonelyplanet

 facebook.com/ lonelyplanet

 instagram.com/ lonelyplanet

 youtube.com/ lonelyplanet

 lonelyplanet.com/ newsletter